Elements in Landscape

I0802319

Elements in Landscape

Areas, Distances, Dimensions

Astrid Zimmermann

Birkhäuser
Basel

Contents

1 Introduction

A hallmark of planning processes is their inclusion of a multitude of demands and desires. In addition to design concerns and conceptual considerations, these typically also include dimensional specifications and parameters that are factored into the design task.

Planning processes must take into account a multitude of demands and desires. In addition to design concerns and conceptual considerations, dimensional specifications and parameters often become part of the design task. These can be a source of inspiration – a starting point for how to particularize a design – and can also be integrated, through an assessment process, in the intended concept. In both cases, an interplay of necessity and exclusion, of logical consequences and inevitable contradictions comes about. Compensating these and finding the optimal balance is the task of the planner.

Almost every design process is accompanied by a multitude of dimensional specifications and parameters. These frequently have an undeniable impact on the spatial or formative design. And for the subsequent use of an outdoor facility, they ensure it will be functional and safe. The sooner that relevant aspects are included in the planning process, the better they can be integrated into a design idea. Subsequent efforts to make modifications can be avoided that way, as can planning deficiencies.

Elements in Landscape is an extract of the reference work *Planning Landscape,* newly conceived in a handy format as a tool and planning aid that provides assistance in the process of designing landscape architecture.

Inasmuch as pertinent governmental regulations exist, the data presented is based on the applicable European or international regulations. For topics that are subject to varied regulations at a national level, German standards and legislation are taken as the basis. In individual cases, these are supplemented by the regulations of other countries.

Since stipulations can also differ at the regional or local level, it is not always possible to make generally applicable statements. In such cases, the information presented here should be taken as guidelines.

The use of plants, which is an extensive field of study in itself, can only receive limited treatment

within the framework of this book. An emphasis is given here to woody plants and to the use of plants in relation to built structures.

2 Human Measure

Almost every design project addressed by planners is based in some way on human measure. This can pertain to people and their proportions – human scale – as well as the aspects of sensory and social perception. Whereas human dimensions modulate the form of the individual object, the parameters of visual and auditory perception constitute a basis for the formation of space.

2.1 Basic Human Measurements

Because the basic measurements that serve as an initial aid for planning can only express average values for human dimensions and other measures, they should also be applied creatively and consciously. For the dimensioning of spaces for play and physical activity or the design of seating, these measurements represent basic standard values for reference, which can be modified as needed by taking the expected use into account.

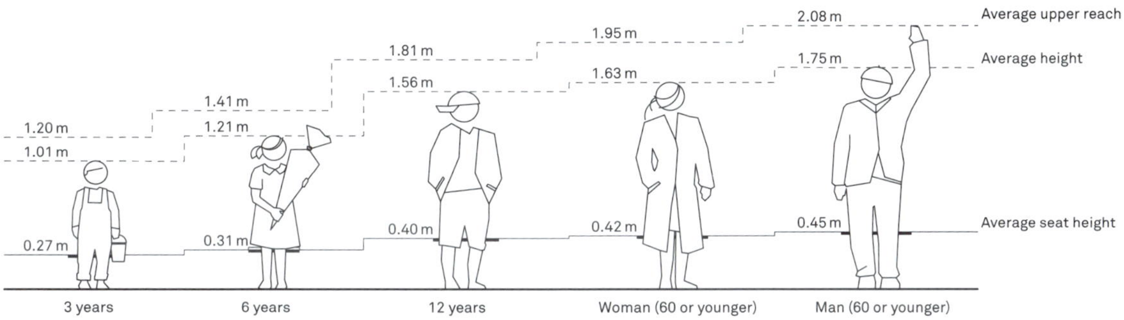

Figure 2.1 Human scale – heights of different age groups

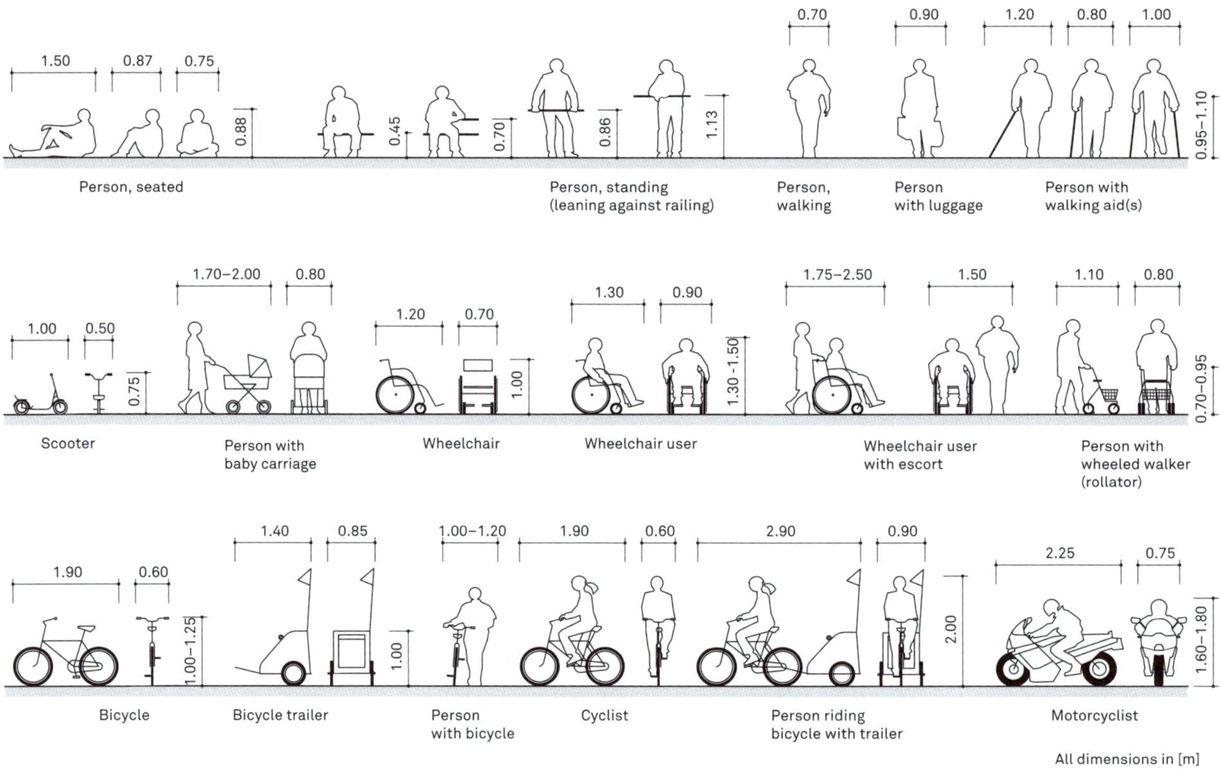

Figure 2.2 Dimensions of traffic participants (without maneuvering space)

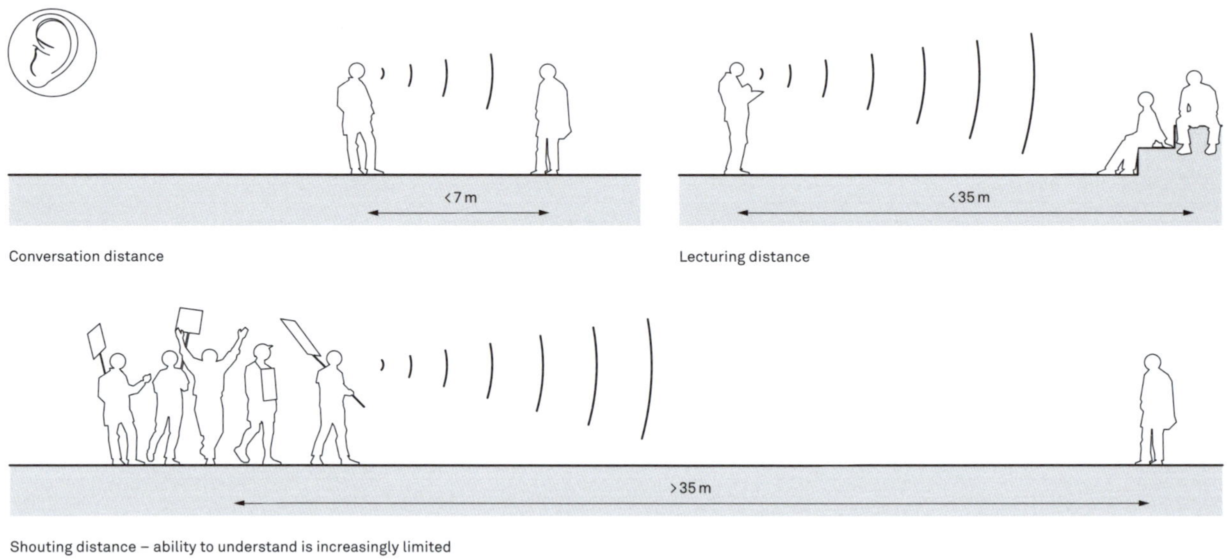

Figure 2.3 Distance of perception – hearing (Source: Jan Gehl, *Life Between Buildings*, 1987)

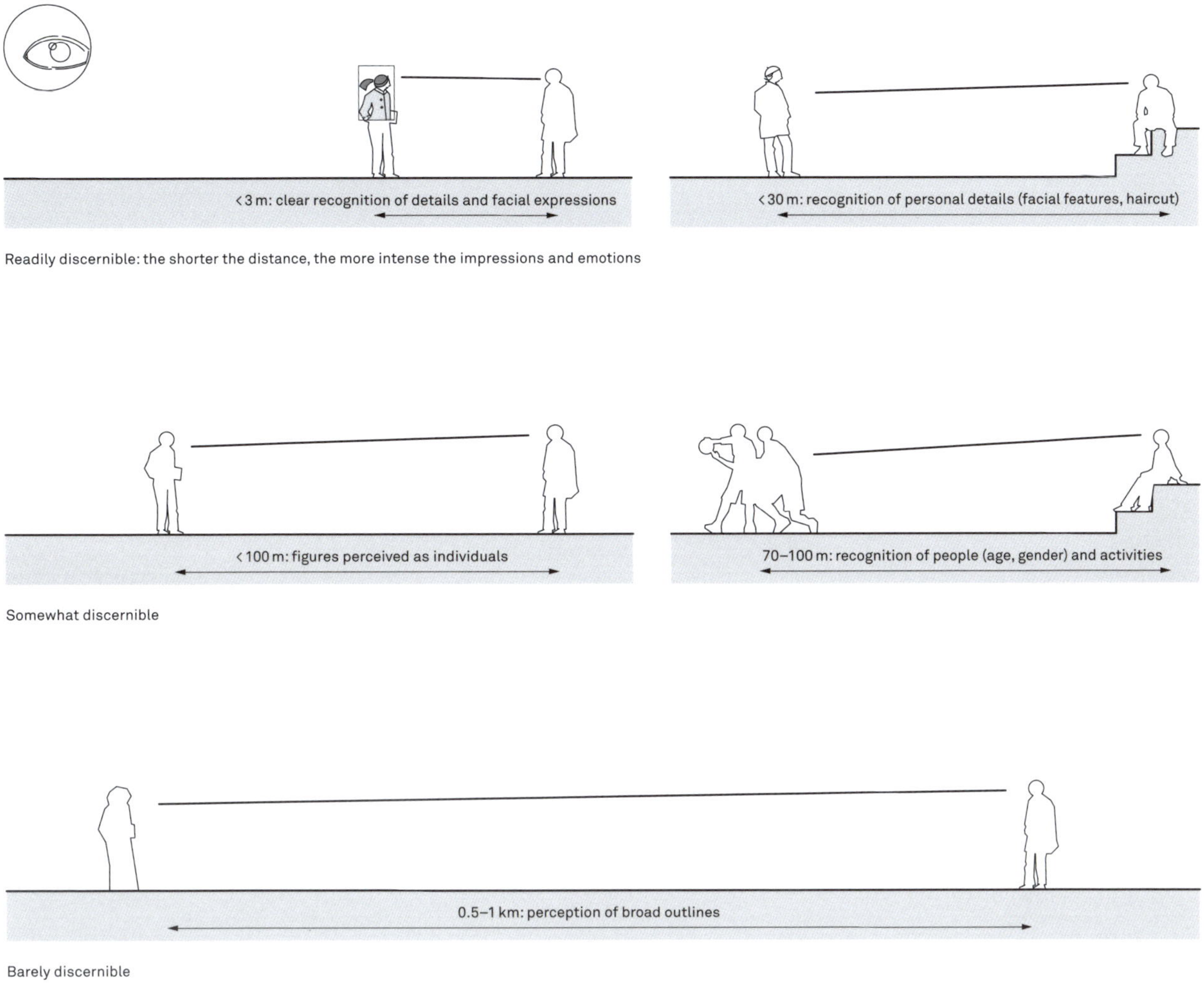

Figure 2.4 Distance of perception – hearing (Source: Jan Gehl, *Life Between Buildings,* 1987)

2.2 Quantifying Need

For the planning of open spaces, there are no high-level statutory requirements for the size and quantity of particular green spaces.

How much open space does a person need? Standard values can offer guidance when planning, but they can seldom replace a precise determination of requirements.

While also taking into account any possible local regulations, the following requirement figures can be used as recommended standard values.

Open space/reference value	Standard value/requirements	Minimum size	Remarks
Generally accessible public open spaces			
Parks/green spaces • Local (serves nearby residents)	 6 m²/resident [a] 3.5–4 m²/resident [b]	 1 ha 2,000 m² 5,000 m² (Berlin)	 • Maximum 500 m walking distance
• Serves entire residential area	3–6 m²/resident [b]	10,000 m²	• Small parks, urban green spaces, youth playgrounds • Especially children's playgrounds, open spaces in apartment complexes, and tenant gardens
• Neighborhood	7 m²/resident	10 ha	• Community park, 1,000 m walking distance
• District-level	7–8 m²/resident [b]	5 ha	• District parks, parts of green corridors
• Regional	7 m²/resident	75 ha	• District park, up to 5 km away via public transit
Parks	6–7 m²/resident [c] 8 m²/resident for 0.2 FAR ≤15 m²/resident for 1 FAR	2–25 ha [b] (*urban greenery* 0.5 ha; *urban garden* 0.1–0.2 ha)	
Purpose-related public open spaces			
Total requirement for play and sports areas • Up to 2,500 residents • 2,500–10,000 residents • Over 10,000 residents • District-level	4 m²/resident (D) 3.5 m²/resident (A) 5 m²/resident 3.5 m²/resident 2.5 m²/resident 3.5 m²/resident [b]	6 ha	• Net area = area usable for sports • District sports facility (example)
Sports fields	6 m²/resident (gross area) [a]		• Relative to the entire metropolitan area; sports areas excluding gymnasiums
Gymnasiums (indoor facilities)	0.2 m²/resident (net area) [c]		
Outdoor swimming pools/ bathing waters	1 m²/resident [a] or 0.05–0.15 m² water surface per resident [c]		• Relative to the entire metropolitan area; public and private pools
Play areas in general (DIN 18034) • Local, within detached development • Local, within attached development • Neighborhood • Regional		 500 m² 5,000 m² For large-scale, near-natural areas up to 10,000 m² 10,000 m²	• Areas usually comprise multiple play areas

Table 2.1 Standard values for urban open spaces (per area, resident, or dwelling unit)
(Sources: [a] Landschaftsprogramm HH [Hamburg landscape program], 1997 [b] Gälzer 2001/City of Vienna [c] Richter 1981)

Open space/reference value	Standard value/requirements	Minimum size	Remarks
Play areas for children to age 5 or 6	Minimum 30 m² [b] 0.75 m²/resident 0.5 m²/resident (net area) 60–225 m² gross area 40–50 m² usable play area [c]		
Play areas for children from ages 6 to 12	Minimum 500 m² [b] 0.75 m²/resident 0.5 m²/resident (net area) [c] 675–1,200 m² gross area		
Play areas for youth age 12 and older	0.75 m²/resident 0.5 m²/resident (net area) 800–3,750 m² gross area 1 m²/resident (average) [c]		
Play areas for adults	1.5 m²/resident		
Cemetery areas	5 m²/resident 3.5–5 m²/resident		• Relative to the entire metropolitan area; public and sectarian cemeteries
Parking	1 parking space per 1.1–1.2 dwellings		
Semipublic and semiprivate open spaces			
Schoolyards	5 m²/student (excluding sports areas)	–	–
Preschools, daycare centers, orphanages	Minimum 600 m² usable area; grass-covered area min. 300 m², hard-surfaced playing area min. 200 m², 10 m²/child [b]		• Boundary enclosure 1.5 m high
Retirement homes	0.45–0.5 m²/resident [c]		
Hospitals	0.8–1.2 m²/resident or 80–150 m² per bed 1–1.7 m²/resident [c]		
Allotment gardens	1 allotment garden for each 7–10 dwelling units with no garden of their own 1 allotment garden per 7 dwelling units for apartments 2.8 m²/resident for 0.2 FAR, up to 15 m²/resident for 1 FAR; 10–17 m²/resident [c]	320 m²; Facility: 1.8–4.5 ha	• Maximum size: 400 m² (D) 650 m² (A)
Gross residential land	70–150 m²/resident		
Net residential land	45–75 m²/resident		
Children's play and recreation areas on residential lots			
Playgrounds for small children (to age 5)	2 m²/dwelling [a]	30 m²	• As per Hamburg building code (HBauO) for buildings with 3–5 dwelling units on the premises
Children's play and recreation areas	10 m²/dwelling [a]	150 m²	• As per Hamburg building code (HBauO) for buildings with more than 5 dwelling units on the premises; incl. playground for small children (30 m²), on the property or nearby

Table 2.1 (Continuation) Standard values for urban open spaces (per area, resident, or dwelling unit)
(Sources: [a] Landschaftsprogramm HH [Hamburg landscape program], 1997 [b] Gälzer 2001/City of Vienna [c] Richter 1981)

Standard width [m]	Options for use & design
3–5 m	Path
5–10 m	Path + planting
10–30 m	Path + road + planting; path + grass; path + seating; ball court (lengthwise) + planting; promenade + trees
30–100 m	Children's playground, lawn for play and sunbathing, small sports facility, possibly an allotment garden site
100–500 m	Play and sports facility, allotment garden site, cemetery, urban gardens of all types, green corridors with recreation facilities
500–1,000 m	Sports stadium, cemetery, amusement park, public park, bodies of water, woods, orchards, open-air gardening, and special facilities, e.g., equestrian sports, zoo
>1,000 m	Horticulture, arable fields and pastures, woods, recreational areas (landscape portions)

Table 2.2 Standard widths of green connections and green corridors (Source: Gälzer, 2001)

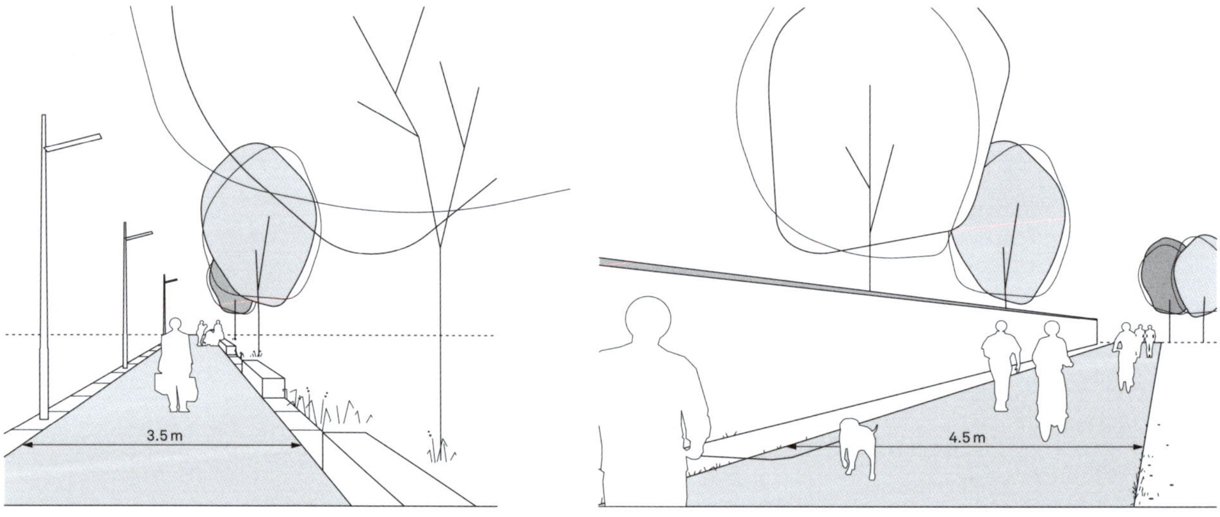

Figure 2.5 Exemplary widths of green connections

Green connection with walkway and play area at the side

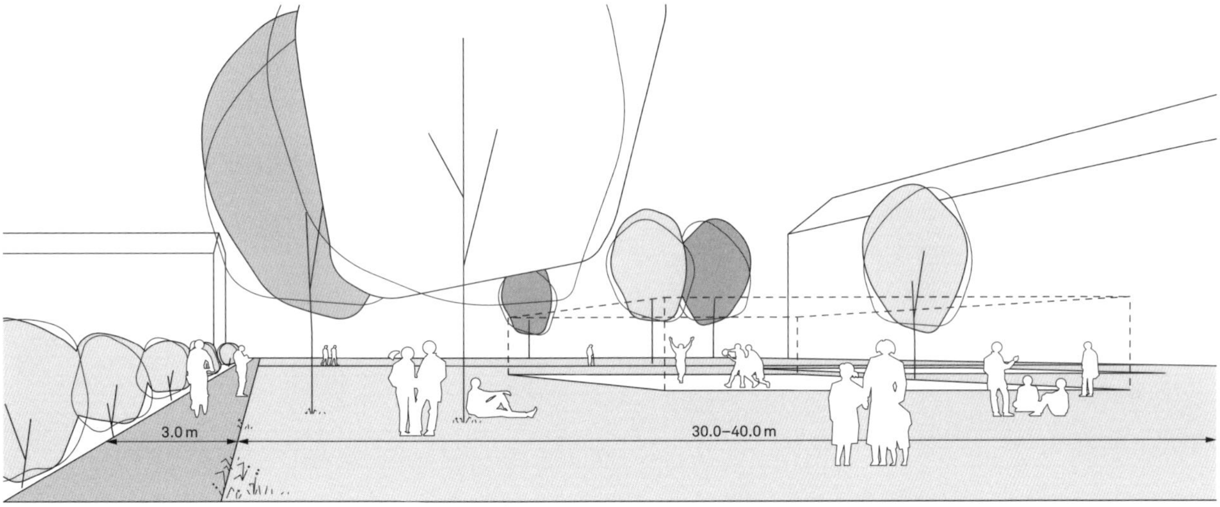

Green connection with walkway and small sports fields at the sides

3 Topography

The basis for every design in landscape architecture is an engagement with the existing elevations on the site. Even on flat ground, slight variations in the grading can be required to ensure adequate drainage.

3.1 Grading

The basis for all grading decisions is an exact knowledge of the topographic circumstances. For this purpose, corresponding plans of the existing conditions should be consulted when available.

Existing elevations at specific locations that cannot be modified are restrictions that can affect the planning. These include:

- Elevations within the root zone of existing trees
- Defined elevations along adjacent properties and roads
- Existing and finished elevations of adjacent buildings
- and other structures
- Minimum coverages for existing pipes/ducts as needed (e.g., protection from frost or excessive loading)

Country	Designation	Abbreviation	Gauge datum as reference value
Germany (DHHN92)	Meter über Normalhöhennull* [meters above normal height null]	m. ü. HNH	Amsterdam
Austria	Meter über Adria [meters above Adriatic Sea]	m. ü. Adria	Trieste 1875
Switzerland, Liechtenstein (LN02)	Meter über Meer [meters above sea level]	m. ü. M.	Derived from the tide gauge at Marseille > Datum is a rock outcrop in Lake Geneva known as the Repère Pierre du Niton (373.6 m above the tide gauge at Marseille)
Belgium	meter boven Oostends Peil [meters above Ostend ordnance datum]	m O. P.	Ostend
France (NGF-IGN69)	mètres au-dessus du niveau de la mer [meters above sea level]	m	Marseille
Great Britain	meters above sea level	MASL/m. a. s. l.	Newlyn
Italy	metri sul livello del mare [meters above sea level]	m s. l. m.	Genoa
Netherlands	meter boven/onder NAP [meters above/below Amsterdam Ordnance Datum]	m NAP	Amsterdam
Poland	metry nad poziomem morza [meters above sea level]	m n. p. m.	Braşov
Spain	metros sobre el nivel del mar [meters above sea level]	msnm	Alicante
Czech Republic	metrů nad mořem [meters above sea level]	m n. m.	

* Introduced throughout Germany in 1993 in the course of reunification; before: DHHN12/m ü. TBD (West Germany) and SNN76/m ü. HN (East Germany)

Table 3.1 Official height reference systems in Europe

Wear surface/type of use	Minimum slope	Maximum slope	Remarks	Guidelines
Categorized by surface				
Concrete and asphalt pavement	1.5 %		≥ 2.5 % for roads	
Pavers of precast concrete or fired brick	2.5 %	–	Cross slope	DIN 18318
Cobblestones and other natural stone paving blocks	3 %			
Slabs of concrete or natural stone	2 %			
Water-bound and other unbound paving	3 % (2 %)	5 %		
Permeable paving (pavers with gravel or grass joints, grass paving blocks, etc.)	1 %	5 %		FLL guideline "begrünbare Flächenbefestigungen" [Greenable surface pavements]
Categorized by use				
Public access roads (up to 50 km/h), longitudinal slopes	–	8 % (12 %)		RASt 06
at road intersections	–	4 %		
Cross slope of public roadways				
Concrete and asphalt pavements	2.5 %	Typically 5 %	If cross slope cannot be maintained: drainage gradient ≥ 2 %	RAS-Ew*
Stone paving	3 %		If cross slope cannot be maintained: drainage gradient ≥ 3 %	
Ramps and approaches to garages and parking spaces	–	15 % (short ramps maximum 20 %)	At changes in slope with a difference of 8 % or more, a flat or curved transition is required Ramp cross slopes should be avoided (maximum 2 % for drainage)	EAR 05
Walkways, longitudinal slope	–	12 % (15 %)	On short sections: 15 %, maximum 20 %; alternatively or in addition: ramp stairs	
Walkways, cross slope	–	Typically 2.5 %		EFA 02
Bikeways, longitudinal slope	–	6 % (5 % for wear surfaces without binding agents)	Greater width needed; with more than 3 % slope, an asymmetric division of the cross section is expedient	ERA 10
Bikeways, cross slope	2.5 %	≤ 4 %	With low planarity the cross slope of 2.5 % should be increased to 3 %	ERA 10
Paths for inline skaters, longitudinal slope	–	12 %	Longer distances with slopes ≥ 3 % will already limit the performance of inexperienced skaters	Deutsche Verkehrswacht e.V.
Accessible paths and paved spaces, longitudinal slope	–	≤ 3 %	≤ 8 % is also possible on short segments	DIN 18040-1
		≤ 4 %	4 % over maximum length	DIN 18040-1
		≤ 6 %	One intermediate landing with maximum 3 % slope at least every 10 m	DIN 18040-1

* ERA: *Empfehlungen für Radverkehrsanlagen* [Recommendations for cycling facilities]; RAS-Ew: *Richtlinie für die Anlage von Straßen – Teil: Entwässerung* [Directive for the construction of roads: Drainage]

Table 3.2 Recommended minimum and maximum slopes as functions of surface and use

Wear surface/type of use	Minimum slope	Maximum slope	Remarks	Guidelines
Accessible paths, cross slope	–	≤2%	Acc. to DIN 18040-1 ≤2.5%; maximum 6% at driveway approaches to lots; no cross slope on ramp runs	DIN 18024-1 & 18040-1
Seating areas, esp. with tables (e.g., terraces)	1%	2%		
Sports fields	0.5%	1%	With clay/artificial turf surfacing ≥0.8%	DIN 18035-4
Tennis courts	0.5%	0.5%		DIN 18035-5
Grass playing fields	1%	5%		
Lawns	1%	–		
Grass embankments in outdoor facilities	–	33%		

* ERA: *Empfehlungen für Radverkehrsanlagen* [Recommendations for cycling facilities]; RAS-Ew: *Richtlinie für die Anlage von Straßen – Teil: Entwässerung* [Directive for the construction of roads: Drainage]

Table 3.2 (Continuation) Recommended minimum and maximum slopes as functions of surface and use

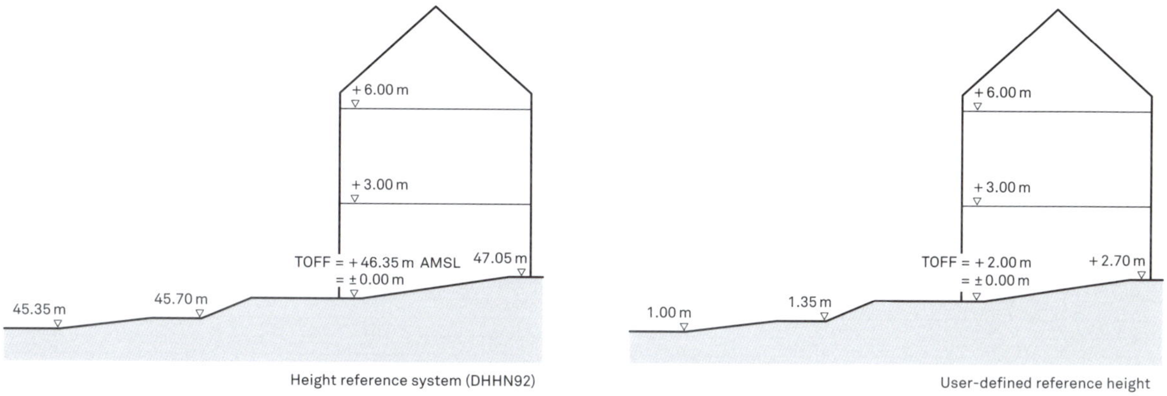

Figure 3.1 Finished elevations based on a height reference system and user-defined datum

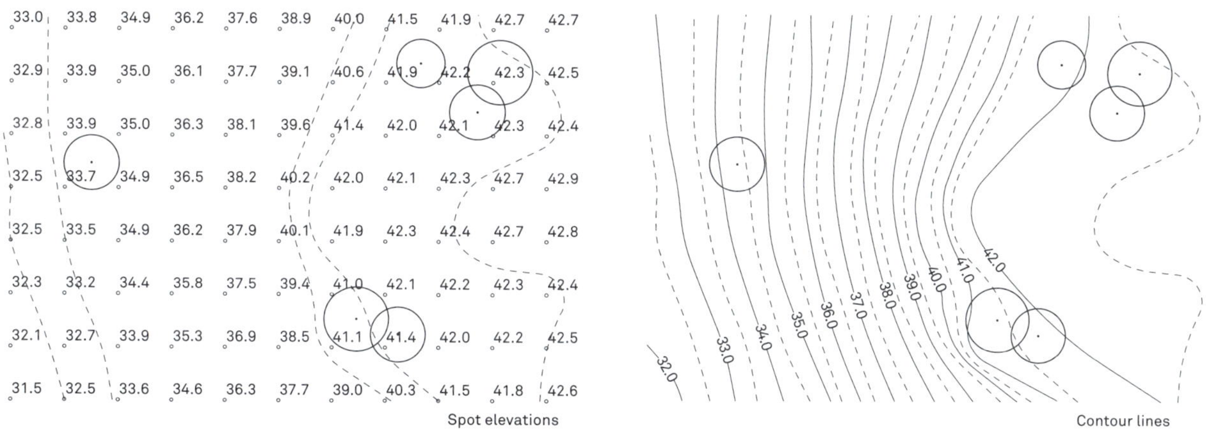

Figure 3.2 Representation of the terrain conditions using spot elevations, contour lines, and a contour model

3.2 Drainage

The goal of drainage planning is to drain stormwater away from path surfaces as quickly as possible and to divert it away from buildings.

Paved surfaces in particular must be designed for direct drainage of stormwater in order to ensure that they can be used safely regardless of the weather and to prevent damage from occurring to existing buildings due to water infiltration. On hilly as well as flat terrain, this circumstance places high demands on the planning, hence it should be taken into account from the very beginning.

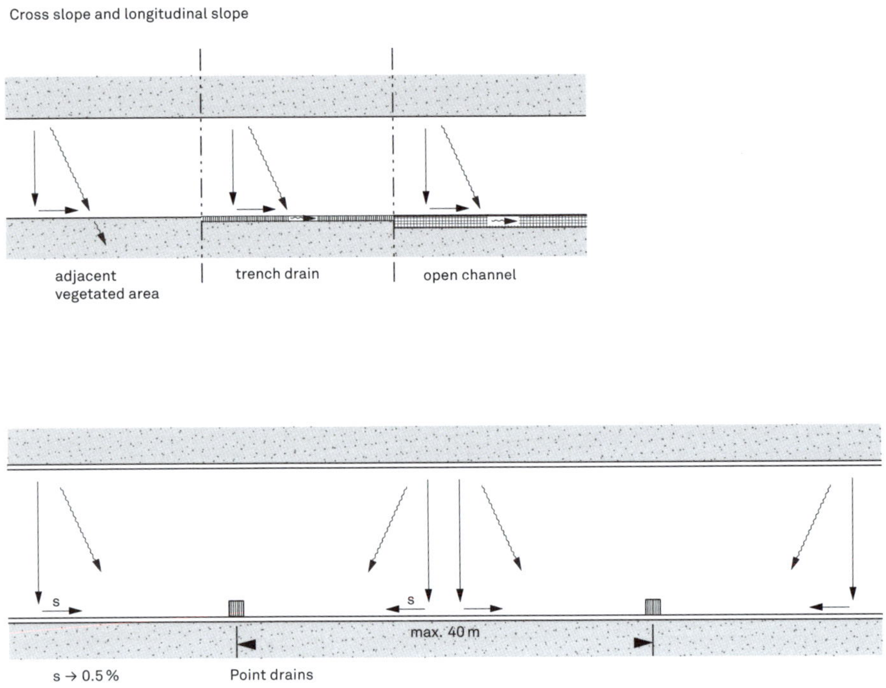

Figure 3.3 Examples of linear drainage

3.2 Drainage

Cross slope

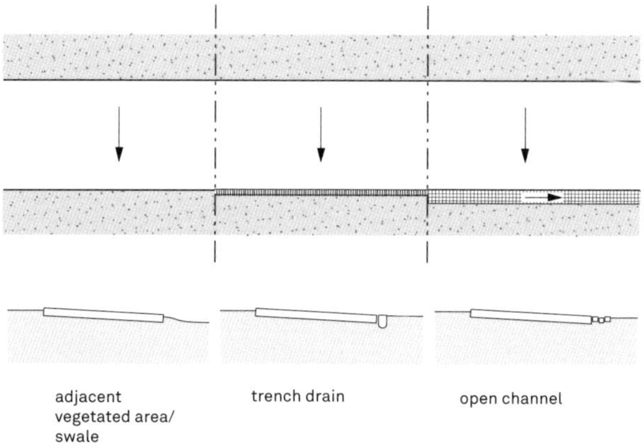

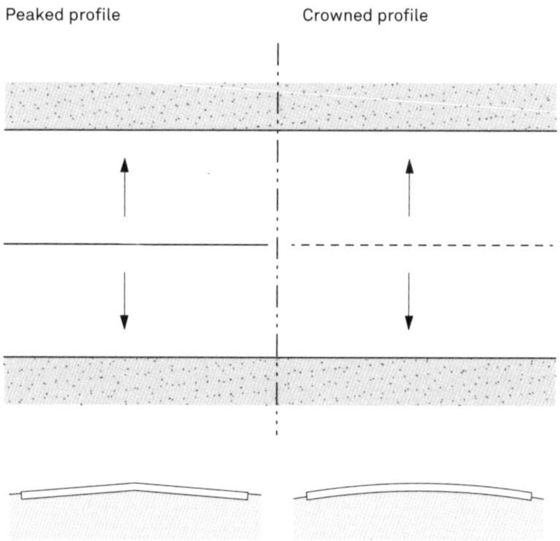

Longitudinal slope

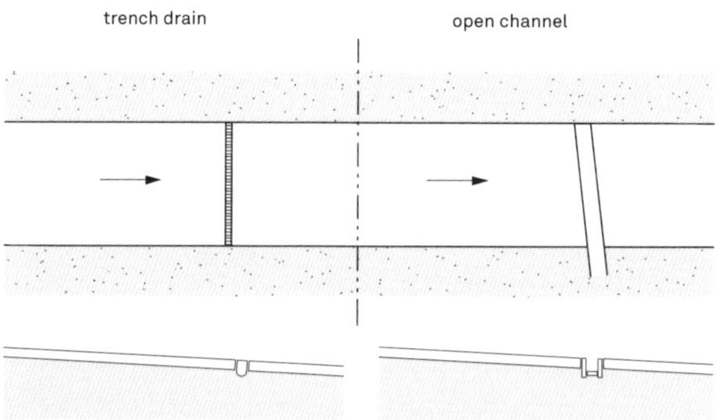

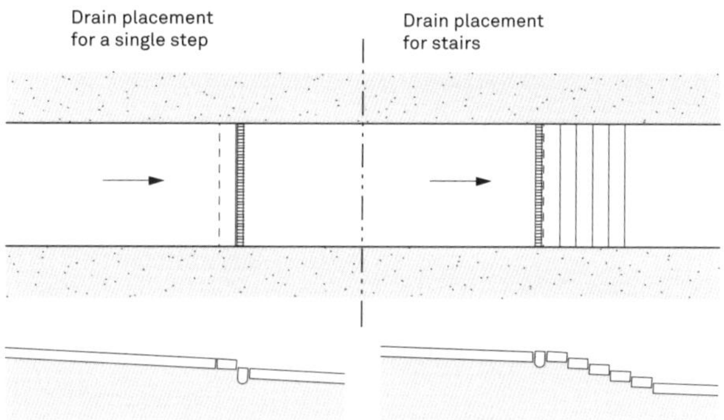

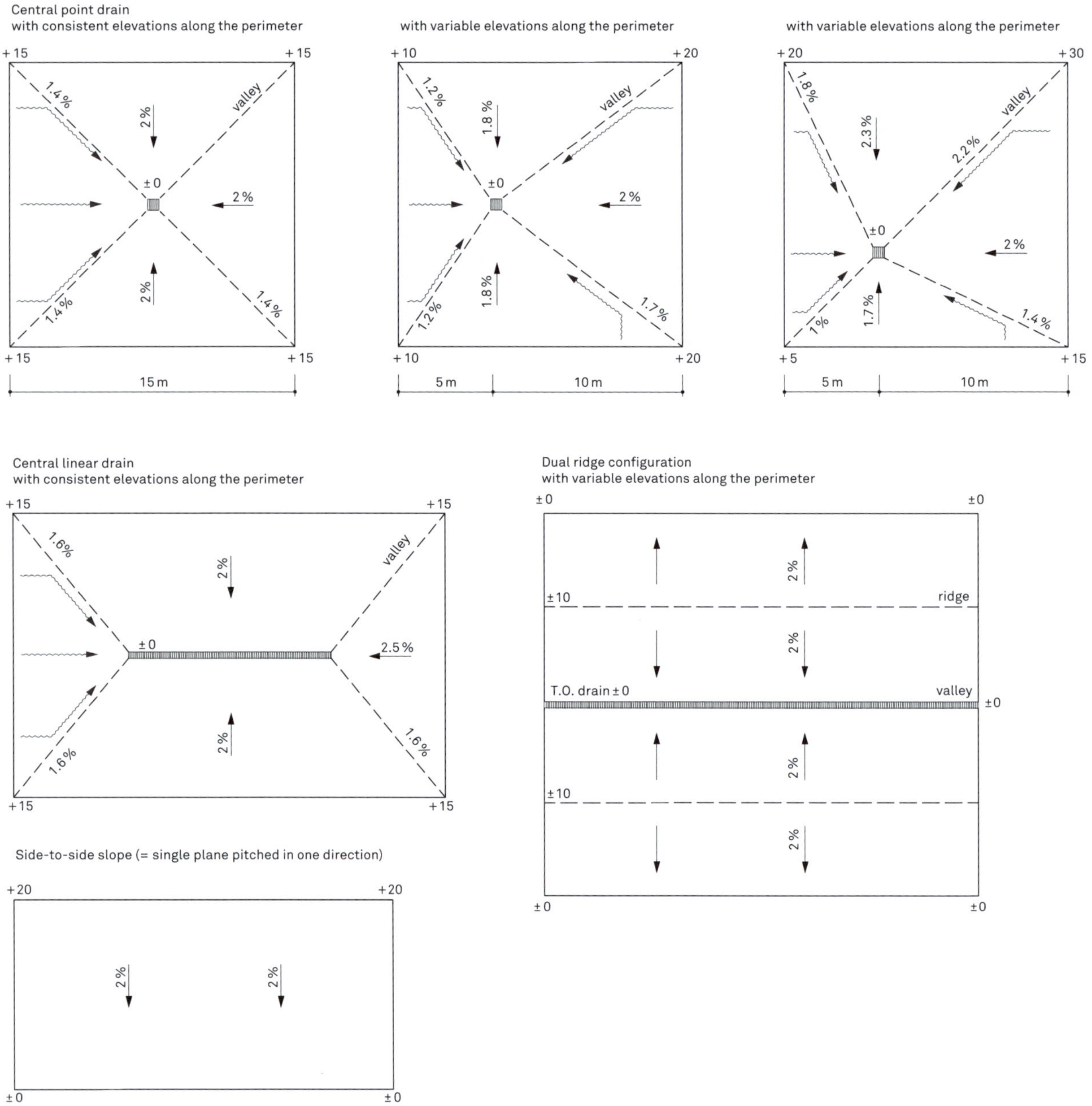

Figure 3.4 Exemplary drainage patterns for plazas and sports fields

3.2 Drainage

Hipped configuration
with consistent elevations along the perimeter

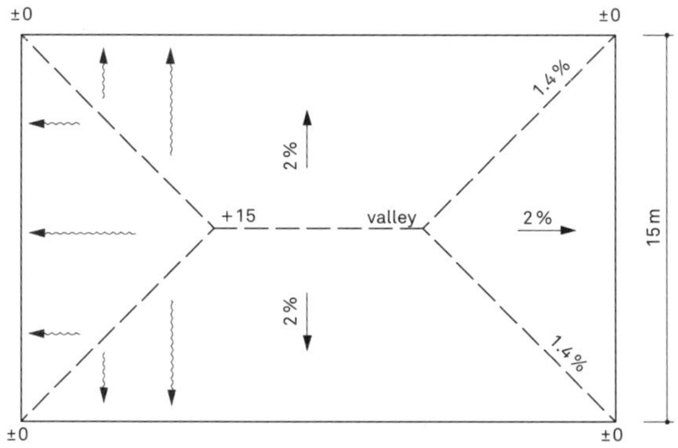

with variable elevations along the perimeter

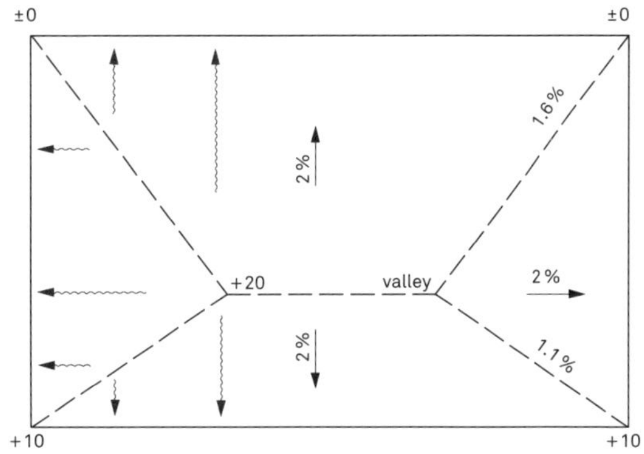

Football pitch with hipped configuration

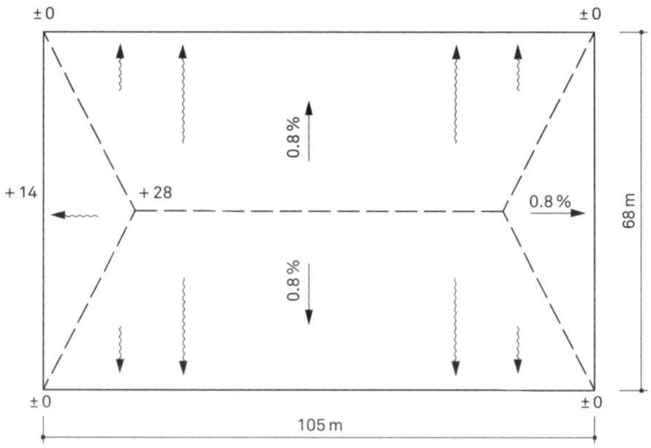

Grass soccer field with traditional central (longitudinal) crown

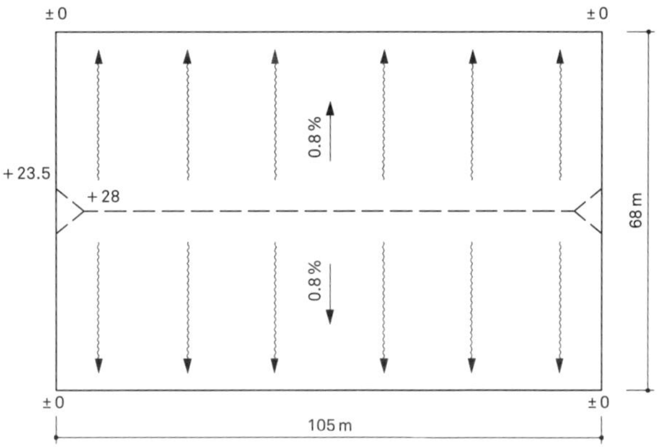

Tennis court, treshing floor with side-to-side slope

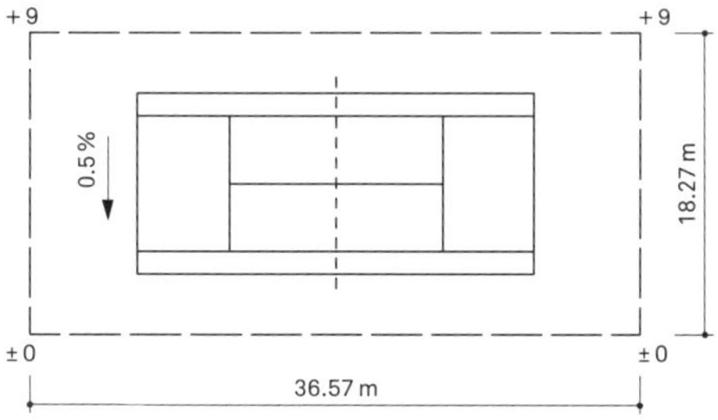

4 Circulation

Requirements for paths and circulation areas are derived from the nature and frequency of their use and must, in addition, be adapted to their specific location, whether in a garden, park, supra-regional green corridor, or alongside public roadways. When planning public open spaces, it is particularly important to take into account the needs of pedestrian and bicycle traffic, including people with reduced mobility. In public spaces, on private access roads, and in parking lots, motorized traffic poses unique demands that must be accommodated through functional design that also pays regard to pertinent regulations (including road traffic regulations such as Germany's Road Traffic Ordinance, the StVO).

For roads, prime importance is given to the functional separation of lanes for different means of transport, such as pedestrian, bicycle, and private motor vehicle traffic as well as public transit, with parallel areas.

4.1 Walk- and Bikeways

When designing pedestrian paths that give access to parks and green spaces, many different path widths can result from varied functions and the anticipated frequency of use. Specific requirements apply to sidewalks that are adjacent to roadways.

The accessible design of walkways encompasses diverse measures. To facilitate a person's orientation along their path, tactile paving surfaces in contrasting colors should be used to structure the walkway. Additionally, the main circulation route must be designed to be free of obstacles. In addition, the design of pedestrian crossings with depressed curbs and tactile paving surface indicators is of major importance. Separated crossing points take advantage of differentiated curb heights. Curb heights of 6 cm and more constitute a clear boundary between sidewalk and roadway.

When designing bikeways, a distinction is made between on-road bikeways, which follow the roadway, and off-road bikeways (e.g., separately routed in parks or as bike trails, and also running parallel to the road but separated from it by a median). The path width is determined by two factors: whether the path carries one- or two-way traffic; and its frequency of use.

With 500 motor vehicles/hour on roadway widths up to 6 m or with 800–1,000 motor vehicles/hour on roadways that are 7 m wide, bicycle traffic can be accommodated directly on the roadway. On two-lane roads, however, designated advisory bike lanes should be incorporated for bicycle traffic (lane as separately marked area of the roadway).

When bikeways are situated in the roadside space, they are to be distinctly differentiated from the walkway by means of 0.3 m wide delineator strips (with tactile and visual contrast). Bikeways adjacent to the roadway are preferably designed for one-way traffic. The safety clearances presented in **Table 4.4** can also be applied analogously to pedestrian traffic. The Guideline for Rural Road Construction (RLW 75/88) specifies a minimum width of 1 m for bikeways, and 1.6 m with two-way traffic. For high-traffic bike trails, widths from 2 m to 2.5 m must be chosen to establish a balance of comfort, safety, and minimal disturbance of the traffic participants.

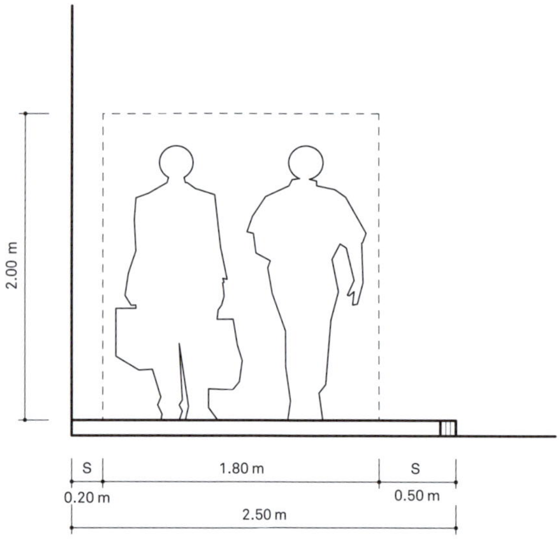

Figure 4.1 Standard width of a roadside space (as per RASt 06)

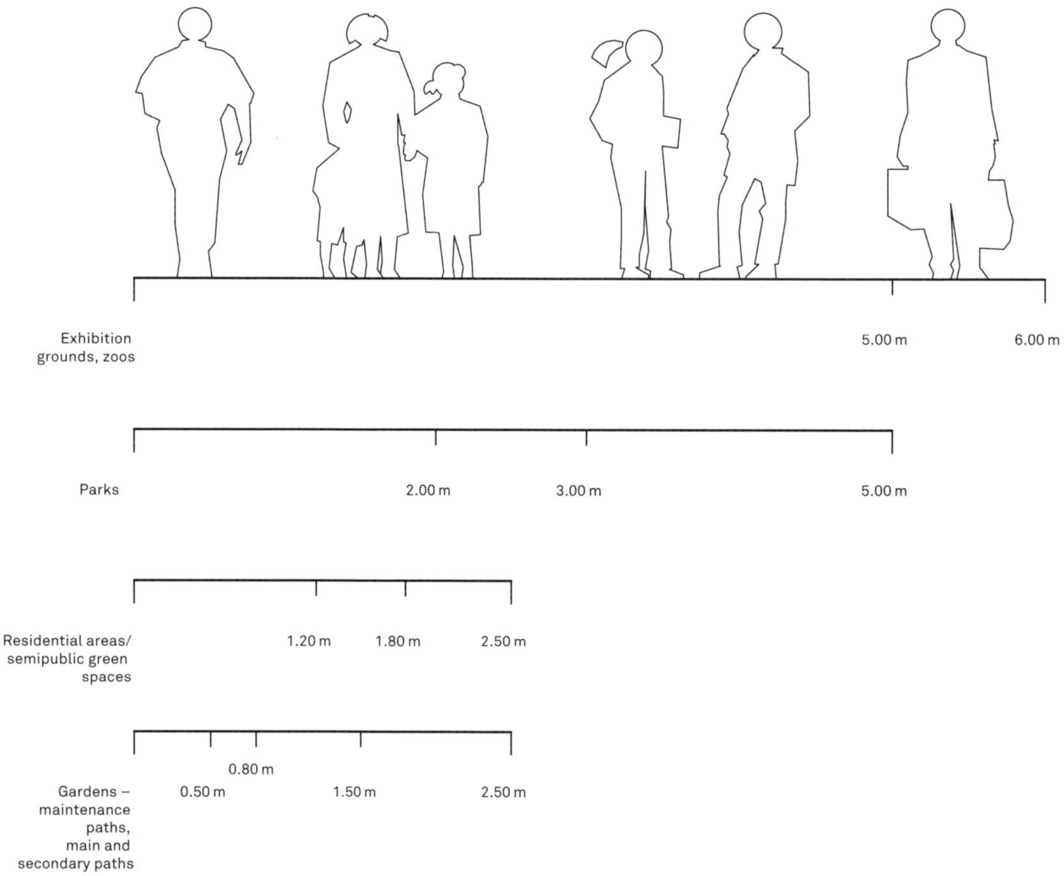

Figure 4.2 Space requirements for walkways

Category/function	Width (standard values)
Gardens	
Main paths	1.5–2.5 m
Secondary paths	0.8–1.5 m
Maintenance paths, not barrier-free	0.5 m
Access to public and semipublic buildings / semipublic green spaces / residential areas	
Main paths	1.8–2.5 m
Secondary paths	1.2–1.8 m
Parks	
Main paths (including shared use by bicycle traffic)	3–5 m
Secondary paths	2–3 m
Exhibition grounds, zoos	
Main paths	5–6 m

Table 4.1 Guideline values for path widths in outdoor facilities

Roadside space requirements	Space required
Standard width for walkways	2.5 m
plus ...	**+**
Areas for children's play	≥2 m
Spaces for lingering in front of store windows	≥1 m
Median strip without trees	≥1 m
Median strip with trees	≥2–2.5 m
Benches	≥1 m
Waiting areas at bus stops	≥2.5 m
Display shelves in front of stores	1.5 m
Parking spaces for two-wheeled vehicles Parking angle 90°/100 gon Parking angle 45°/50 gon	 2 m 1.5 m
Vehicle overhang with rows of perpendicular or angled parking	0.7 m

Table 4.2 Standard values for the additional space required in roadside space due to special requirements and uses (as per RASt 06)

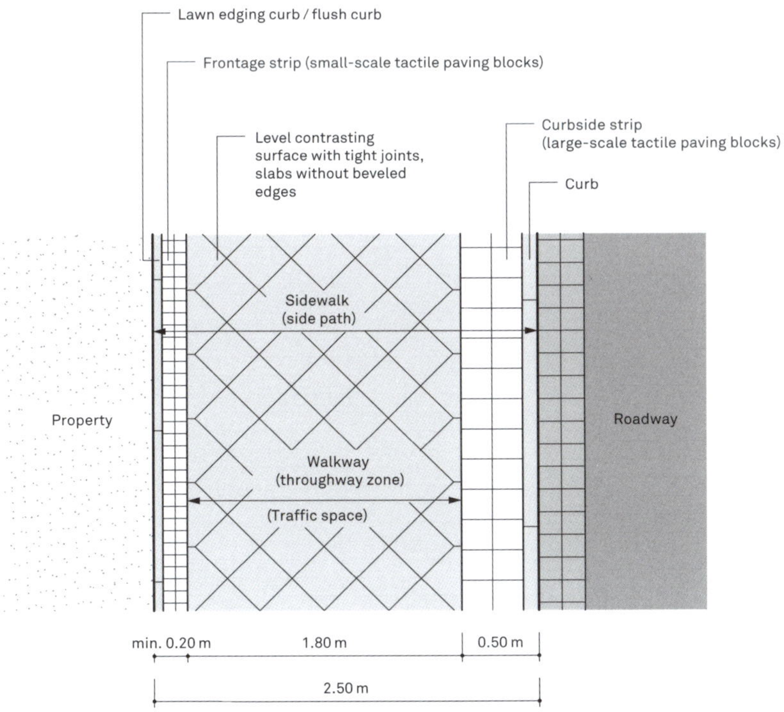

Figure 4.3 Tactile and visually tangible sidewalks

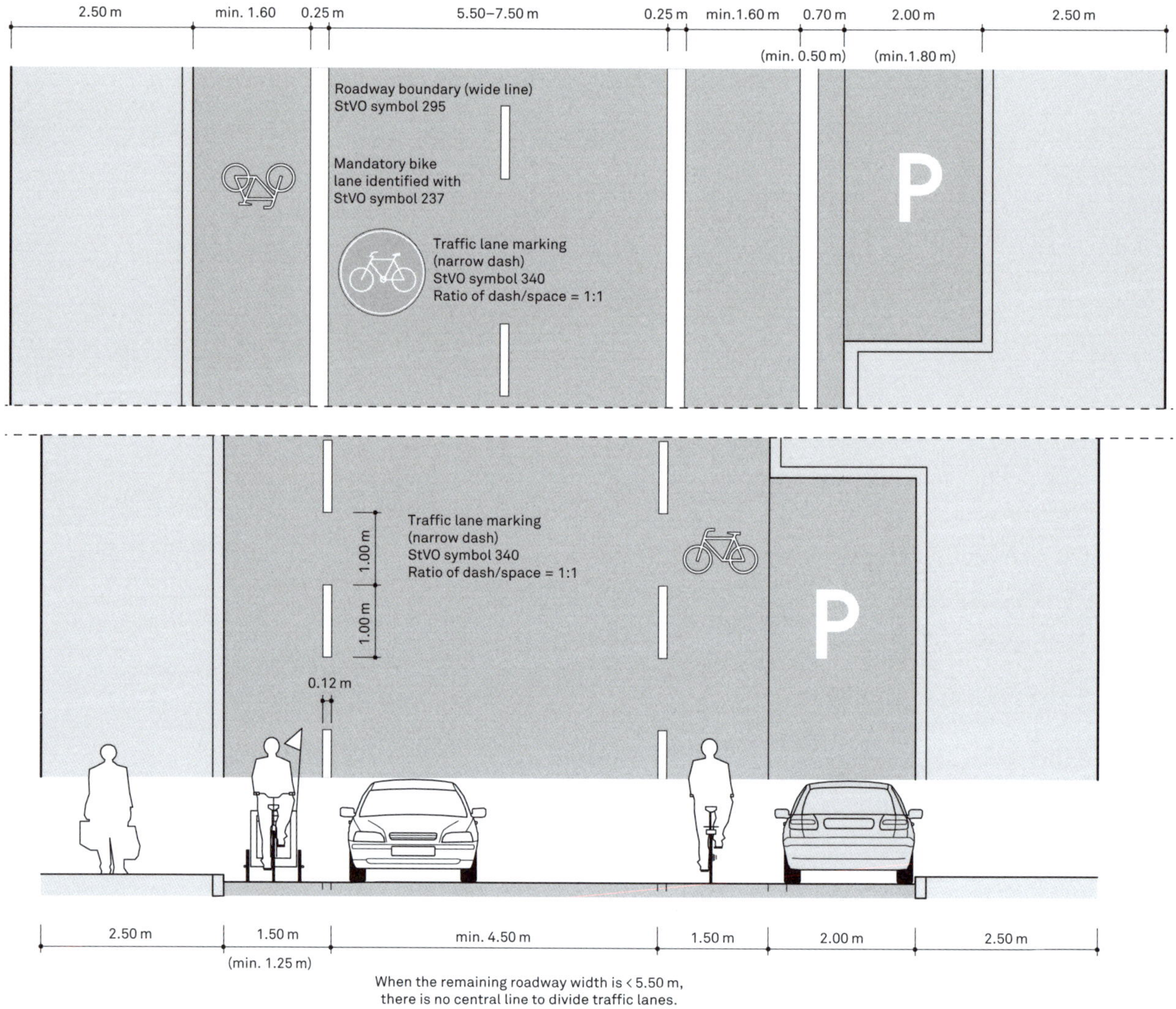

Figure 4.4 Arrangement of advisory bike lanes (multipurpose lanes in Austria) and mandatory bike lanes for bicycle traffic on the roadway

Facility type	Path width	Width of dividing strip		
		Along roadway	Along parallel parking spaces	Along angled/perpendicular parking spaces
On the roadway				
Advisory bike lane	1.50 m (minimum 1.25 m)	–	Safety clearance: 0.25–0.50 m (no markings required)	Safety clearance: 0.75 m
Mandatory bike lane	1.85 m (incl. markings)	–	0.50–0.75 m (marked as continuous strip)	0.75 m (marked as continuous strip)
Adjacent to the roadway				
One-way bikeway	2.00 m (1.60 m*)	0.50 m (can include overhang strip)	0.75 m	1.10 m (can include overhang strip)
Two-way bikeways on both sides	2.50 m (2.00 m*)	0.75 m (at permanent fixtures or with high traffic volume)		
Two-way bikeway on one side	3.00 m (2.50 m*)			
Shared pedestrian and cycle path (within built-up areas)	≥2.50 m (dependent on pedestrian and bicycle traffic volume, see **Table 4.8**)			
Shared pedestrian and cycle path (outside built-up areas)	2.50 m	1.75 m on rural roads		

* for low bicycle traffic volume

Table 4.3 Dimensions of bikeways accompanying roads (per RASt 06)

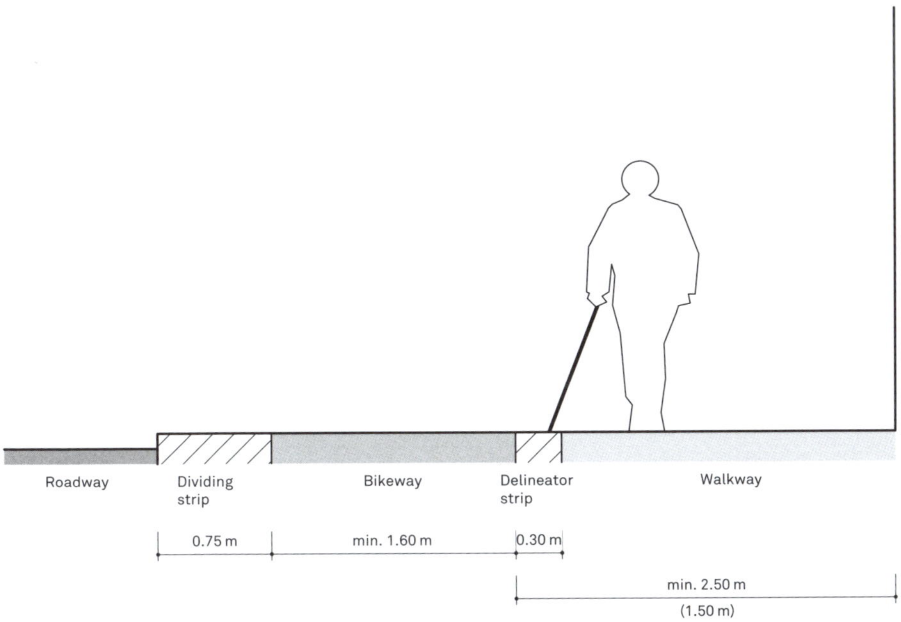

Figure 4.5 Delineator strip between bikeway and walkway

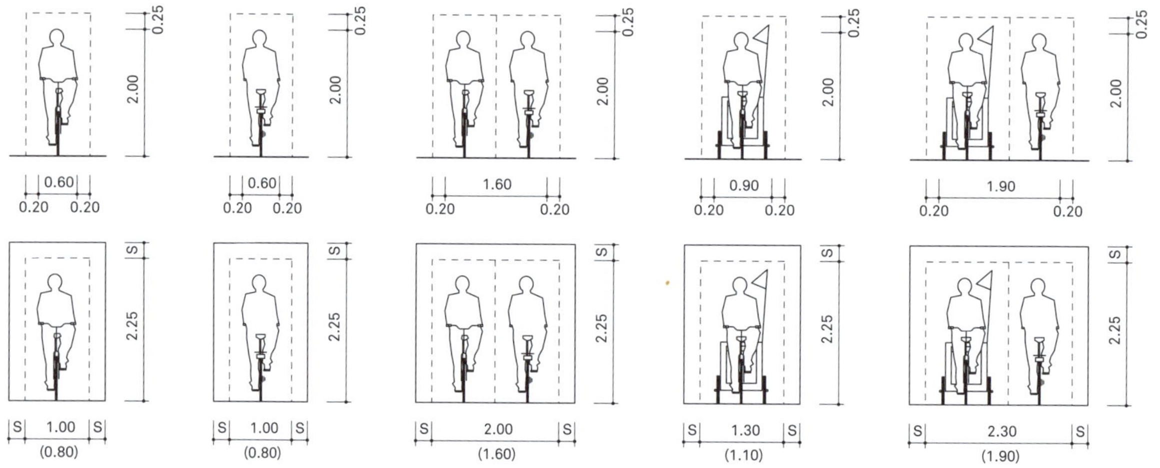

All dimensions in [m]

Figure 4.6 Space requirements for bicycle traffic with and without safety clearance (S)

Bikeway	Independently routed bikeways (per RLW 75/88) Minimum width	Safety clearance
One-way bikeway	1.00 m	Min. 0.25 m to obstacles on each side
Two-way bikeway	1.60 m; for heavily-used routes: 2.00 m and more	Min. 0.25 m to obstacles on each side

Table 4.4 Dimensions of independently routed bikeways (per RLW 75/88)

Minimum curve radius Asphalt/interlocking concrete pavers [in m]	2.5	5	10	15	20	30
Speed (km/h)	10	16	24	28	32	40

Table 4.5 Necessary minimum curve radii for bikeways with a cross slope of 2.5 % as a function of speed

Speed [km/h]	Minimum curve radius [m]		Crest radius min H_K [m]	Sag radius min H_W [m]	Stopping distance with wet surface
	Asphalt/interlocking concrete pavers	Unbound paving			
20	10	15	40	25	15
30	20	35	80	50	25
40	30	70	150	100	40

Table 4.6 Radii and stopping distances as a function of speed for the layout of off-road bikeways

Slope [%]	Max. length of ascending slope	Height difference
12	8.00 m	0.96 m
10	20.00 m	2.00 m
6	65.00 m	3.90 m
5	120.00 m	6.00 m
4	250.00 m	10.00 m
3	> 250.00 m	> 10.00 m

Table 4.7 Acceptable lengths of ascending slopes for bikeways (per ERA 10, supplemented)

Maximum roadside traffic at peak hours*	Necessary width aside from dividing strip
70 (P + C) / h	≥2.5–3 m
100 (P + C) / h	≥3–4 m
150 (P + C) / h	≥4 m

* The number of cyclists should not exceed one-third of the total traffic load.

Table 4.8 Shared pedestrian and cycle paths along streets (Source: RASt 06)

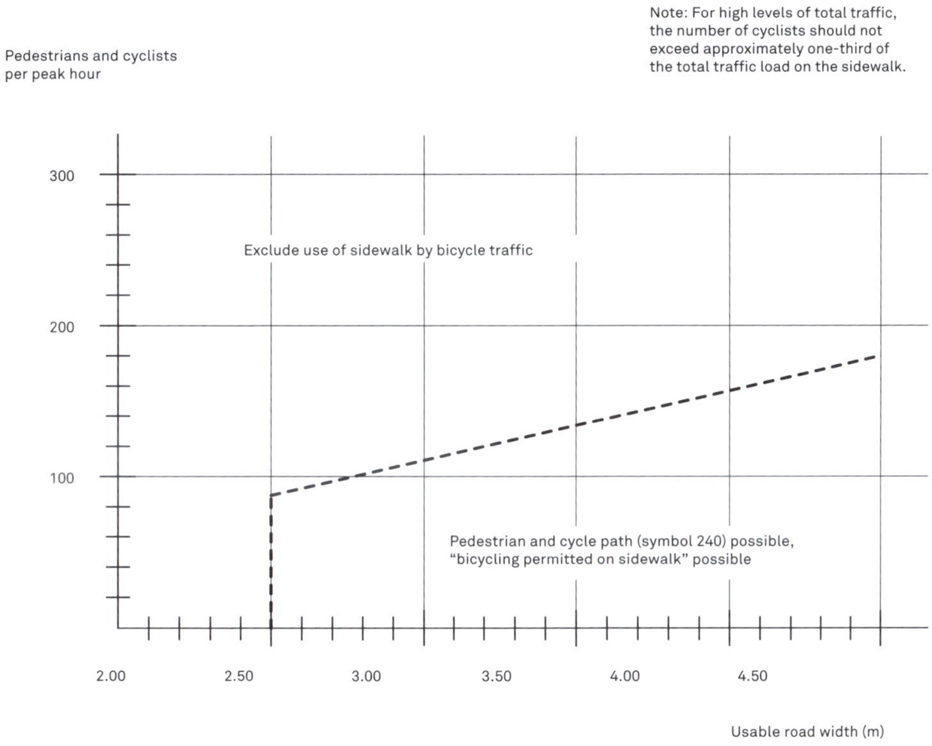

Figure 4.7 Application limits for implementing off-road shared paths for pedestrians and cyclists, in accordance with ERA-R2 recommendations for bicycle facilities

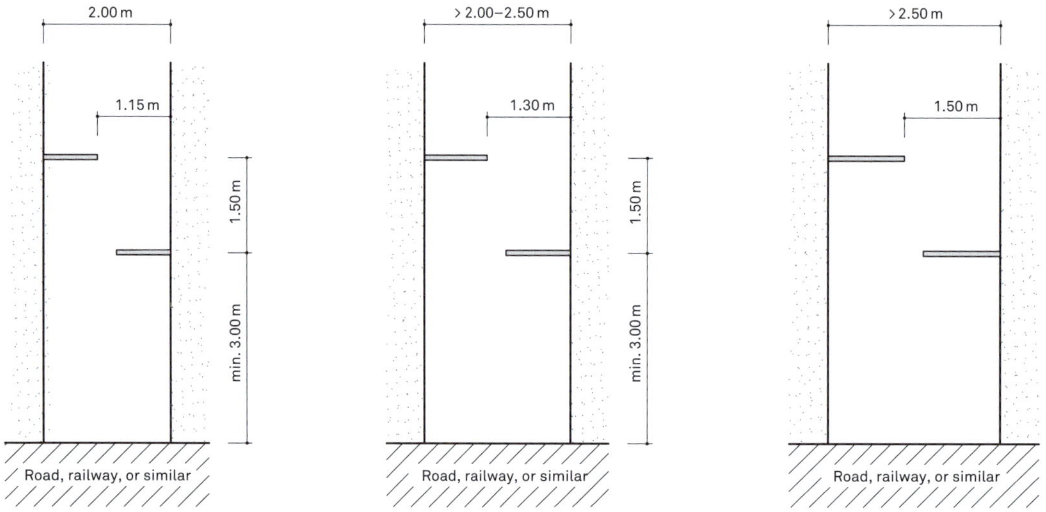

Figure 4.8 Cycle barriers in off-road pedestrian and cycle paths

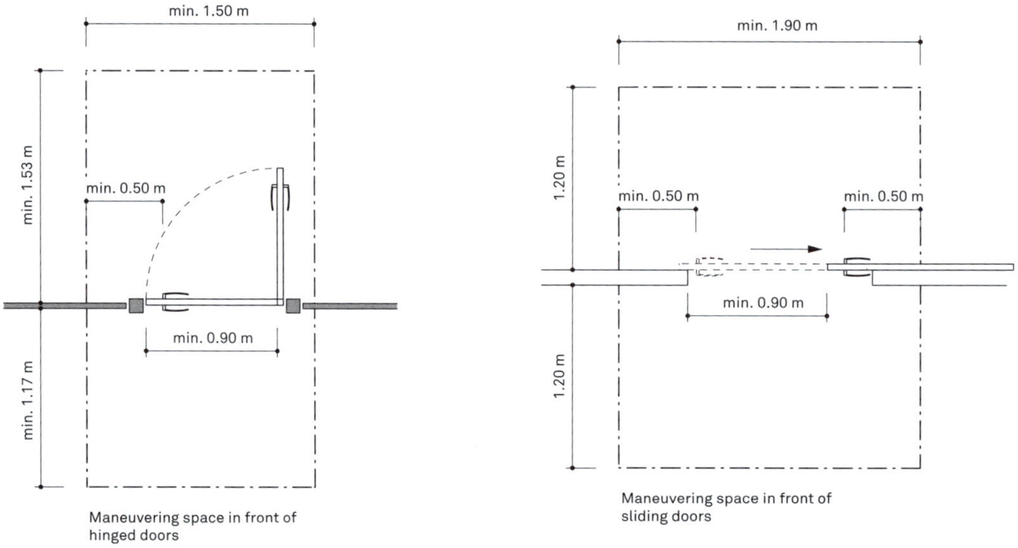

Figure 4.9 Maneuvering spaces in front of doors and gates

4.2 Streets

When designing roads for motorized traffic, a distinction is made between the principles of separation and mixture. When the lanes are physically segregated, one can speak of a separation principle. If, on the other hand, multiple means of transport come together on one and the same roadway surface, one can speak of a mixing principle.

How and in what form the roadway is laid out depends on the traffic volume, any additional presence of public transportation, the routing of bicycle traffic, and functional requirements arising from how the road is used. The dimensioning of the roadway is based upon the traffic spaces and clear spaces of the traffic participants. In Germany, the width of the roadway that is needed is determined in accordance with the "Richtlinien für die Anlage von Stadtstraßen" (RASt 06) [Guidelines for urban road design]. The two-lane roadway covers a wide range of potential motor vehicle traffic volumes.

Depending on the requirements for use and the traffic volume, a combination of the traffic spaces of the various traffic participants, the necessary safety clearances and the roadside spaces result in different cross sections for the street space.

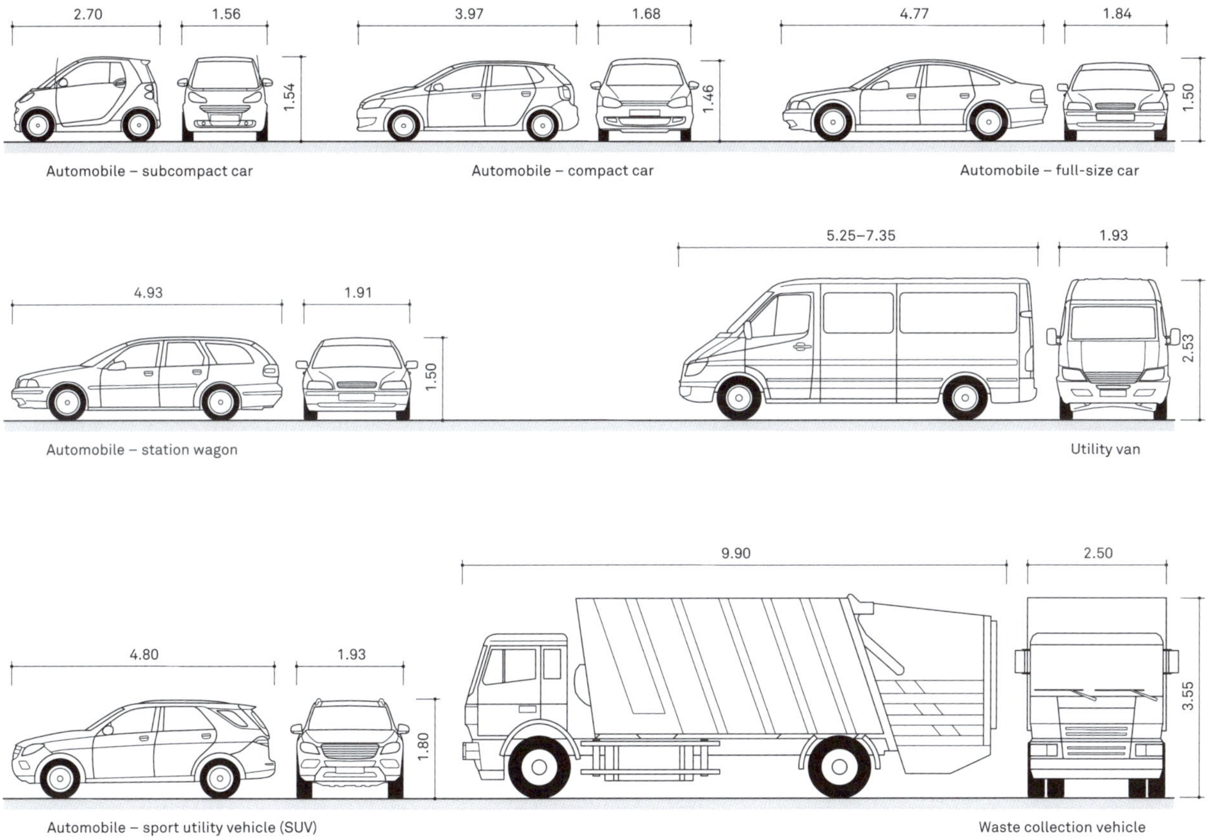

Figure 4.10 Dimensions of traffic participants (without maneuvering space)

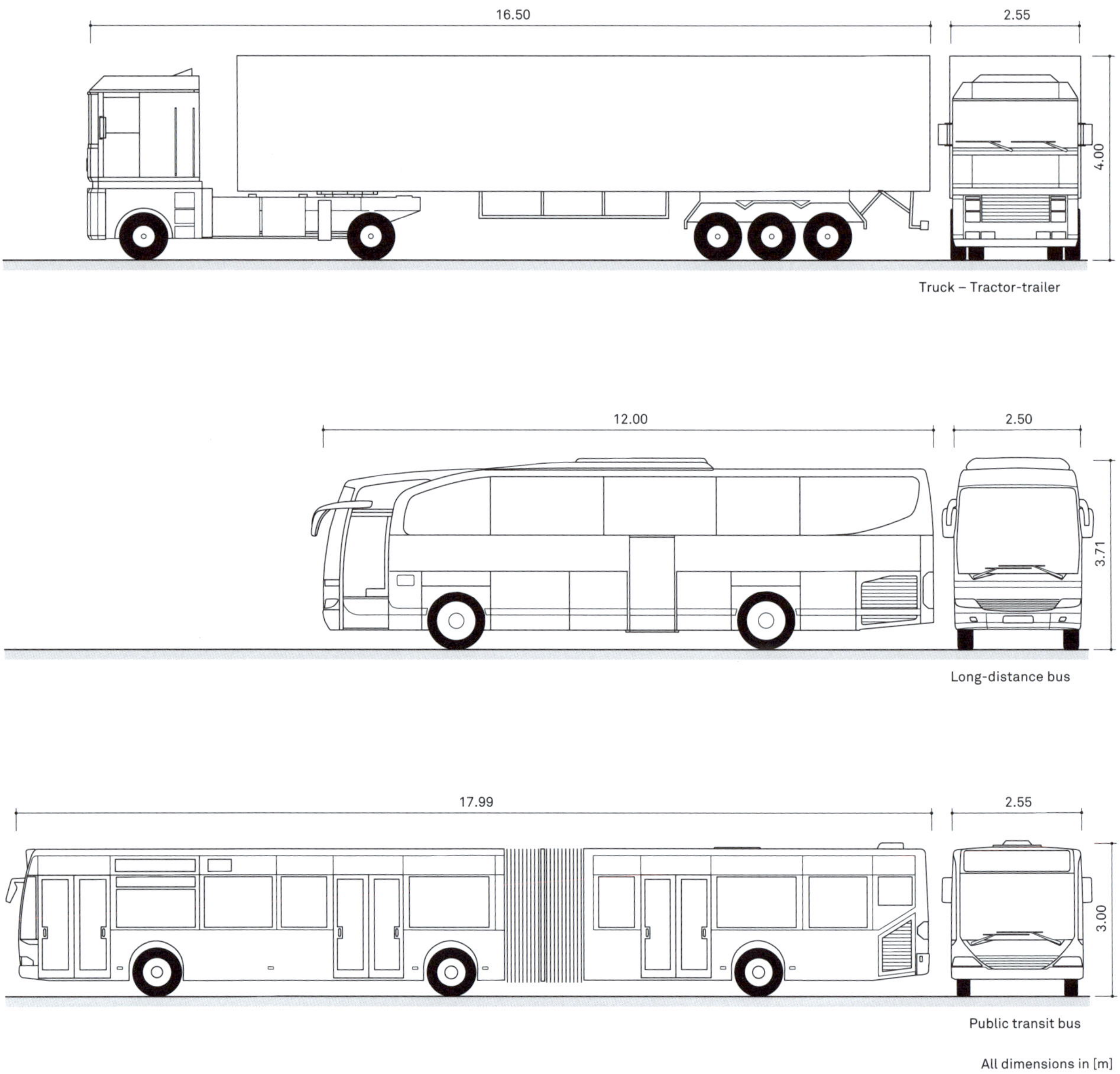

Figure 4.10 (Continuation) Dimensions of traffic participants (without maneuvering space)

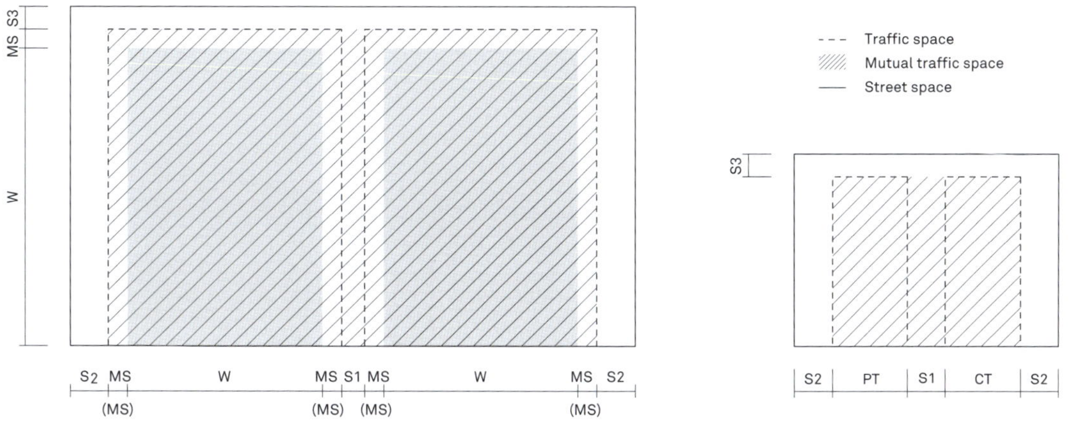

W Vehicle width/ Dimensions of the traffic participant
MS Maneuvering space to account for movement during travel
(MS) Restricted maneuvering space

S1 Average safety clearance
S2 Vertical safety clearance
S3 Horizontal safety clearance

PT Pedestrian traffic space
CT Cyclist traffic space

Figure 4.11 Composition of the space required for motor vehicles, pedestrians, and cyclists, per RASt 06

Traffic participant	Dimensions – average values (W) in cm		Maneuvering space in cm		Traffic space in cm	
	Width	Height	MS	(MS)	Width	Height
Pedestrian*	100 (80)	200	–	–	100 (80)	200
Wheelchair user, without change of direction*	110	–	–	–	110	–
Person with white cane*	120	200	–	–	120	200
Person with baby carriage*	100	200	–	–	100	200
Inline skater	180	210	–	–	180	210
Bicyclist*	100 (80)	225	–	–	100 (80)	225
Bicyclist with trailer*	130 (110)	225	20	10	130 (110)	225
Horseback rider	130	270	≥20	–	170	290
Motorcyclist	90**	180	20***	–	130	200
Car*	175**	150	25	15	225 (205)	200
Truck*	255**	400	25	20	305 (295)	450
Public transit bus*	255**	300	25	20	305 (295)	350
Streetcar (tram)*	265**	(420–) 500	30	(420–) 500	325	560

* as per RASt 06 ** without side mirrors *** disregarding tilted position while taking curves

Table 4.9 Traffic spaces of individual traffic participants, including their maneuvering space B and restricted maneuvering space (B)

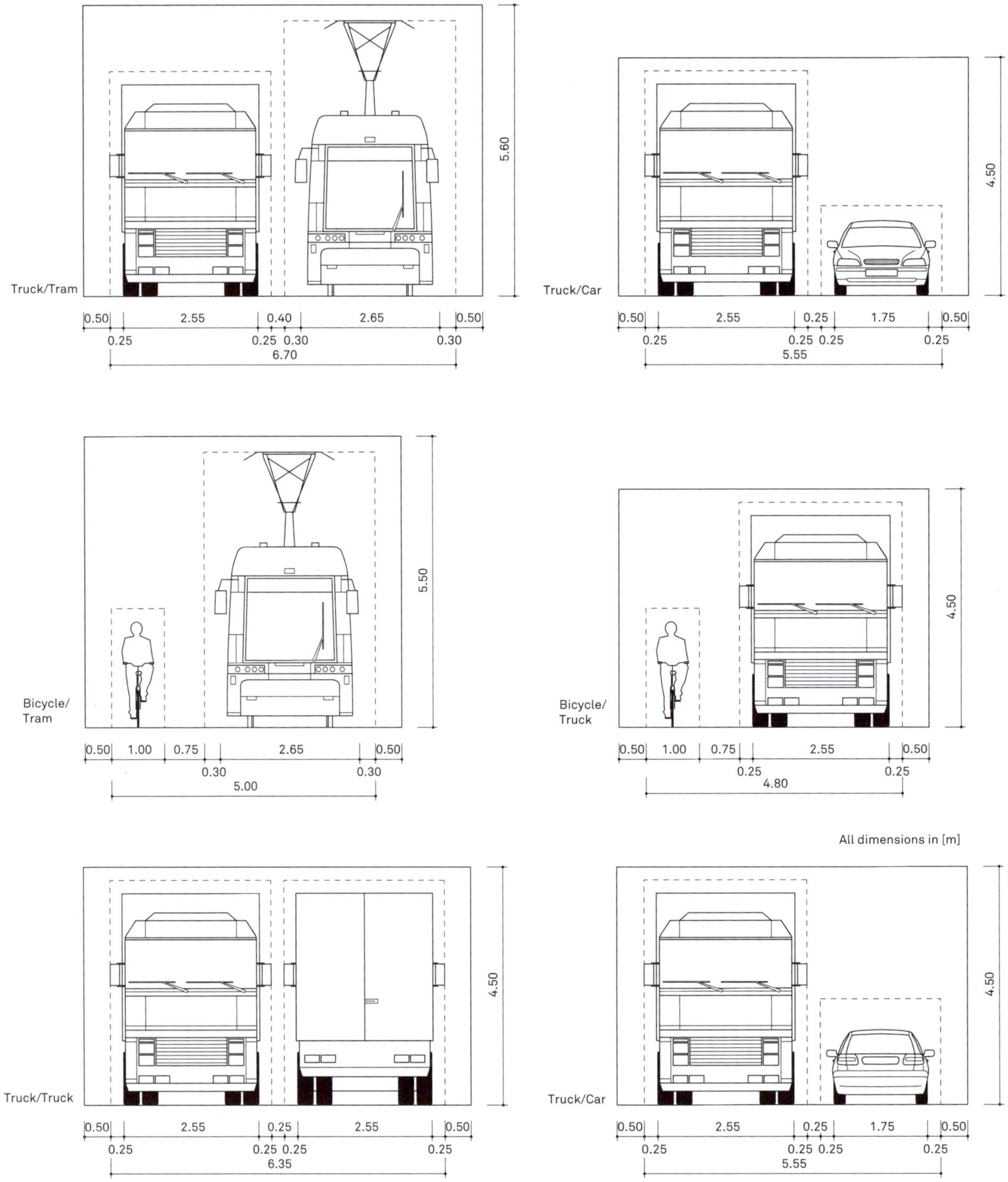

Figure 4.12 Composition of traffic spaces and clear spaces for oncoming, side-by-side, and passing traffic (as per RASt 06)

Bus/Bus

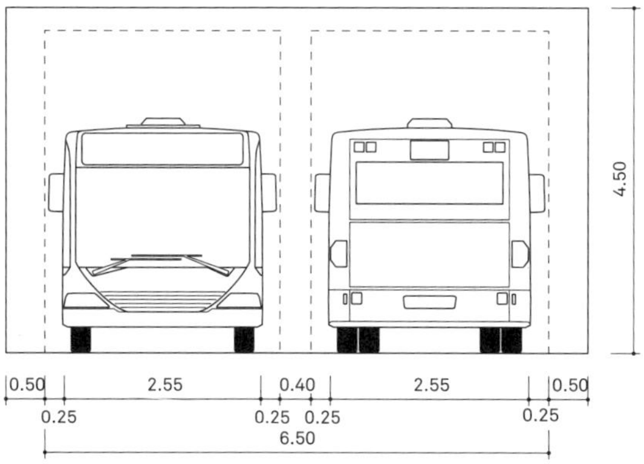

Utility van/
Utility van

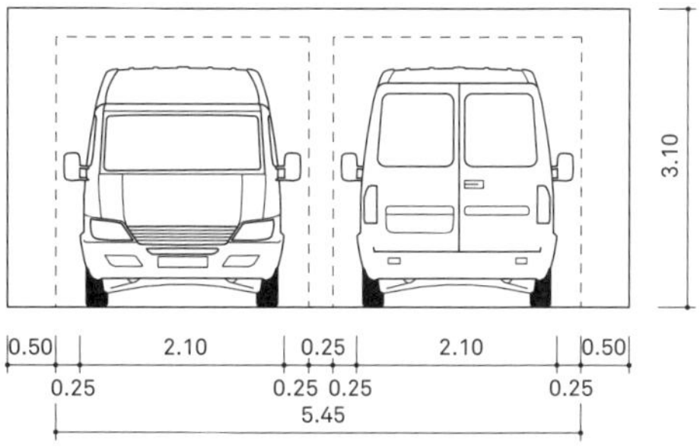

Utility van/
Car

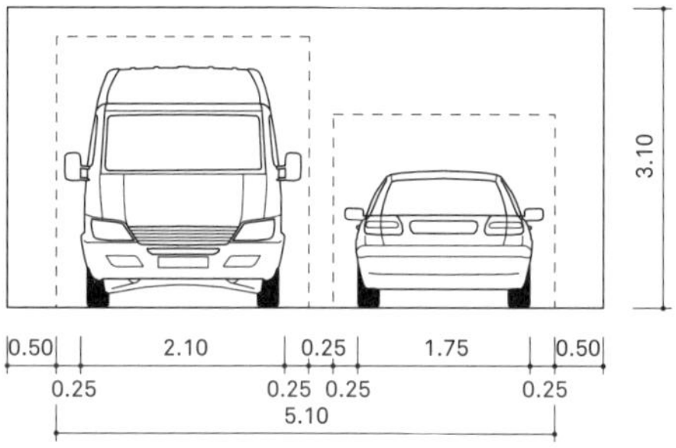

Car/Car

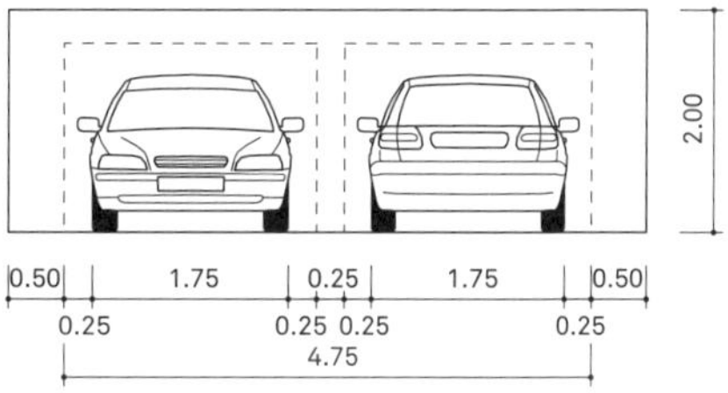

Utility van/
Bicycle

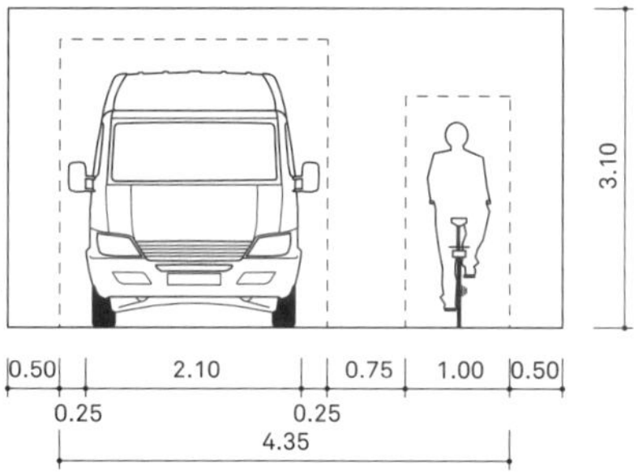

Car/Bicycle

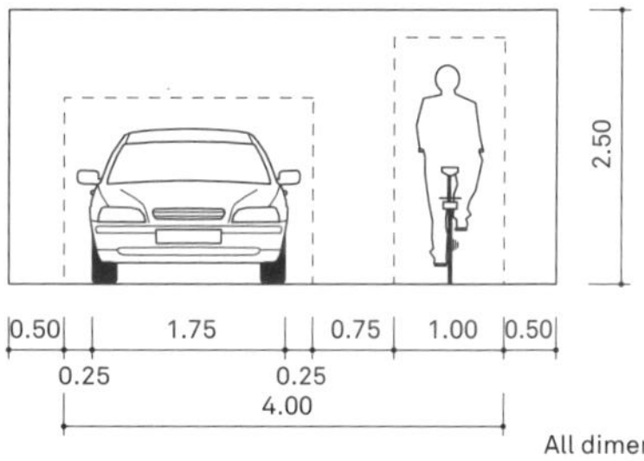

All dimensions in [m]

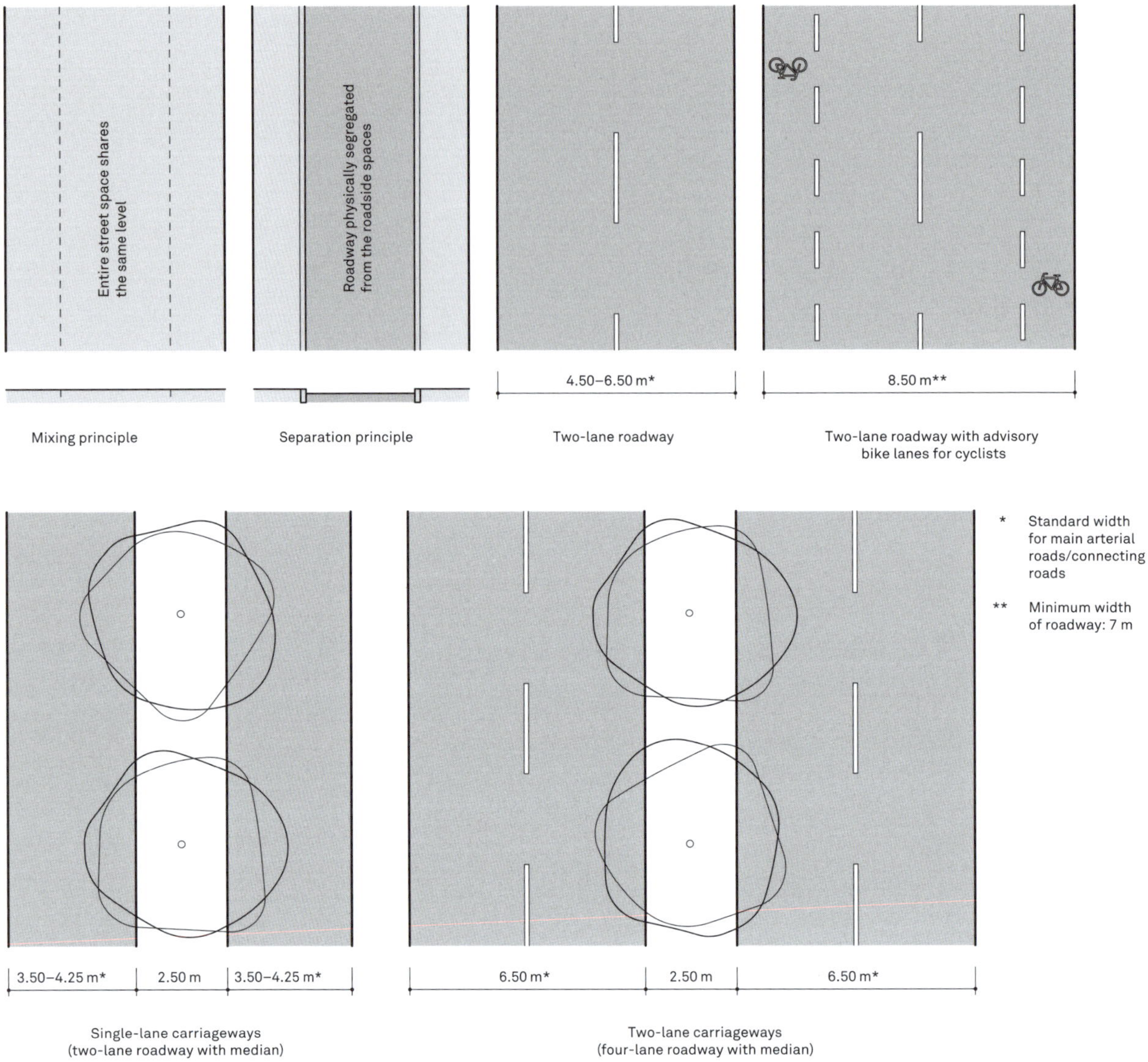

Figure 4.13 Roadway types

Application	Roadway width, main arterial road	Roadway width, connecting road
Single-lane carriageway / one-way street		
Typical case (with cyclists using the roadway)	4.25 m (where available space is limited: 3 m)	3.5 m (where available space is limited: 3 m)*
Bicycle traffic on roadway in opposed direction	Not applicable	3.5 m (3 m with sufficient turnout opportunities)
Roadway with advisory bike lane	3.75 m (2.25–1.5 m) with minor truck traffic	Does not generally occur
Two-lane roadway		
Typical case	6.5 m **	4.5–5.5 m
With public transit bus service	6.5 m **	6.5 m
Limited public transit bus service and minor use requirements***	6 m	6 m
Low frequency of encounters with truck traffic	5.5 m (at reduced speed)	–
High frequency of encounters with bus and truck traffic	7 m	–
With advisory bike lanes for cyclists	7.5 m with 1.5 m advisory bike lanes on both sides 7.5 m with 1.25 m advisory bike lanes on both sides in confined conditions****	
Two-lane carriageway	**Roadway width**	
Typical case	6.5 m	
Low frequency of bus or truck traffic	6 m (with limited available space: 5.5 m)	
Bus or truck traffic dominates	7 m (only in cases where continuous side-by-side travel should be ensured)	
Local residential streets and alleys		
Local residential street (Separation principle)	4.75 m (delivery vehicles permitted)	
Local residential alley (Mixed principle)	3 m (delivery vehicles and parking in adjacent areas permitted)	

* Requirements stemming from winter maintenance shall be checked individually ** With this dimension, obligatory mandatory cycling facilities are ordinarily to be provided *** For example, solely provides access **** Not adjacent to frequently used parking lanes

Table 4.10 Dimensions for one- and two-lane roadways as well as divided carriageways, local residential streets and local residential alleys, as per RASt 06

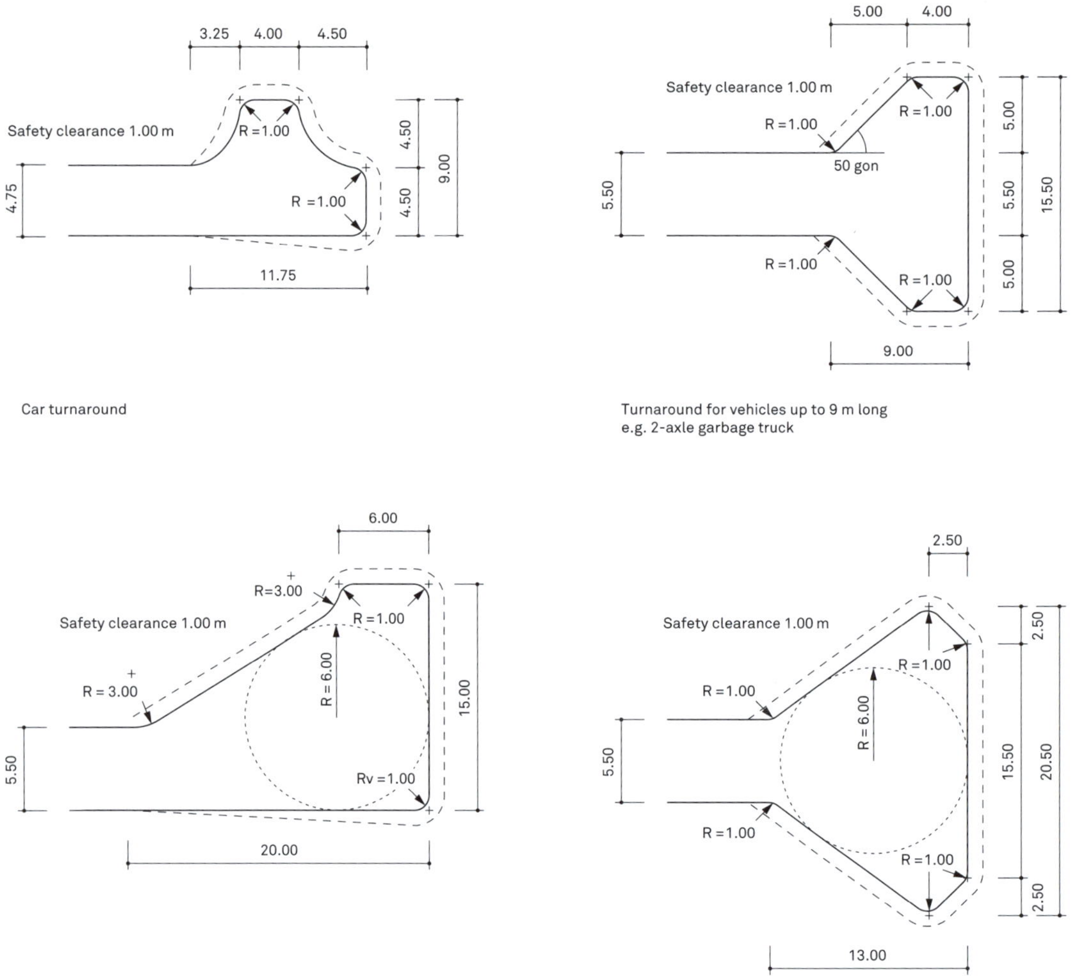

Car turnaround

Turnaround for vehicles up to 9 m long
e.g. 2-axle garbage truck

Single-sided turnaround and hammerhead turnaround for vehicles up to 10 m long
e.g. 3-axle garbage truck

All dimensions in [m]

Figure 4.14 Hammerhead turning areas and turning circles for cars and trucks

Configuration	Height	Function	Areas of application
High curb	10–14 cm (maximum 20 cm)	Separation of roadway/walkway (roadside bikeway)	Non built-up main arterial roads, built-up four- and multilane main arterial roads
	8–12 cm	Division of roadway or parking lane from walkway (roadside bikeway)	Two-lane main arterial roads, connecting roads
Half-height curb	4–8 cm	Division of roadway from walkway (roadside bikeway) or roadway from parking lane	Two-lane main arterial roads, connecting roads
Low curb	0–4 cm	Division of roadway from walkway (roadside bikeway) or from parking lane	Two-lane main arterial roads with low traffic volumes, connecting roads, depressed curb at crossing points for pedestrians, wheelchair users (≤3 cm), cyclists*

* For cyclists, a flush curb represents the optimal alternative; deviations are only permitted in exceptional cases. Along segregated bikeways, a flush curb shall always be provided.

Table 4.11 Areas of application of varied curb heights

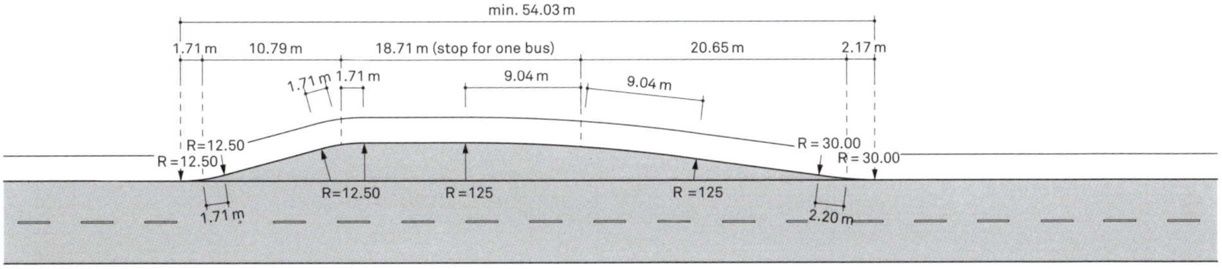

Bus bay, stop for one bus

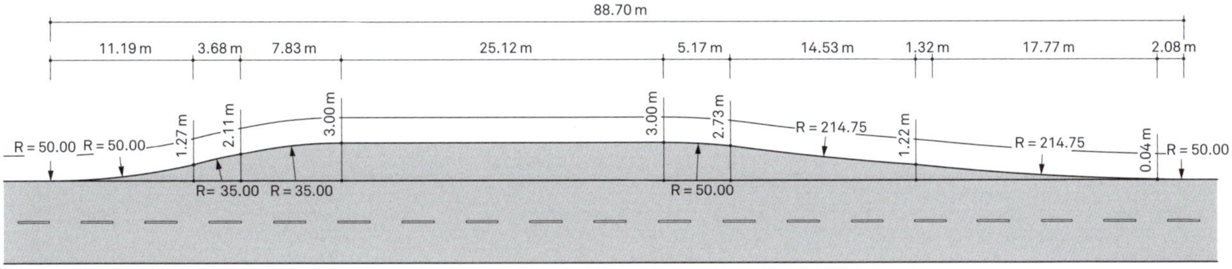

Bus bay with barrier-free accessibility for boarding and exiting by enabling the bus to pull up parallel to the curb

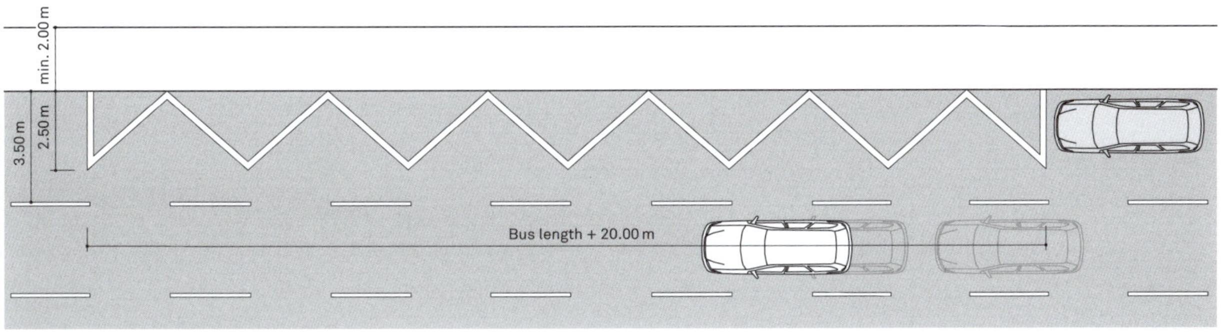

Curbside bus stop within parallel parking lane

Figure 4.15 Dimensions of bus bays and curbside bus stops

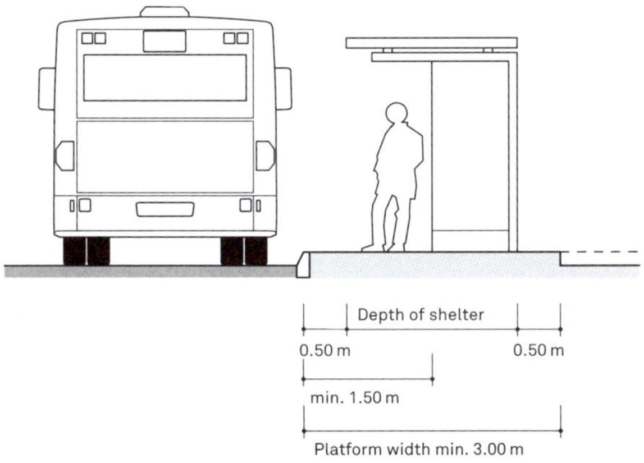

Figure 4.16 Dimensions of waiting areas and islands with shelters

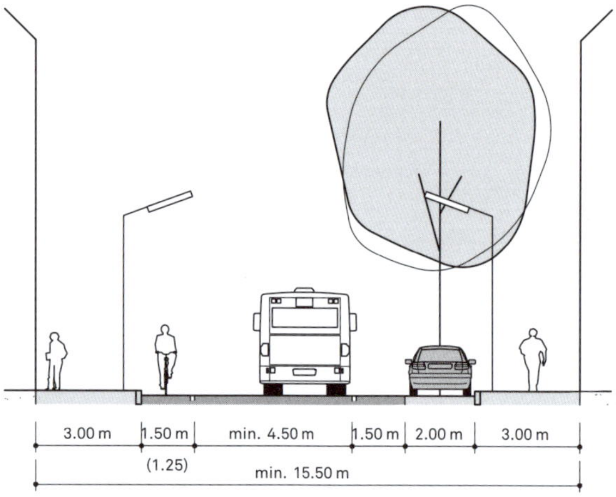

Neighborhood street (400–1,000 cars per hour) with advisory bike lanes for cyclists

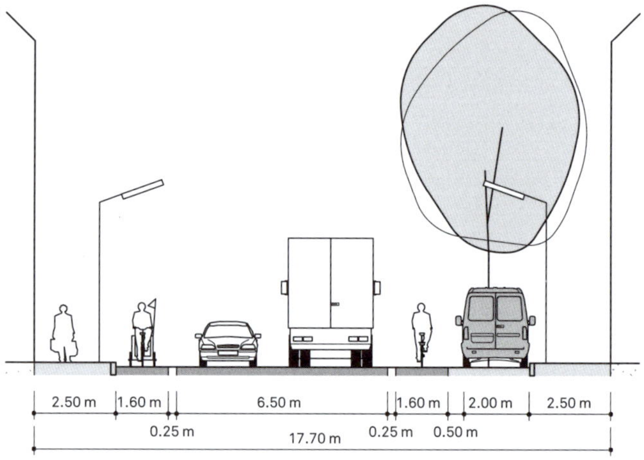

Neighborhood street (800–1,800 cars per hour) with mandatory bike lanes

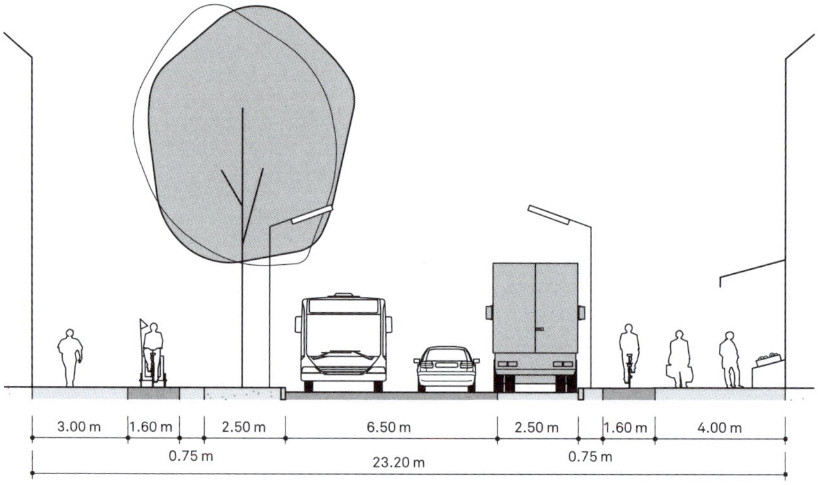

Local commercial streets (800–1,800 vehicles per hour) with parking and delivery, public transport, and accompanying roadside bikeway

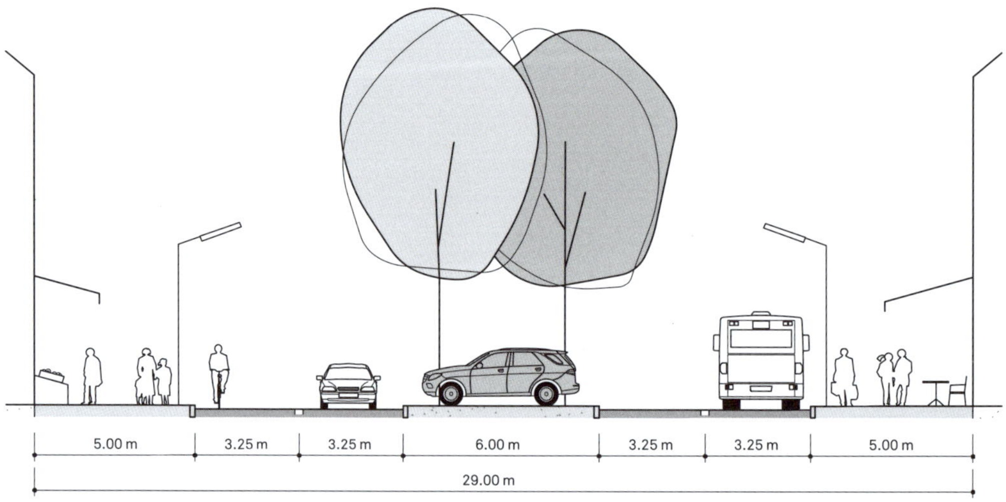

All dimensions in [m]

Main shopping street (800–1,800 vehicles per hour) with designated bus lanes (bicycling permitted) and median strip

Figure 4.17 Street space cross-sections for different usage requirements

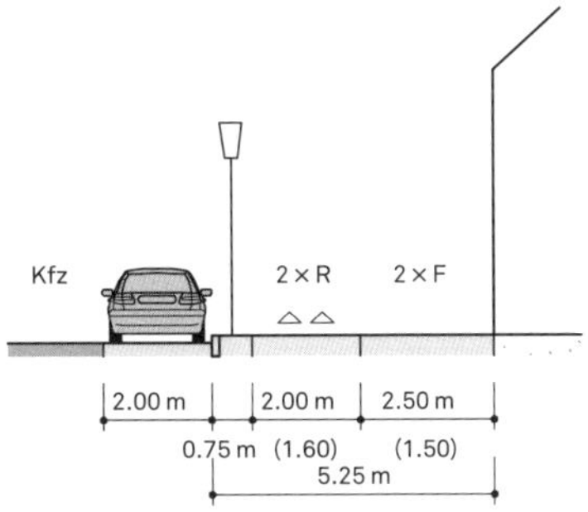

Bikeway adjacent to the roadway and parallel parking

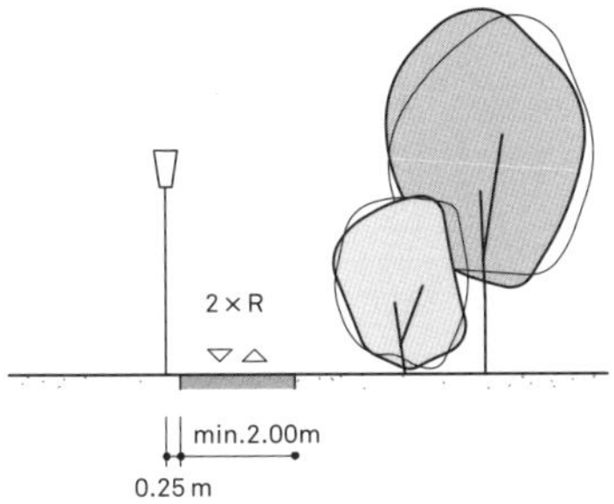

Independently routed two-way bikeway

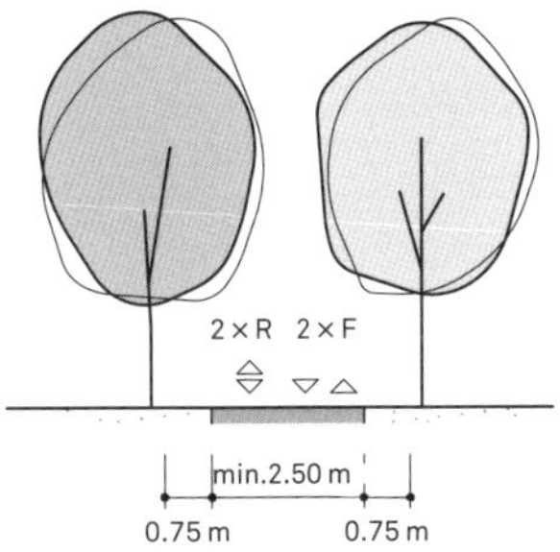

Combined pedestrian and bike path

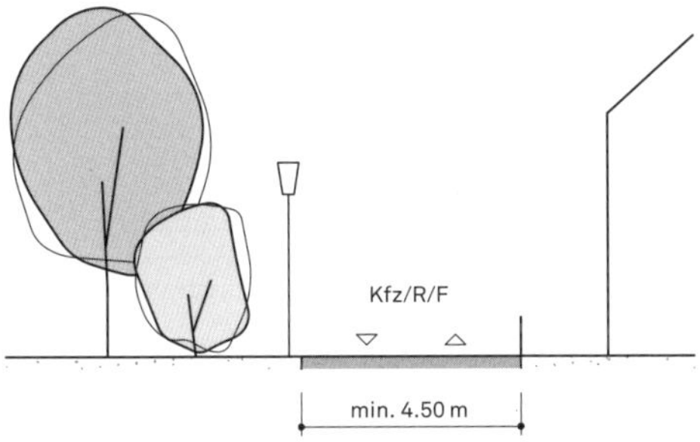

Residential lane (<400 vehicles per hour) used as gathering place, mixed principle

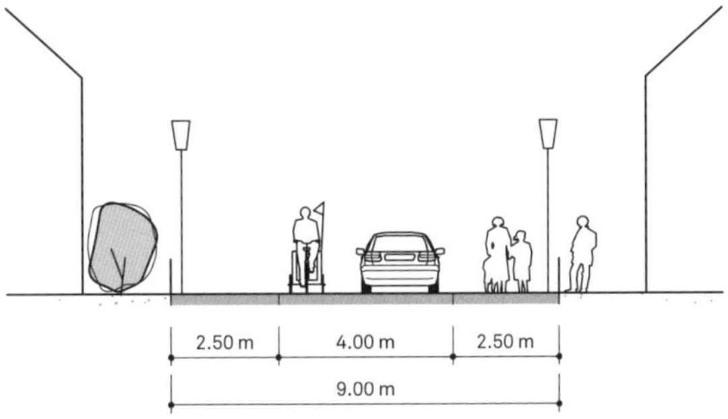

Residential lane (<400 vehicles per hour) used as gathering place, mixed principle

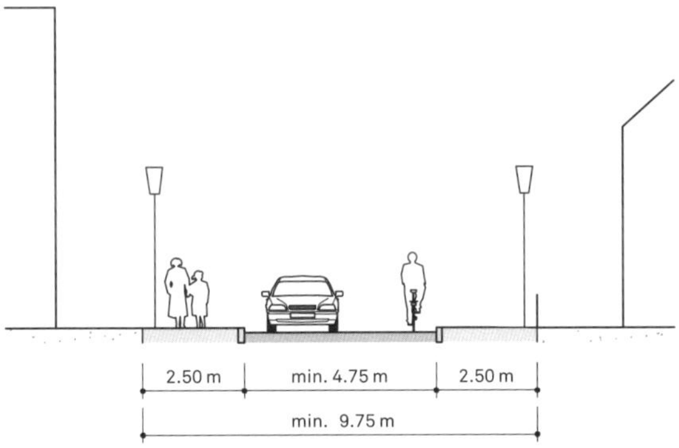

Residential street (<400 vehicles per hour) used as gathering place, separation principle

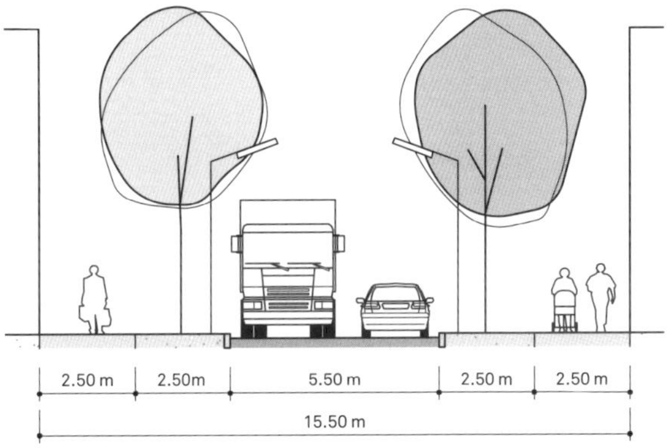

Residential street (<400 vehicles per hour) with roadside vegetation strip, separation principle

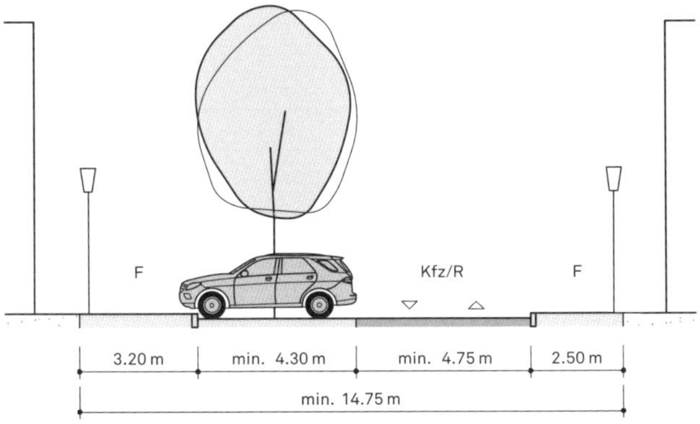

Residential street (<400 vehicles per hour) with perpendicular parking, separation principle

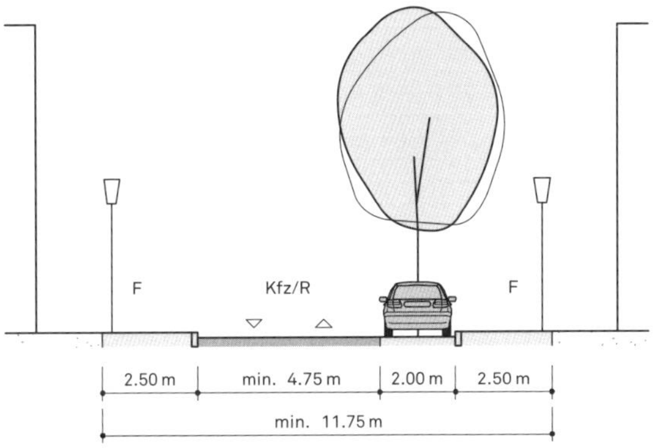

Residential street (<400 vehicles per hour) with parallel parking, separation principle

4.3 Parking Lots for Bicycles and Motor Vehicles

For buildings and other built structures where vehicular traffic is to be expected, automobile parking spaces and bicycle parking spaces of a suitable character are to be provided in sufficient quantity and size, under consideration of the local traffic conditions and available public transit alternatives.

Whereas quantitative specifications for automobile parking spaces are increasingly absent from the legal standards, the provision of bicycle parking and of automobile parking for people with disabilities has gained special emphasis.

Facility type	**Quantity** Bicycle spaces	Car spaces	Accessible parking spaces*
Residential buildings			
Apartments	1 per 30 m² total living area or2 per apartment	1 per apartment < 160 m², 2 per apartment ≥ 160 m²	Minimum 1, when apartments must be accessible
Multifamily houses with more than ten apartments		0.8 per apartment	
Weekend and vacation houses	1 per apartment	1 per apartment	
Children's residences and youth homes	0.5 to 1 per bed or 10 per 15 residents	0.6 to 1 per 15 beds	
Student dormitory	0.5 to 1 per bed or 0.7 per resident	1 per 3 beds or 0.2 per resident	
Retirement home, assisted living facility	1 per 10 beds 0.7 per resident 1 per 5 apartments	1 per 10 beds 0.2 per resident	
Visitors to private apartments	1 per 200 m² total living area		
Office and administration buildings, doctors' offices, workplaces			
Offices and administration	1 per 60 m² usable area 0.7 per 40 m² usable area 1 per 100 m² GFA >4,000 m² office floor area → 1 per 200 m² GFA 1 per 70 m² usable area	1 per 40 m² usable area	
Spaces with substantial visitor traffic (customer service desks, dispatch rooms, consultancies, doctors' offices, etc.)	1 per 40 (50) m² usable area	1 per 25 m² usable area	
Offices, workshops, and manufacturing plants (per EAR 05)	0.3 per workstation		
Sales areas in sales outlets			
Retail stores, commercial buildings	For < 400 m² → 1 per 50 m² sales area For > 400 m²–800 m² → 1 per m² sales area min. 4 parking spaces For > 800 m² → 1 per 100 m² sales area, min. 10 parking spaces	1 per 40 (100) m² sales area	
Shopping centers	1 per 80 (100) m² sales area	1 per 15 (100) m² sales area	

* Unless indicated otherwise, at least 1 %–3 %, but at least two, of the required total number of parking spaces shall be accessible spaces, and where possible, stalls that allow rear exit from the vehicle should be provided.

Table 4.12 Requirements for bicycle and automobile parking spaces, with guideline and average values as determined from various parking statutes (relevant valid building regulations must be observed!)

Facility type	Quantity		
	Bicycle spaces	Car spaces	Accessible parking spaces*
Places of assembly (except sports facilities) and churches			
Places of assembly (theaters, concert halls, movie theaters, etc.)	1 per 15 (20) attendees or movie theater, auditorium: 1 per 10 seats theater, concert hall: 1 per 50 seats	1 per 7 (10) visitors/seats	1 per 200 seats, minimum 1 per facility
Churches	1 per 20 attendees or 1 per 50 seats	1 per 30 visitors/seats	1 per 200 seats, minimum 1 per facility
Sports facilities			
Sports venues without spectator seating with spectator seating	1 per 250 m² sports area plus 1 per 30 spectator seats or 1.5 per 400 m² sports area plus 1 per 15 spectator seats or 1 per 20 spectators (local), 1 per 50 spectators (supra-local, e.g., stadium)	1 per 800 m² sports area plus 1 per 30 spectator seats or 1 per 400 m² sports area plus 1 per 15 spectator seats	1 per 200 spectators, but min. 1 (for minimum 100 spectators)
Multipurpose gyms without spectator seating with spectator seating	1 per 30 m² floor area; plus 1 per 15 spectator seats or 2 per 200 m² sports area plus 1 per 15 spectator seats Without: 1 per 250 m² sports area With: 1 per 10 spectator seats	1 per 80 m² floor area; plus 1 per 15 spectator seats or 1 per 200 m² sports area plus 1 per 15 spectator seats	1 per 200 spectators, but minimum 1 (for minimum 100 spectators)
Outdoor swimming pools	2 per 200–300 m² lot area or 1 per 50 m² lot area	1 per 200–300 m² lot area	
Indoor swimming pools without spectator seating with spectator seating	1 per 7 lockers 1 per 10 spectator seats 2 per 10 lockers	1 per 10 lockers 1 per 15 spectator seats	
Tennis courts, squash facilities without spectator seating with spectator seating	2 per court; plus 1 per 10 spectator seats	2 per court; plus 1 per 15 spectator seats	
Dance schools, fitness centers, saunas, solariums, etc.	1 per 50 m² usable area or 1 per 5 lockers	1 per 5 lockers	
Restaurants and lodging establishments			
Snack stands without seating	1 per 15 m² usable area	1 per 20 m² usable area	
Beer garden	1 per 2 seats or 1 per 20 m² usable area		
Restaurants of local significance	1 per 7–10 seats or 1 per 20 m² usable area		1 per 200 patron seats, but a minimum of 1 (for a minimum of 100 patrons)
Restaurants of regional significance	1 per 18 m² usable area	1 per 9 m² usable area	

* Unless indicated otherwise, at least 1 %–3 %, but at least two, of the required total number of parking spaces shall be accessible spaces, and where possible, stalls that allow rear exit from the vehicle should be provided.

Table 4.12 (Continuation) Requirements for bicycle and automobile parking spaces, with guideline and average values as determined from various parking statutes (relevant valid building regulations must be observed!)

Facility type	Quantity Bicycle spaces	Car spaces	Accessible parking spaces*
Restaurants and lodging establishments			
Hotels, pensions, sanatoriums, etc.	1 per 3 lodging rooms; for attendant restaurant operation additional 1 per 15 m² usable area (full-serve restaurant) or 1 per 20 m² usable area (snack outlet without seating) or 1 per 20 beds	1 per 10 lodging rooms; for attendant restaurant operation additional 1 per 12 m² usable area (full-serve restaurant) or 1 per 15 m² usable area (snack outlet without seating)	1 per 200 beds, but a minimum of 1 (for a minimum 100 beds)
Youth hostels	1 per 4–5 beds	1 per 10 beds	
Medical institutions			
Hospitals, private clinics	1 per 20 beds	1 per 4 (5) beds	1 per 200 beds, but min. 1 (for min. 100 beds)
Elderly nursing home	1 per 40 beds 0.5 per 12 beds 1 per 30 beds	1 per 8 beds 1 per 12 beds	
Schools, youth training centers			
Elementary schools	1 per 3 students 5 per 20 student slots 1 per 5 students 0.1 per student	1 per 50 students 1 per 20 student slots	1 per 200 seats/student slots, but a minimum of 1 per facility
Other general education schools, vocational schools	1 per student	1 per 40 students, plus 1 per 10 students over 18 yrs. old	
Special needs schools (for people with disabilities)	1 per 15 students	1 per 30 students	
Colleges and universities	1 per 5 students 3 per 10 student slots 0.6 per student	1 per 6 students 2 per 10 student slots	1 per 200 seats/student slots, but a minimum 1 per facility
Preschools, daycare centers, etc.	1 per 15 children (daycare spaces) or 1 per group/group room	1 per 30 children (daycare spaces) 1 per 30 visitors	
Commercial facilities			
Trade shops and industrial businesses	1 per 70 (up to 200) m² usable area 0.4 per 2 workplaces 1 per 200 m² GFA 1 per 5 workers	1 per 70 m² usable area	
Warehouses, storage yards	1 per 150 m² usable area or 0.4 per 2 workplaces	1 per 150 m² usable area or 1 per 2 workplaces	
Auto repair shops	1 per 100 m² usable area	1 per 100 m² usable area	
Other			
Allotment gardens	1 per 3 plots	1 per 30 plots	
Cemeteries	1 per 1,000 m² lot area 1 per 1,500 m² lot area	1 per 2,000 m² lot area, but min. 10	

* Unless indicated otherwise, at least 1 %–3 %, but at least two, of the required total number of parking spaces shall be accessible spaces, and where possible, stalls that allow rear exit from the vehicle should be provided.

Table 4.12 (Continuation) Requirements for bicycle and automobile parking spaces, with guideline and average values as determined from various parking statutes (relevant valid building regulations must be observed!)

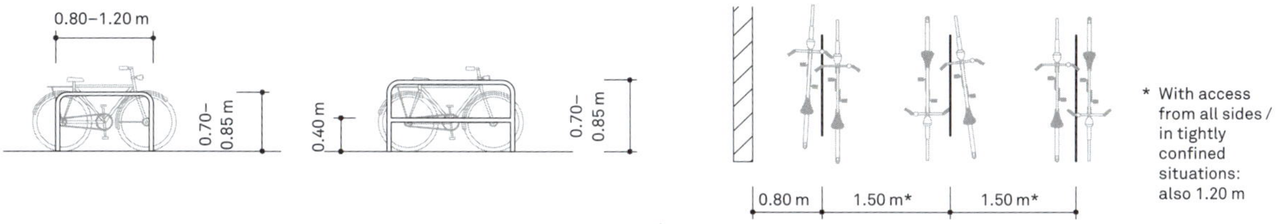

Figure 4.18 Dimensions and alignment of inverted U bike racks with/without crosspiece

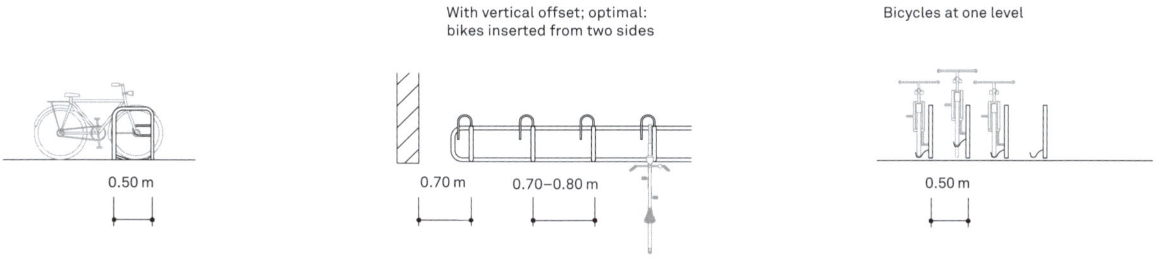

Figure 4.19 Dimensions and alignment of U-shaped racks with front wheel bracket, as multiple rack unit

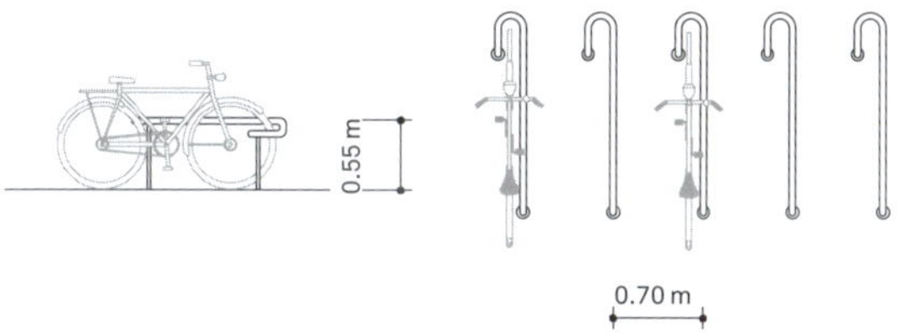

Figure 4.20 U-shaped racks with front bend

	Layout scheme	Area per rack (2 bicycles)	Area per bicycle
A	Perpendicular parking (90°), two rows	4.3 m²	2.15 m²
B	Perpendicular parking (90°), single row	5.2 m²	2.6 m²
C	Diagonal parking (45°), two rows, center aisle with two-way traffic	4.8 m²	2.4 m²
D	Diagonal parking (45°), two rows, center aisle with one-way traffic	4.3 m²	2.15 m²
E	Diagonal parking, single row, aisle with one-way traffic	5.6 m²	2.8 m²

Table 4.13 Space requirements for bicycle parking spaces: inverted U bike racks with 1.5 m spacing

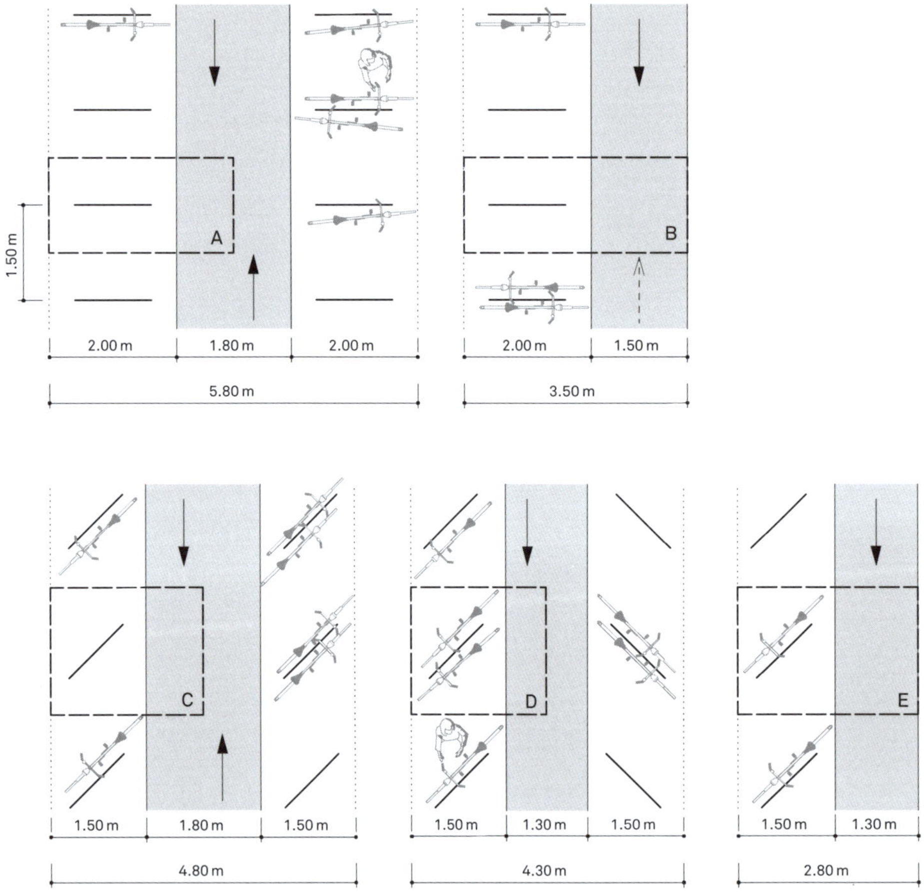

Figure 4.21 Widths of stalls and aisles for perpendicular and diagonal bicycle parking layouts

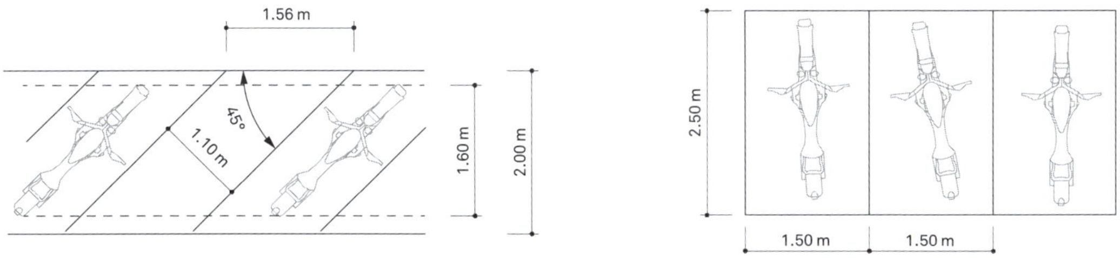

Figure 4.22 Basic dimensions for motorcycle parking

	Parking angle α [gon]	Depth from lane edge t–ü	Width of overhang strip ü	Width of parking stall b	Street frontage length l [m] needed while parking Forward	 Reverse	Lane or roadway width g [m] needed while parking Forward	 Reverse
Parallel parking 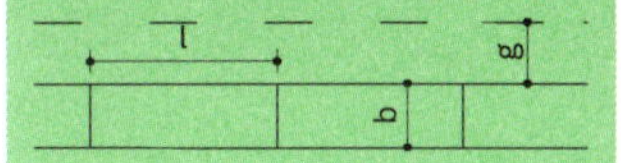	0			2.00 m	6.70 m [1]	5.70 m 5.20 m [2]	3.25 m	3.50 m
Angled parking 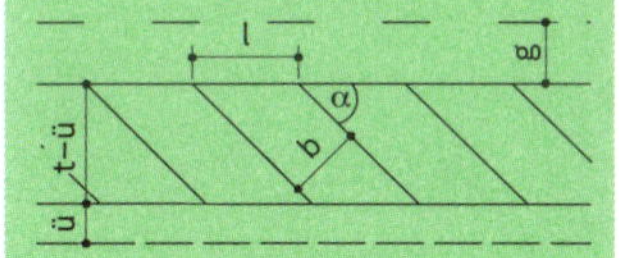	50 (45°)	4.15 m	0.70 m	2.50 m	3.54 m		3.00 m	
	60 (54°)	4.45 m	0.70 m	2.50 m	3.09 m		3.50 m	
	70 (63°)	4.60 m	0.70 m	2.50 m	2.81 m		4.00 m	
	80 (72°)	4.65 m	0.70 m	2.50 m	2.63 m		4.50 m	
	90 (81°)	4.55 m	0.70 m	2.50 m	2.53 m		5.25 m	
Perpendicular parking 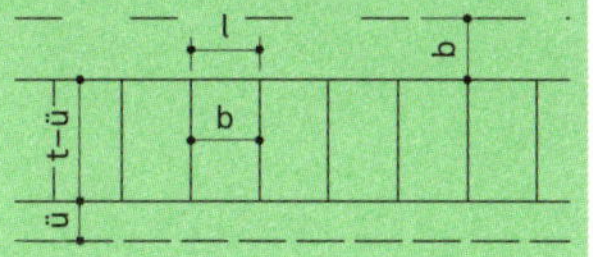	100 (90°)	4.30 m	0.70 m	2.50 m	2.50 m	2.50 m	6.00 m	4.50 m

[1] Only applicable in special cases, for instance to avoid obstructions while reverse parking
[2] Average value without markings

Table 4.14 Dimensions of automobile parking spaces and aisles, for parallel, angled, and perpendicular parking

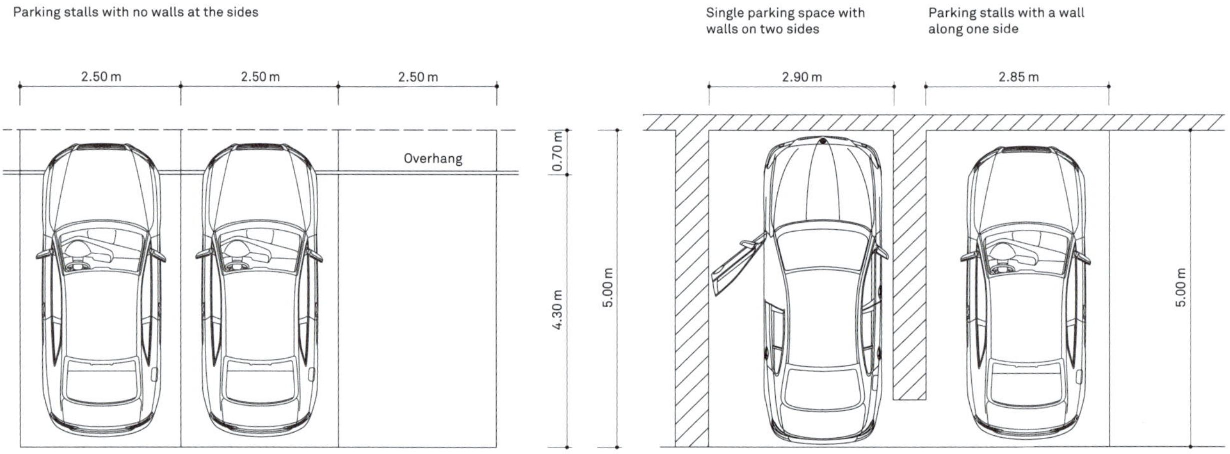

Figure 4.23 Exemplary layout of parking lots with perpendicular and angled parking

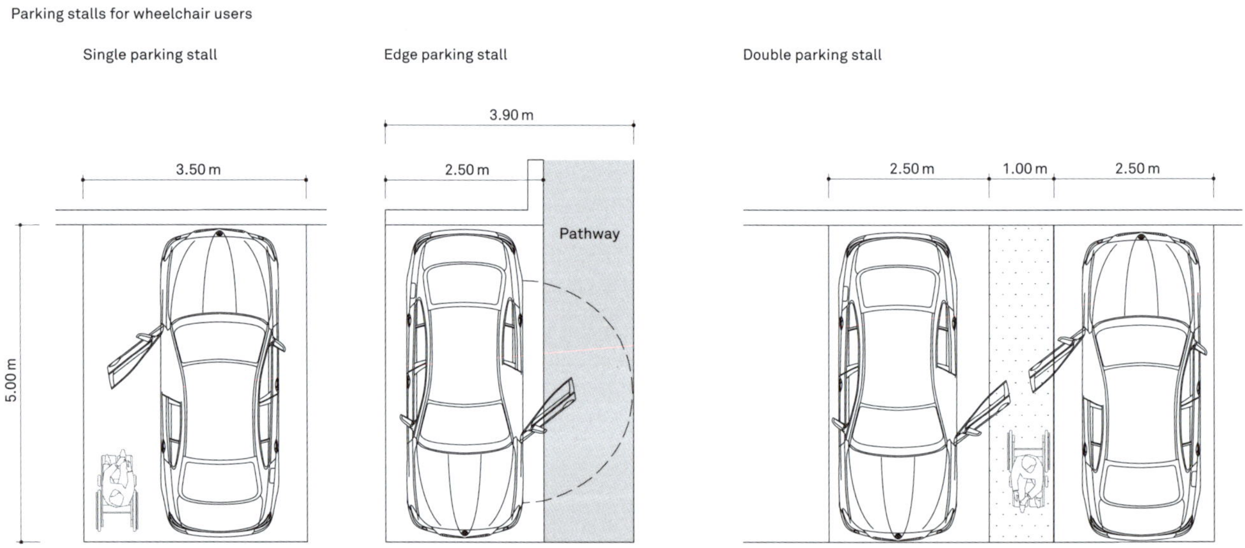

Figure 4.24 Dimensioning of parking stalls for wheelchair users – perpendicular parking

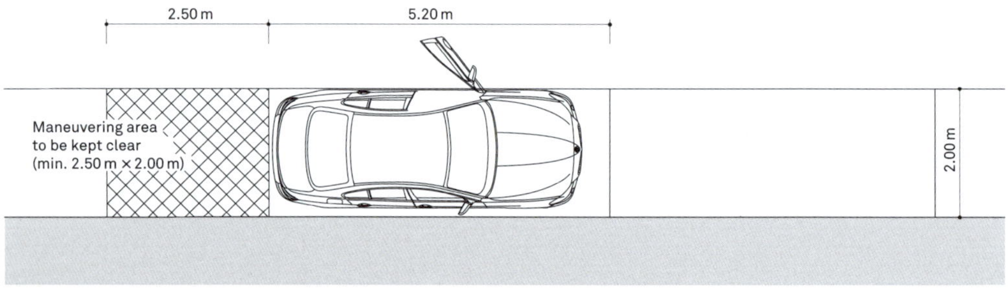

Figure 4.25 Dimensioning of parking stalls for wheelchair users – parallel parking

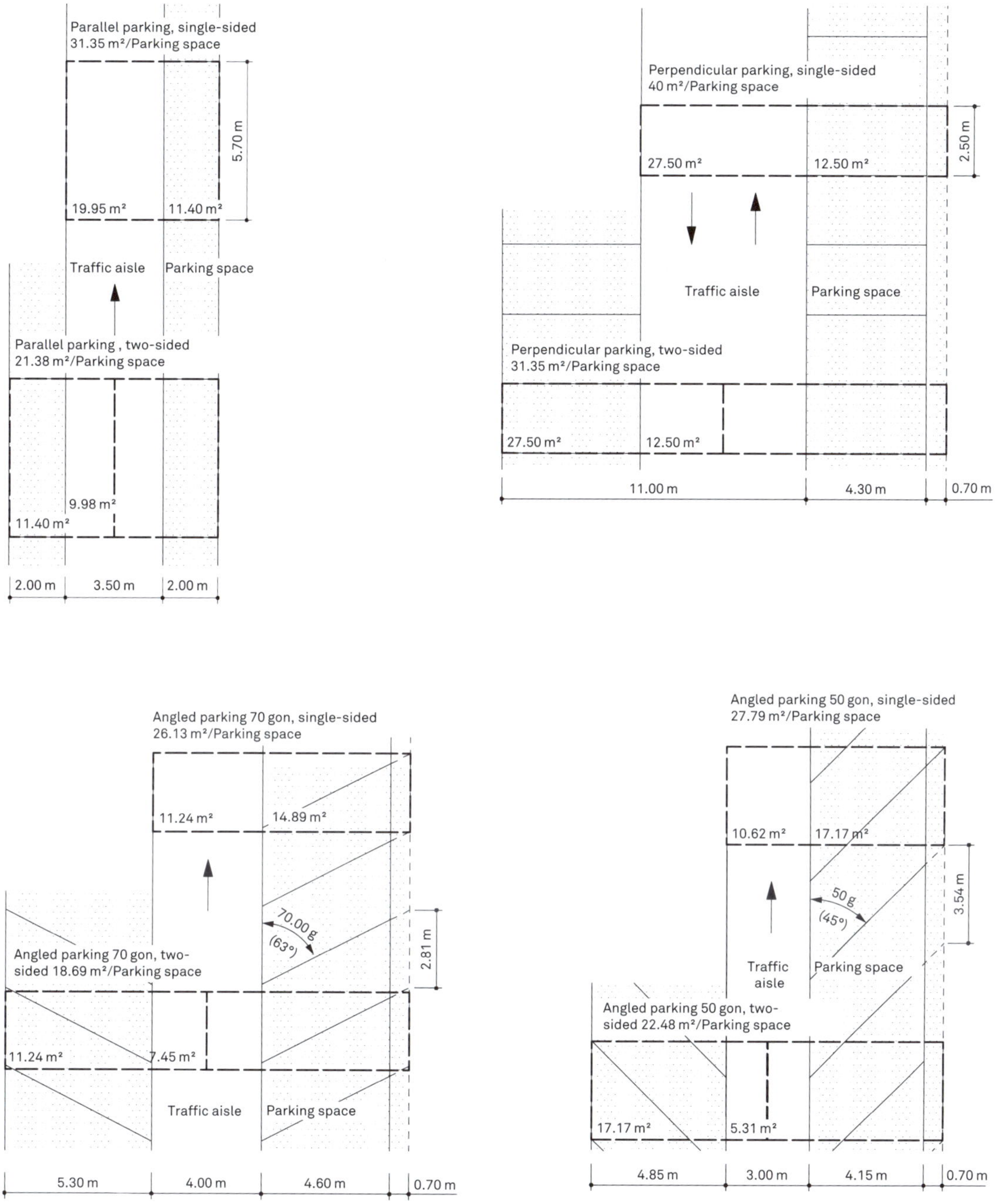

Figure 4.26 Dimensions of parking stalls and space requirements for automobiles in the street space as a function of the parking arrangement

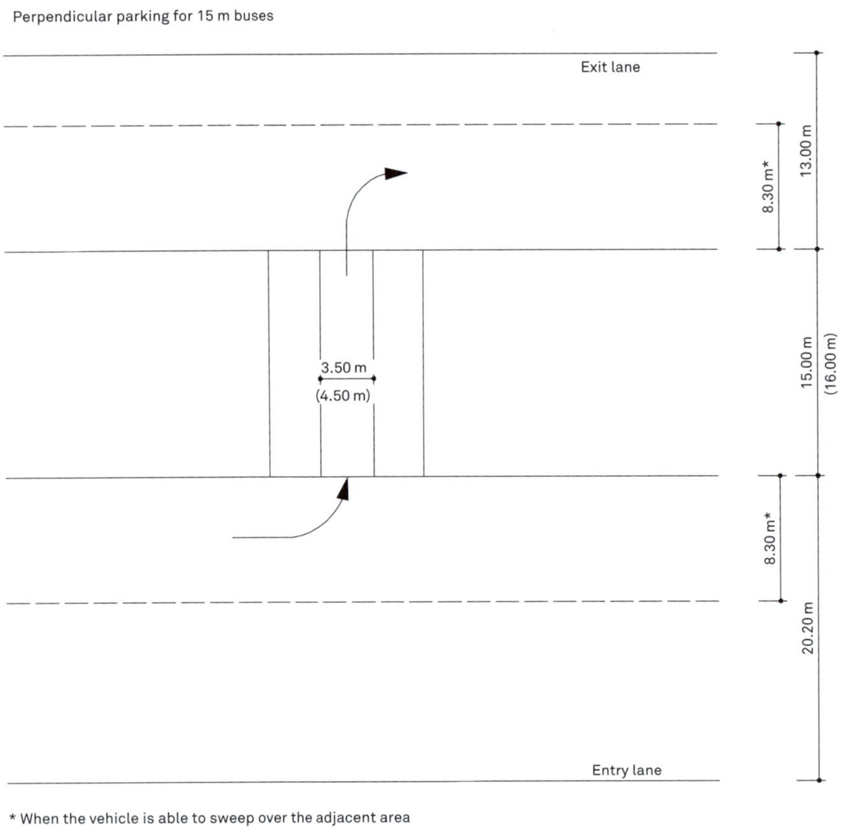

Figure 4.27 Basic dimensions for truck and bus parking – perpendicular spaces

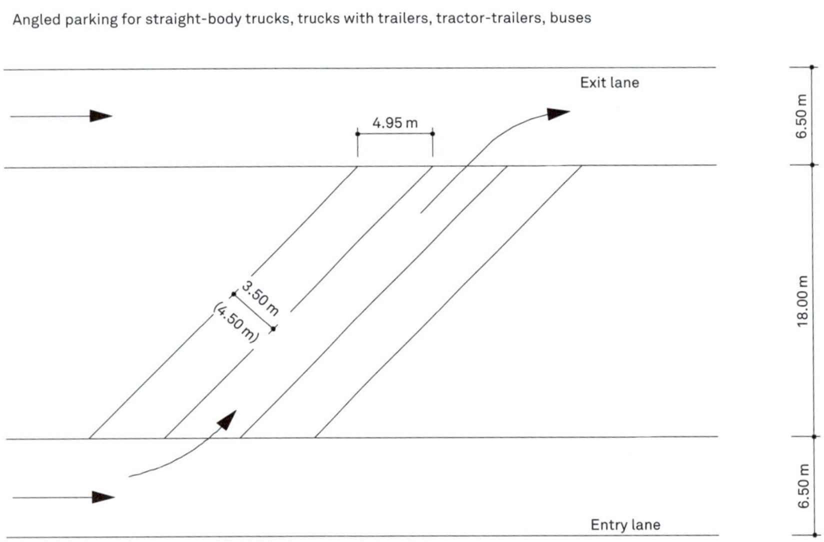

Figure 4.28 Basic dimensions for truck and bus parking – angled spaces

4.4 Ramps and Stairs

When a ramp would have a slope of about 18 % or more, it should be replaced by stairs.

The step dimensions needed for a particular stair are the result of a combination of factors: first, the slope of the ground and second, the riser height (unit rise) and tread depth (unit tread), which are defined in relation to a person's stride length. As the incline, or pitch, increases, however, a person's stride shortens and, vice versa, it gets longer as the pitch decreases. This results in a variable basis for the design of steps. For stairs in and adjacent to buildings, however, the standards used in some countries stipulate a mandatory formula with a constant stride length as the basis for calculation.

The required stair width is dependent on the use, and applicable guidelines must be taken into account for certain uses, such as for assuring access to public buildings or event venues.

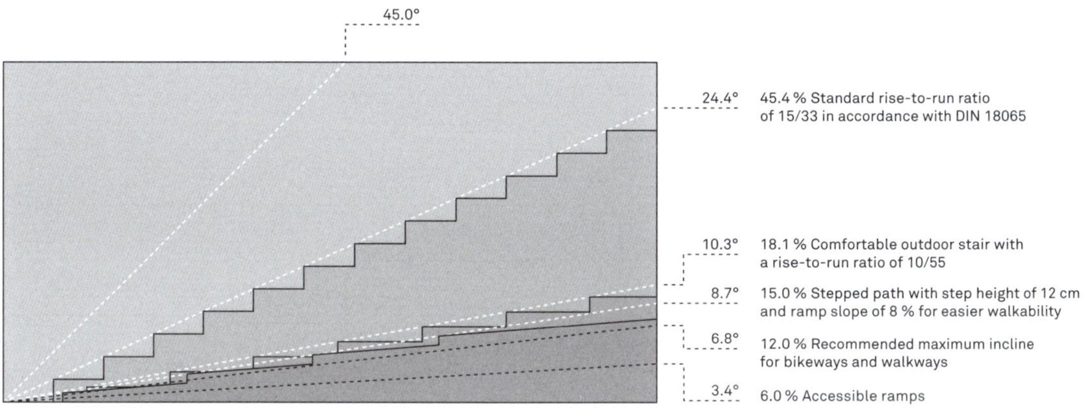

Figure 4.29 Selected inclines of ramps and stairs

Stride	Ground slope	Slope of intermediate landing	Length of landing	Riser height
One intermediate step on each second landing	26 % 24 % 22 %	12 % 11 % 10 %	83 cm 85 cm 89 cm	12 cm 11 cm 11 cm
2 intermediate steps on each landing	20 % 19 % 17 % 15 % 13 %	12 % 11 % 10 % 8 % 7.5 %	175 cm 180 cm 185 cm 190 cm 200 cm	14 cm 14 cm 13 cm 12 cm 11 cm

Table 4.15 Dimensions of stepped paths (Source: Mader 2004)

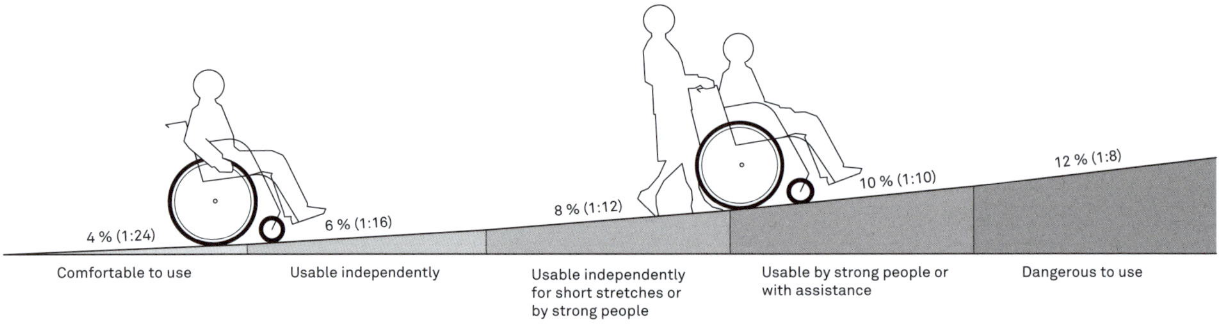

Figure 4.30 Usability of various ramp slopes by wheelchair users

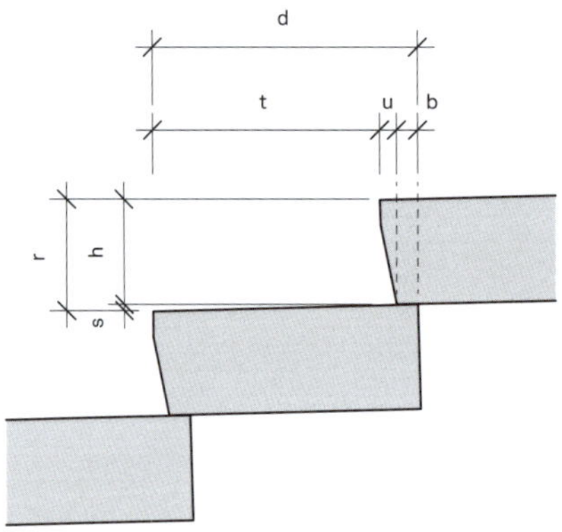

h = height of step (riser)
s = tread slope
r = unit rise
d = depth of step

t = unit tread (unit run)
u = nosing/undercut
b = bearing edge

Riser/tread ratio: r/t
Nominal step size: h/b

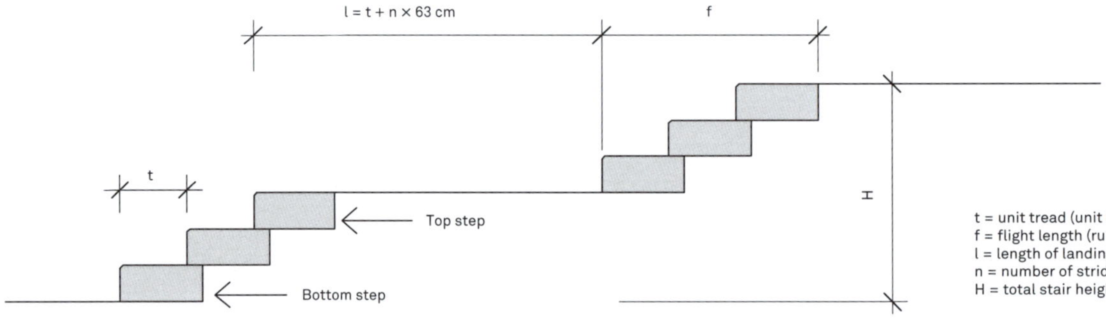

t = unit tread (unit run)
f = flight length (run)
l = length of landing
n = number of strides
H = total stair height

Figure 4.31 Calculating step and landing dimensions

Country	Formula	Applicability	Source
Germany	2r + t = 59–65 cm	At buildings (entrance area and access paths)	DIN 18065
Austria	2r + t = 59–65 cm	At buildings (entrance area and access paths)	ÖNORM B 5371
Switzerland	2r + t = 62–64 cm	At buildings, exterior: risers 13–18 cm and treads 28–35 cm, intermediate landings after 9–12 steps	bfu
France	2r + t = 59–64 cm		Ministère de l'équipement, du Logement, des Transport et du Tourisme
Spain	54 cm ≤ 2r + t ≤ 70 cm	Risers of 10–15 cm are recommended for outdoor grounds	Documento Básico de Seguridad de Utilización (DB-SU)
USA	2r + t = 65–67.5 cm (26–27 inches)	Outdoor premises	Time-Saver Standards

Table 4.16 Stride length formulas for calculating step dimensions

	According to stride length formula for stairs in and adjoining buildings		**Stride length and stride length formulas for outdoor stairs**			
	As per DIN 18065-1		**Recommendation according to Alwin Seifert for $r < 17$**		**Recommendation according to Günter Mader**	
r	Tread (t)	Stride length 2r + t	Tread t = 94 – 4r	Stride length 2r + t	Tread (t)	Stride length 2r + t
9	Not permitted in and adjoining* buildings as per DIN 18065-1		58 cm	76 cm		
10			54 cm	74 cm	50–63 cm	70–83 cm
11			50 cm	72 cm	45–58 cm	67–80 cm
12			46 cm	70 cm	41–53 cm	65–77 cm
13			42 cm	68 cm	38–48 cm	64–74 cm
14	31–37 cm		38 cm	66 cm	36–43 cm	64–71 cm
15	29–35 cm	59–65 cm	34 cm	64 cm	34–39 cm	64–69 cm
16	27–33 cm		30 cm	62 cm	32–35 cm	64–67 cm
17	25–31 cm		–	–	29–32 cm	63–66 cm
18	23–29 cm		–	–	27–30 cm	63–66 cm
19	21–27 cm		–	–	–	–
20**	21–25 cm		–	–	–	–
21 **	21–23 cm		–	–	–	–

* stairs serving as a means of access for a building

** only stairs that are not legally necessary (not part of a rescue route); 20 cm also permitted for residential buildings with max. 2 dwellings

Table 4.17 Rise-to-run ratio of steps

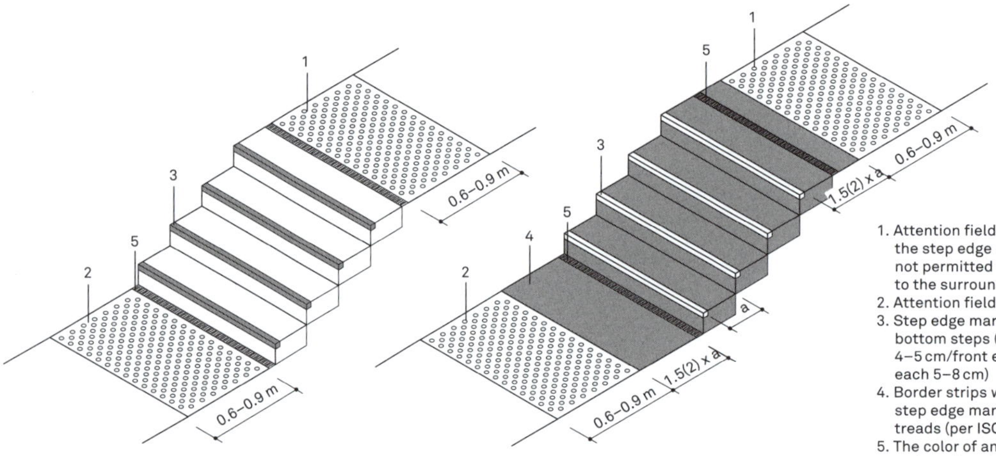

1. Attention field; in order to visually emphasize the step edge markings, these fields are not permitted to exhibit any striking contrast to the surrounding surfaces
2. Attention field optional
3. Step edge markings on at least the top and bottom steps (per DIN 18040-1: top edge 4–5 cm/front edge (1–)2 cm; DIN 18024-1: each 5–8 cm)
4. Border strips with distinct contrast to the step edge markings / same color as the stair treads (per ISO 23599 / DBSV recommendation)
5. The color of any required drainage channel and grating shall be the same as the border strips / in contrast to the step edge markings

Figure 4.32 Attention fields in front of a stair

	Accessible as per DIN 18024-1	User-friendly/functional	Optimized (e.g., for additional use by bicycles)
Maximum longitudinal slope	3 % or 3–6 % on ramps and ways with intermediate landing	3 %–4 %	3 %
Maximum cross slope for surfaces / on ramps	2 % (6 % at driveway approaches to lots)/0 %	1 %/0 %	0 %
Width	1.2 m	1.5 m	≥1.8 m
Maneuvering space / landings at ramps	1.5 m	2.0–3.0 m	≥4.0 m
Spacing of landings	max. 6m (ramps), max. 10m (movement area)	Maximum 10 m	

Table 4.18 Accessible design of inclined surfaces and ramps (Source: Design for All, supplemented)

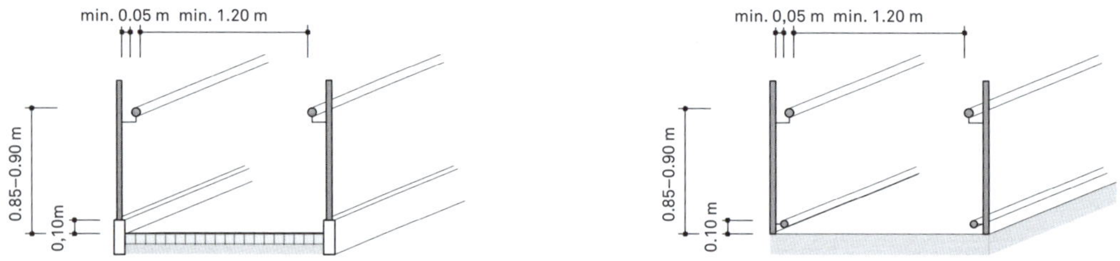

Ramp with curb/wheel deflector

Alternative: ramp with foot rail

Figure 4.33 Ramp cross sections as per DIN 18040-1

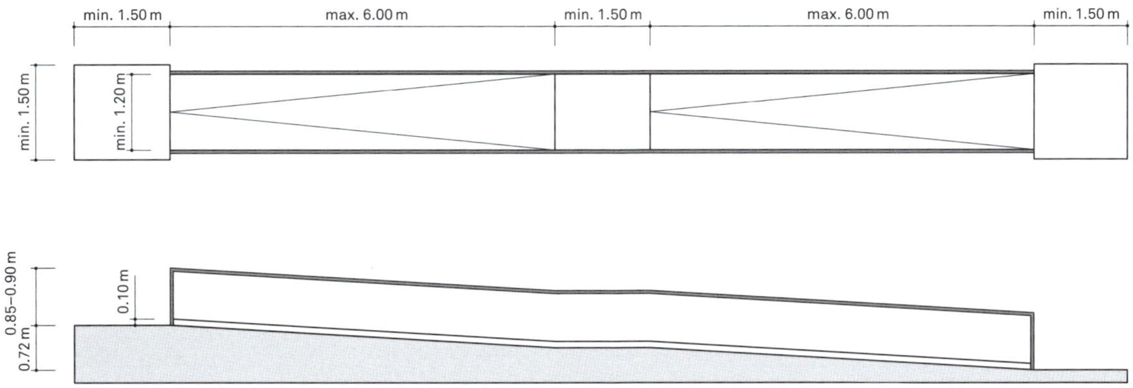

Figure 4.34 Requirements for ramp runs and landings as per DIN 18040-1

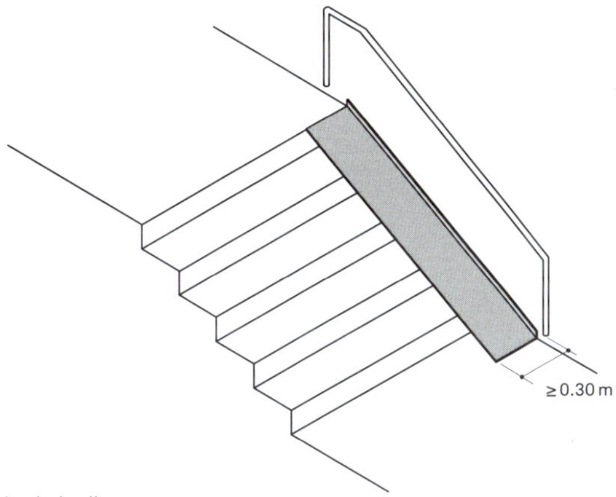

Metal wheeling ramp,
surface-mounted on top of steps

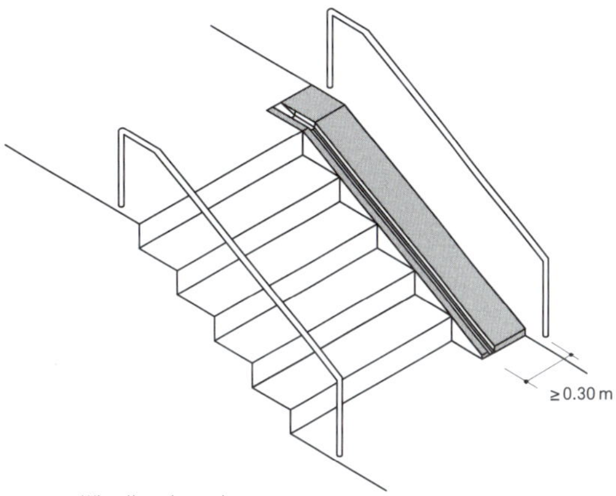

Wheeling channel
(wheel trough)

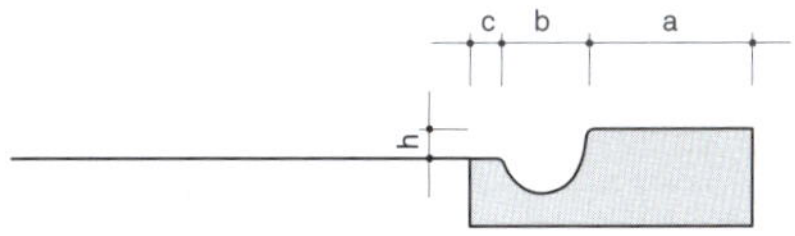

Dimensions of wheeling channels

- a ≥ 20 cm
- b 8–12 cm or 10 cm (for metal stairs)
- c 3–5 cm
- h 3 or 4 cm (for metal stairs)

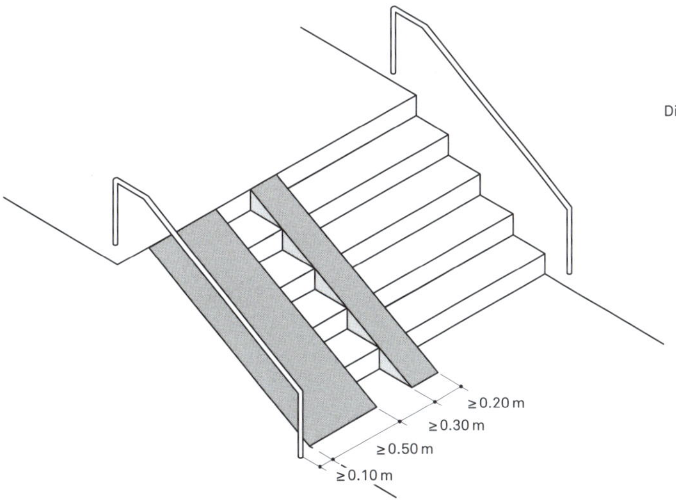

Figure 4.35 Examples of wheeling ramps

5 Vertical Elements

Vertical elements such as fences, railings or boundary enclosures can contribute in various ways to the spatial formation of an open space: depending on their height, layout and/or dimensions, they can have a confining, spatially articulating, or structuring impact. If they fulfill specific functions, for instance as fall protection or as elements for noise abatement and visual privacy, special technical/constructional solutions are generally required.

5.1 Boundary Enclosures

The construction of a boundary enclosure for a plot of land or a particular area can serve to identify property ownership or to prevent (unauthorized) entry or exit. Moreover, special functions are offered by noise barrier walls, privacy walls, and windbreaks.

In open spaces designed for specific purposes, use of a boundary enclosure – as a ball stop fence surrounding sports areas, for example – is of significant importance.

Fences, walls, hedges, trenches, berms, rows of trees, sunken areas, and raised areas all represent possible types of boundary enclosures.

Many areas require a boundary enclosure for a specific purpose. Fences surrounding ball sports areas, for instance, should be at least 3–4 m high, and areas used for dog runs should be enclosed with a fence at least 1 m high, preferably 1.2 m or higher. By contrast, playgrounds can, from a design standpoint, also be enclosed in other effective ways. The enclosure is effective only when ways of leaving the playing area are clearly perceptible for the children. For the purposes of social control, the boundary enclosures of playgrounds should be open and built to a height of 1 m.

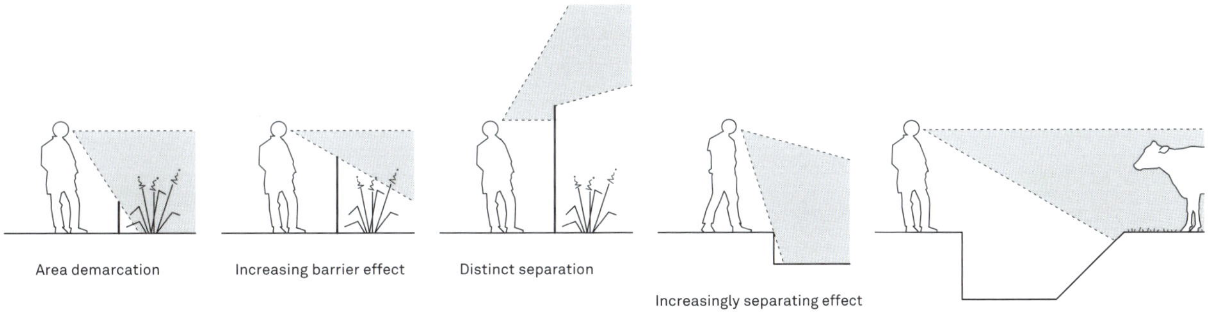

Figure 5.1 Impact of heights (and depths) and their barrier effect

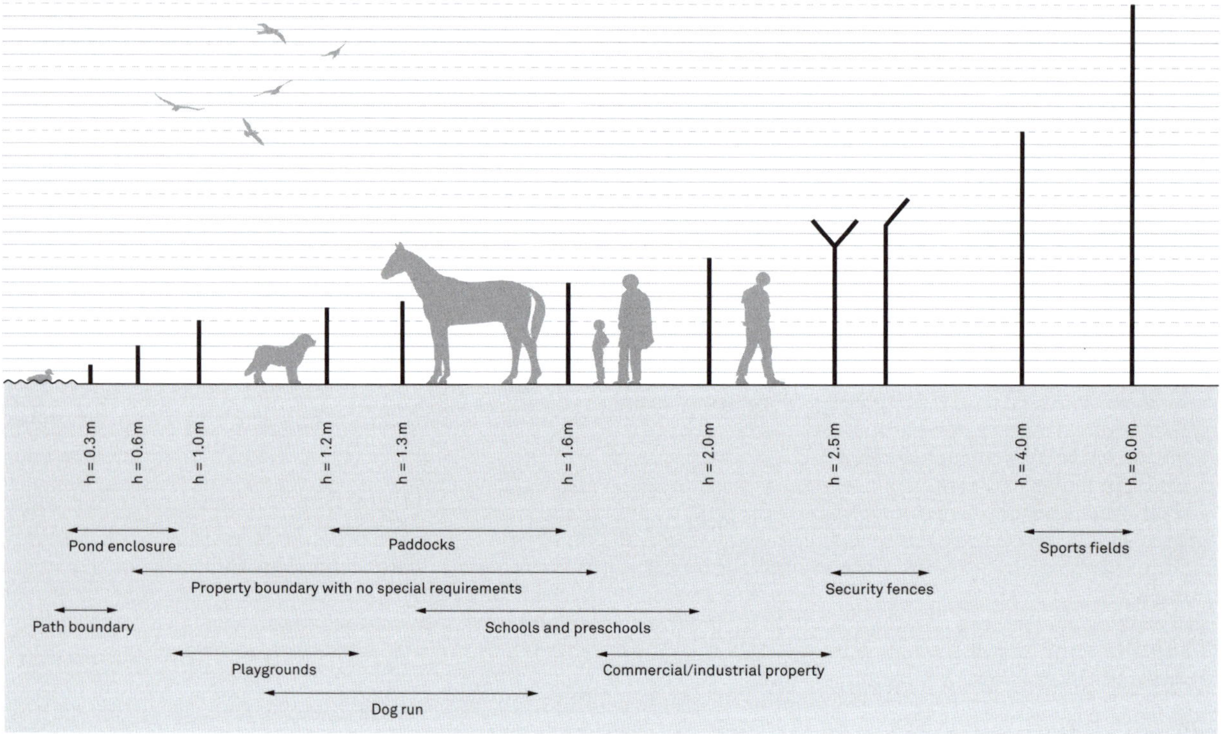

Figure 5.2 Heights (minimum/maximum) of boundary enclosures for specific purposes

Use	Material	Construction method	Special characteristics
Generally-applicable		Size of openings and spaces between horizontal and vertical elements: max. 12 cm (France: 11 cm) or min. 23 cm	
Playgrounds	No restriction	Low or open construction that allows the grounds to be seen. Size of openings and spaces between horizontal and vertical elements: max. 12 cm (France: 11 cm)	Do not use pointed, sharp-edged, or protruding elements or barbed wire as an upper termination. Entries are to be designed so that they are lockable and, if there is nearby moving traffic, so that they cannot be opened by children's hands (for elementary schools and preschools).
Preschools and daycare facilities		Formation as visual screening can be sensible, depending on the situation. Size of openings and spaces between horizontal and vertical elements: max. 12 cm (France: 11 cm)	
School grounds			
Sports facilities for ball sports: tennis etc.	Polyethylene mesh, wire mesh, double wire panels (with noise abatement if applicable)	Recommended configurations for steel welded wire fences: • Up to 2 m high: grid size 50/200 mm • From 2 meters high onward: grid size 100/200 mm • Typical on-center spacing 2,520 mm (post spacing)	

Table 5.1 Fence materials and construction types

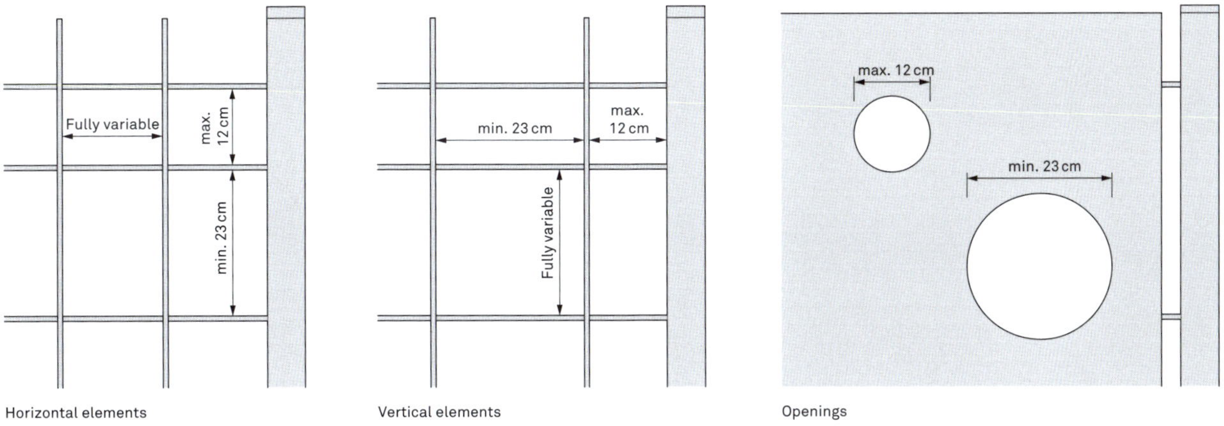

Figure 5.3 Mandatory sizes of openings and spaces between the horizontal and vertical elements of boundary enclosures

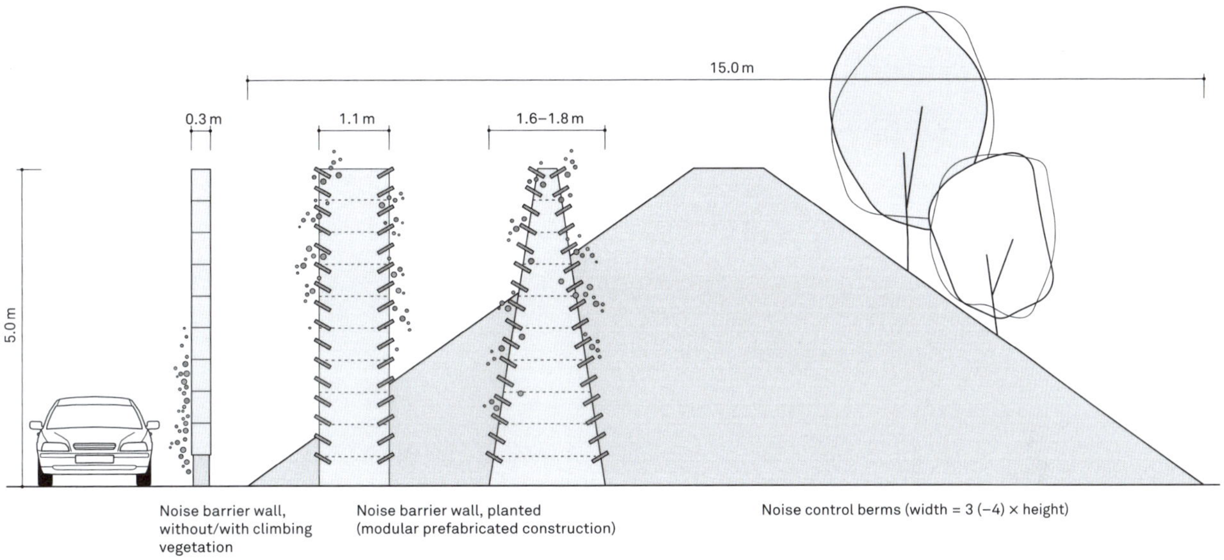

Figure 5.4 Exemplary space requirements for noise abatement measures

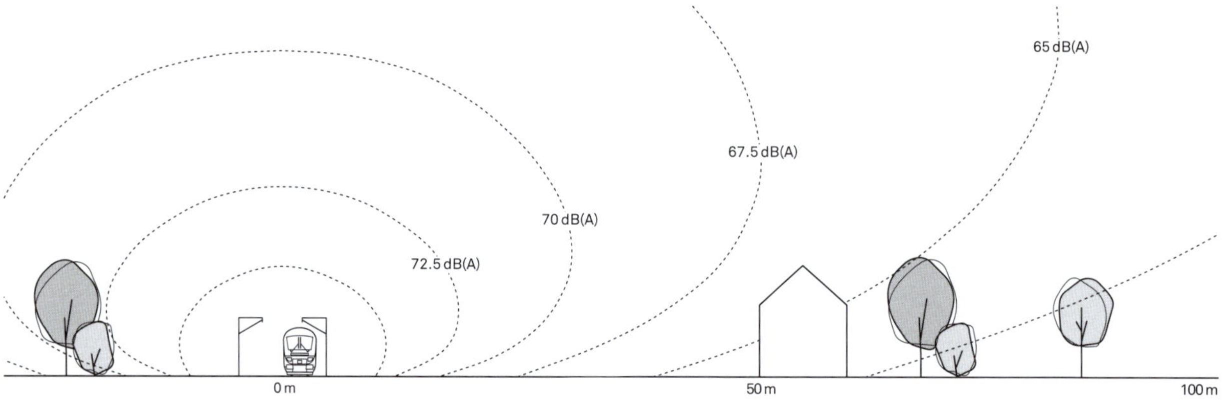

Sound propagation without noise abatement

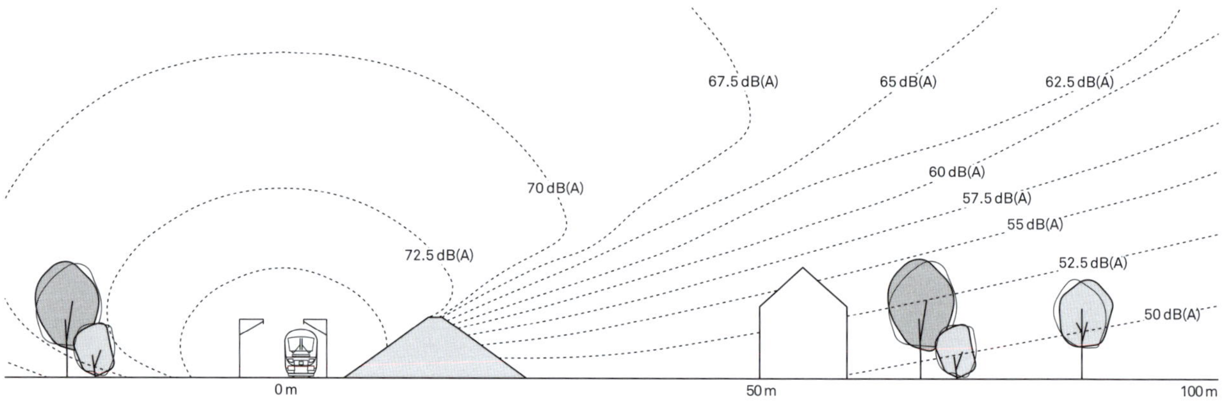

Sound propagation with noise control berms

Figure 5.5 Behavior of sound propagation and acoustic shielding

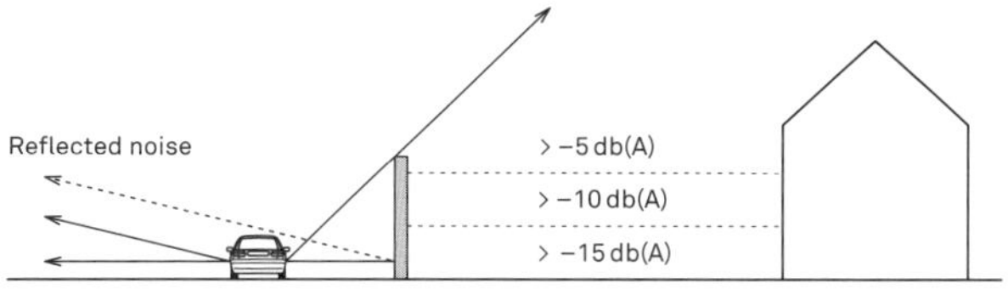
Reflected noise
> −5 db(A)
> −10 db(A)
> −15 db(A)

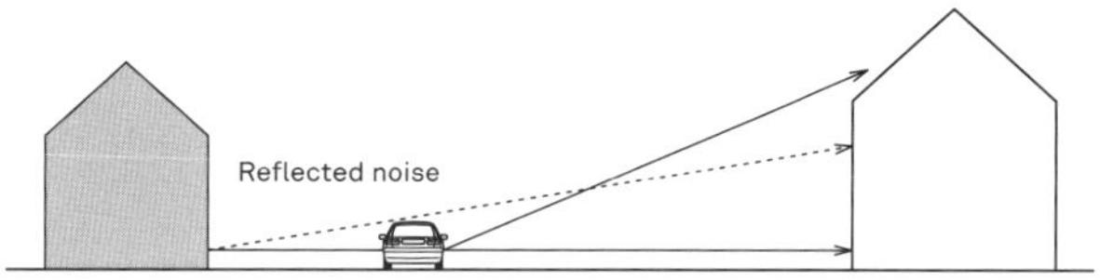
Reflected noise

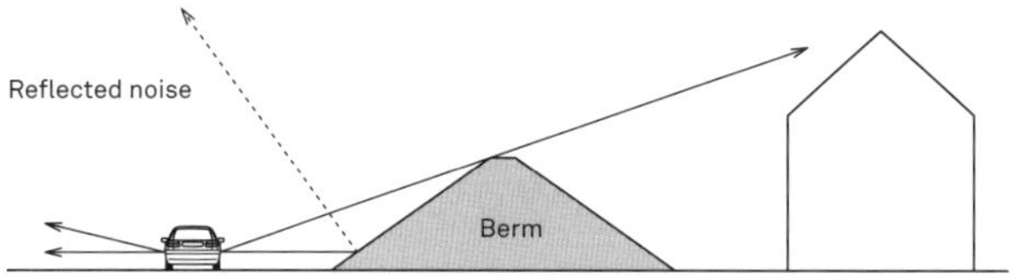
Reflected noise
Berm

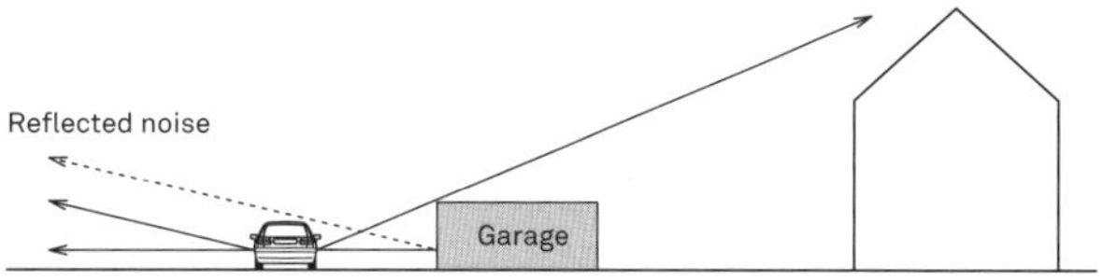
Reflected noise
Garage

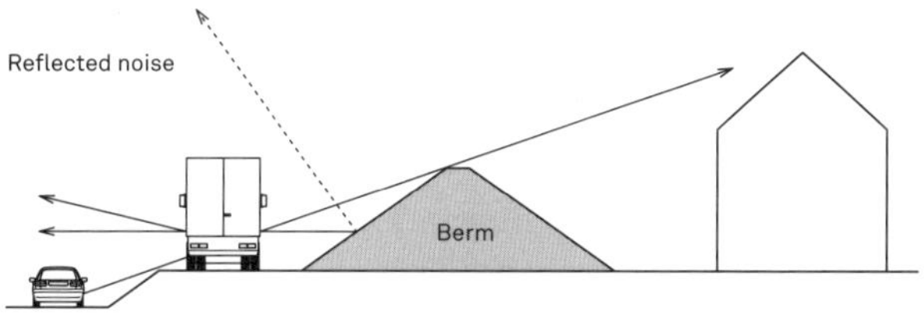
Reflected noise
Berm

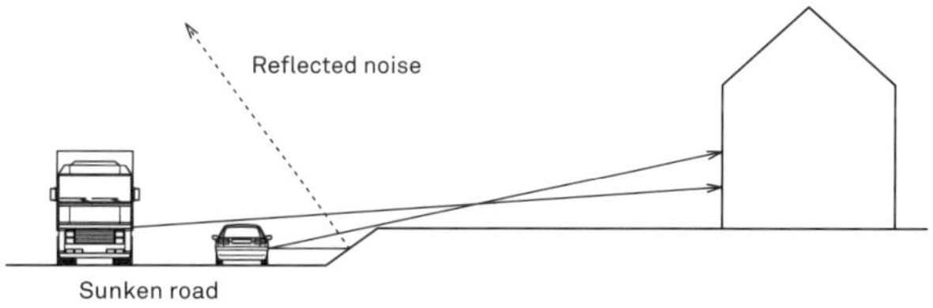
Reflected noise
Sunken road

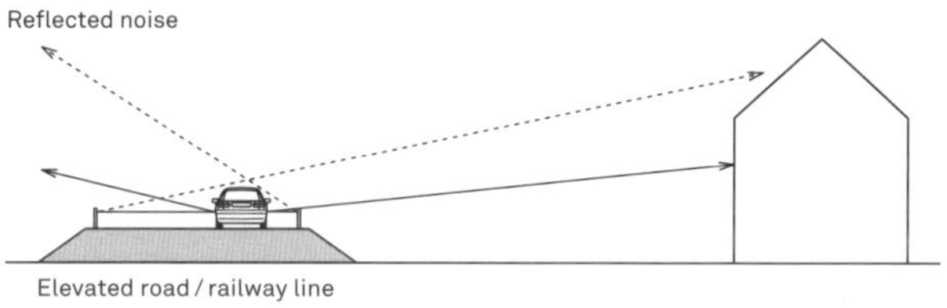
Reflected noise
Elevated road / railway line

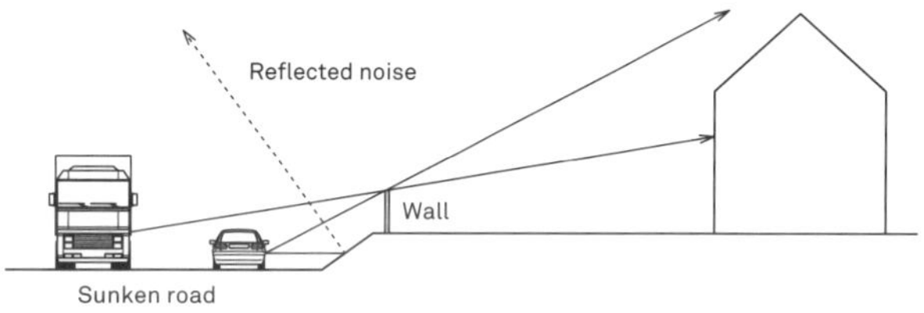
Reflected noise
Wall
Sunken road

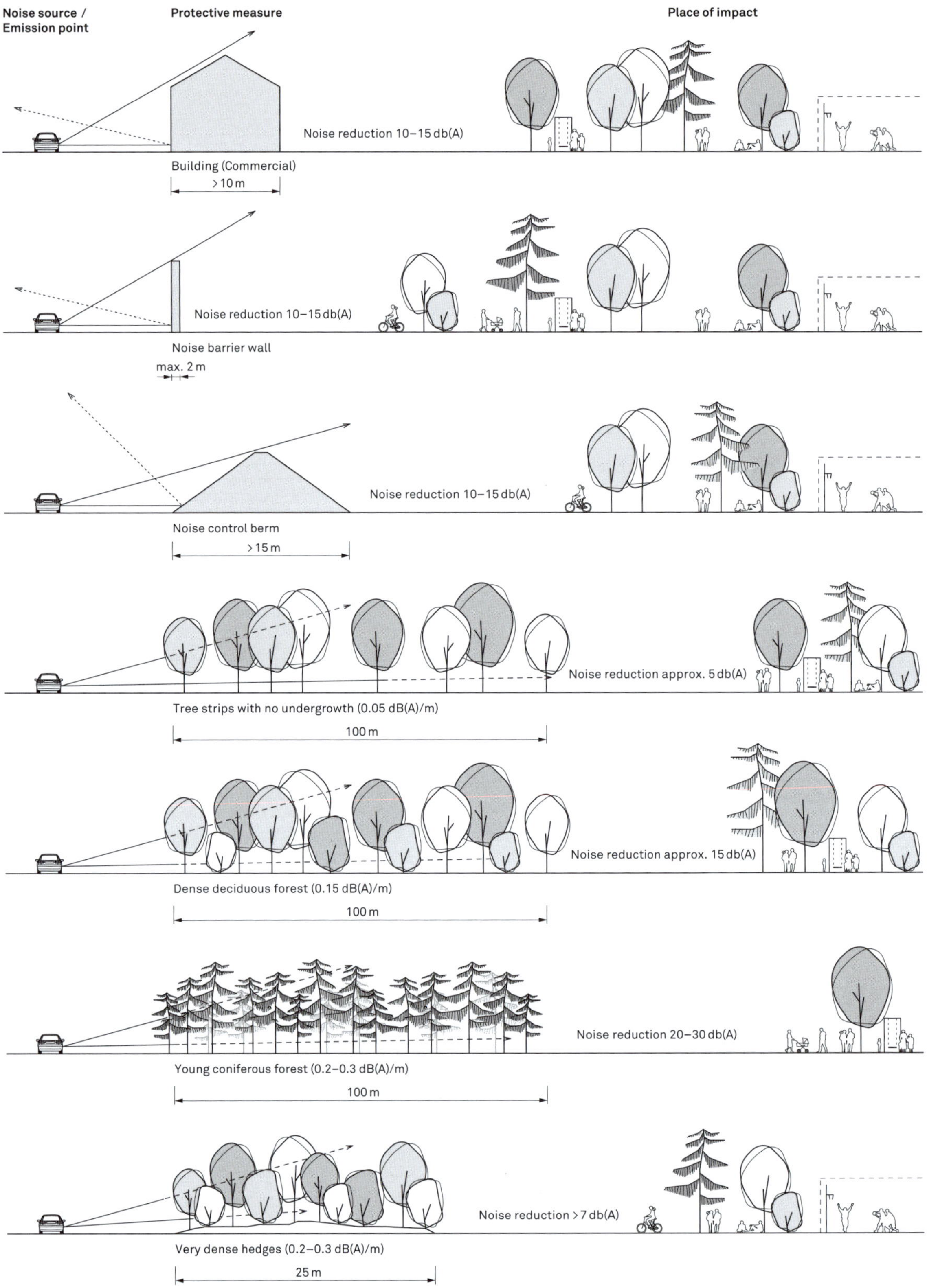

Figure 5.6 Effectiveness of different noise abatement measures

State	Maximum heights of walls / solid boundary enclosures	Maximum heights of open boundary enclosures	Exceptions
Berlin	Up to 2 m, with no height limit in commercial and industrial areas		In undeveloped open areas: open boundary fences with no base, on the premises of an agricultural or forestry operation or in areas used for agricultural purposes
Baden-Württemberg	Up to 1.5 m	Up to 1.5 m	Height of wire fences is not restricted
Bavaria	Up to 2 m, except in undeveloped open areas; Mounds up to a height of 2 m and a maximum area of 500 m²	Up to 2 m, except in undeveloped open areas	In undeveloped open areas: open boundary fences with no base, on the premises of an agricultural or forestry operation or in areas used for agricultural purposes
Brandenburg	Up to 1.5 m high, except in undeveloped open areas	Up to 2 m high, except in undeveloped open areas	In undeveloped open areas: open boundary fences up to 2 m high, with no base, on the premises of an agricultural or forestry operation or in areas used for agricultural purposes
Hesse	Up to 2 m, with no height limit in commercial and industrial areas		Open boundary fences in undeveloped open areas
Lower Saxony	Retaining walls and mounds up to a height of 1.5 m	Up to a height of 2 m, boundary enclosures may only be opaque above a height of 1.8 m if the neighbor grants consent	Boundary fences up to a height of 3.5 m when they enclose garden courtyards and the conditions of § 12 Par. 5 are fulfilled
North Rhine-Westphalia	Up to 2 m high, along public thoroughfares up to 1 m high above grade		In undeveloped open areas on built-up lots or when the construction is granted approval or on the premises of an agricultural or forestry operation or in areas used for agricultural purposes
Saxony	Up to 1.8 m high, with no height limit in commercial and industrial areas		

Table 5.2 Permissible heights (permit-free construction) of boundary enclosures with no property line setbacks from the neighboring lot (selected examples, per respective building codes)

5.2 Handrails, Railings and Parapets

Railings and parapets serve as fall protection along paths, on plazas and squares, bridges, and stairs, and along bikeways. Parapets are primarily opaque constructions made of solid materials, for example masonry or concrete, whereas railings are open structures that might be made of metal or wood. Parapets with a railing as an upper termination are a common combination of both types. For areas where a guard contradicts the intended use, no railing is required. This usually applies to docks, swimming pools, and ponds. A boundary enclosure may be necessary when, for example, a pond or a water basin is located in an area that is frequently visited by children.

Handrails must be affixed wherever there is an uninterrupted series of three steps. For barrier-free access, a handrail is required for two or more consecutive steps. For stair widths greater than 5 m, an additional center handrail shall be provided. The height is measured vertically above the nosing and shall be 90 cm under normal circumstances. For workplaces, a minimum of 100 cm are required.

As a general rule, with a fall height (difference in elevation) of 1 m or more, railings or parapets are required as guards. This also pertains to embankments when these are very steep. The height of the railing or parapet shall in this case be min. 0.9 m (1 m in workplaces). For fall heights of 12 m or more, railings and parapets must be 1.1 m high. Deviating regulations exist, for instance in Bavaria, where a guard is required starting at 0.5 m.

Railings along bikeways or shared pedestrian and bicycle paths should generally be built 1.2 m high.

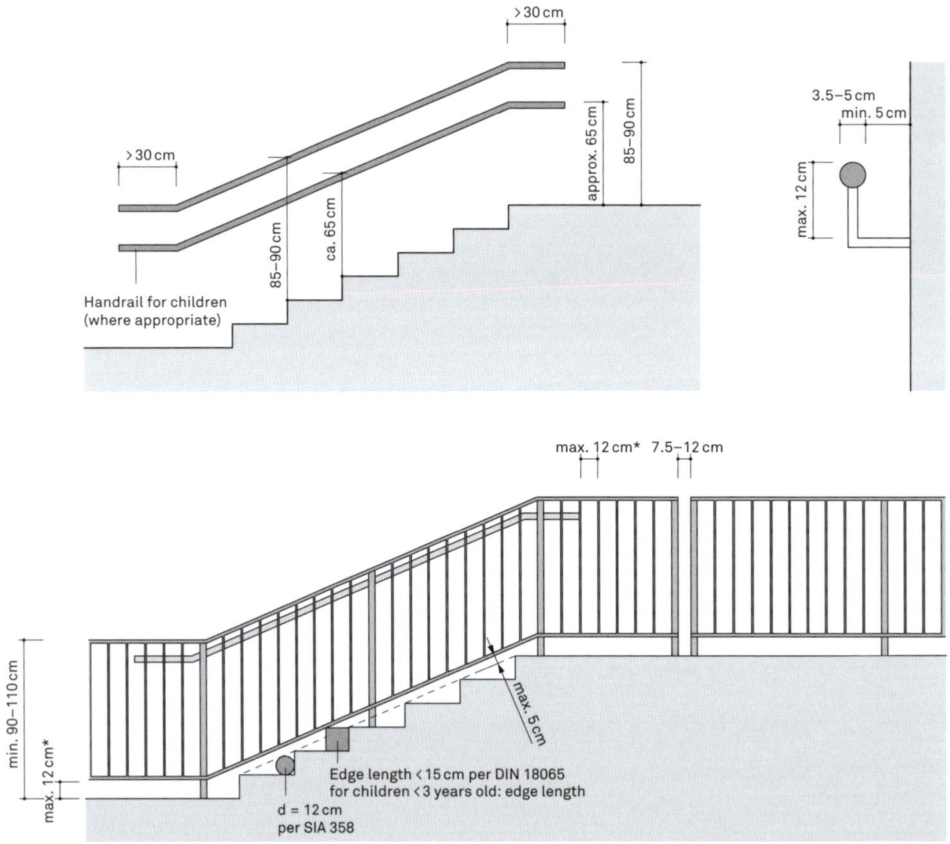

* in day care centers, max. 11 cm (children 3 years and older) or max. 8.9 cm (children under 3 years old)

Figure 5.7 Requirements for stair handrails

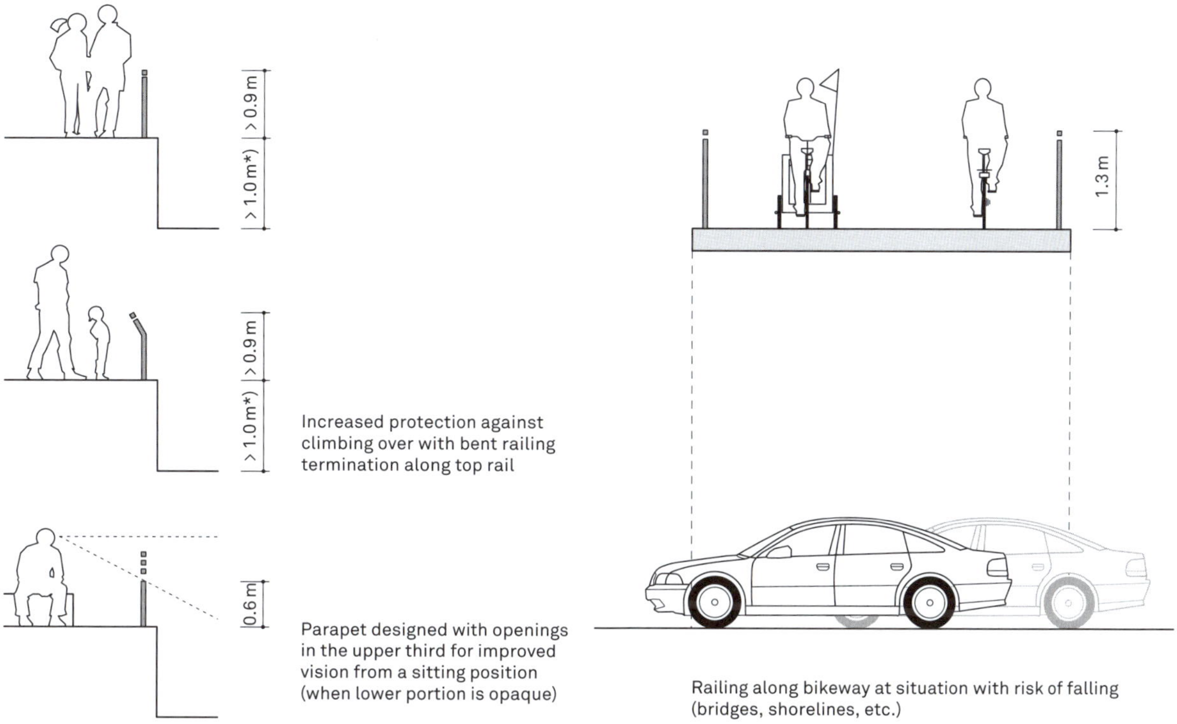

*) Observe state regulations; in Bavaria > 0.5 m

Figure 5.8 Requirements for railings and parapets

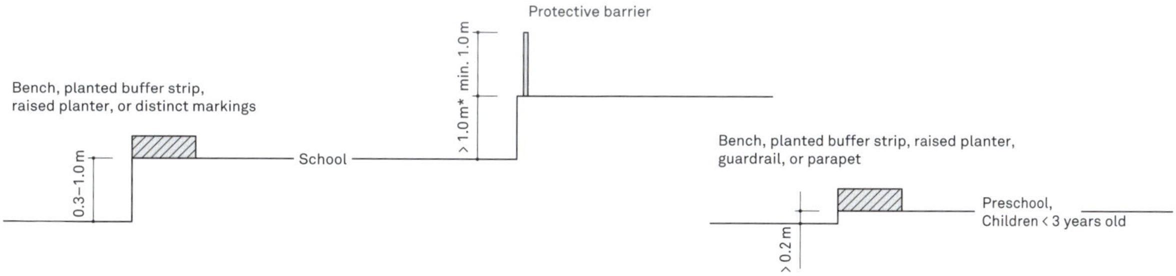

* Per state building codes; in Bavaria > 0.5 m

Figure 5.9 Fall heights and protective measures in schools (left) and preschools (right)

6 Street Furniture

Determining the correct amount of space needed to equip outdoor facilities demands knowledge of standard dimensions and parameters. Seats as well as waste container areas require proper dimensioning that takes into account adequate maneuvering space. Areas that are insufficiently dimensioned can quickly lead to conflicts of use or interference, and hence they should be amply sized. The functionality of an outdoor space is also ensured by providing adequate lighting, which must be appropriate to the use of the space and can be regulated by luminaire spacing and illuminance levels.

6.1 Waste Container Areas

Waste disposal in outdoor facilities has significance in the public sphere mostly in the form of garbage baskets and other waste receptacles that are placed in green spaces and parks, along streets and sidewalks, or at playgrounds and sports fields. In addition, areas for collection containers for glass and other recyclable materials must be provided in the public street space. Finally, corresponding collection points for the temporary storage of household garbage or commercial waste must be provided at buildings.

In planning such waste container areas, attention must be given to their dimensioning, siting, and access.

A refuse collection point must be easily reachable and accessible at all times, both for the residents as well as for the waste removal companies.

A grade-level connection for the approach should be made whenever possible. When ramps are unavoidable, they shall not exceed a slope of 2% – in exceptional cases up to a maximum of 6% – and obstacles such as steps or channels are to be avoided; for large containers (i.e., Dumpsters)

a dropped curb shall be provided.

A paved approach with a minimum width of 1.5 to 1.6 m is commonly provided. For containers up to a volume of 1,100 liters, a minimum width of 1.2 m is sufficient.

Use	Amount/week						
	Residual waste	Paper	Organic	Food waste	Plastic	Metal	Glass
Office per employee	10 L	10 L	1–2 L	–	0.7 L	0.5 L	0.5 L
Daycare facility per 100 children	1,100 L	240 L	120 L	–	–	–	–
School per student	4 L	2 L	0.5 L	–	–	–	–
Nursing home / Hospital per bed	110 L	20 L	2 L	5 L	5 L	2 L	2 L
Restaurant per 100 meals	45 L	15 L	–	15 L	8 L	8 L	8 L
Bed and breakfast per bed	7.5 L	7 L	1 L	–	–	–	–
Hotel ****/***** per bed	85 L	20 L	2 L	5 L	5 L	2 L	2 L

Table 6.1 Orientation values for the waste generated in commercial establishments
(Source: Recommendations of Abfallwirtschaftsbetrieb München (AWM), 2011)

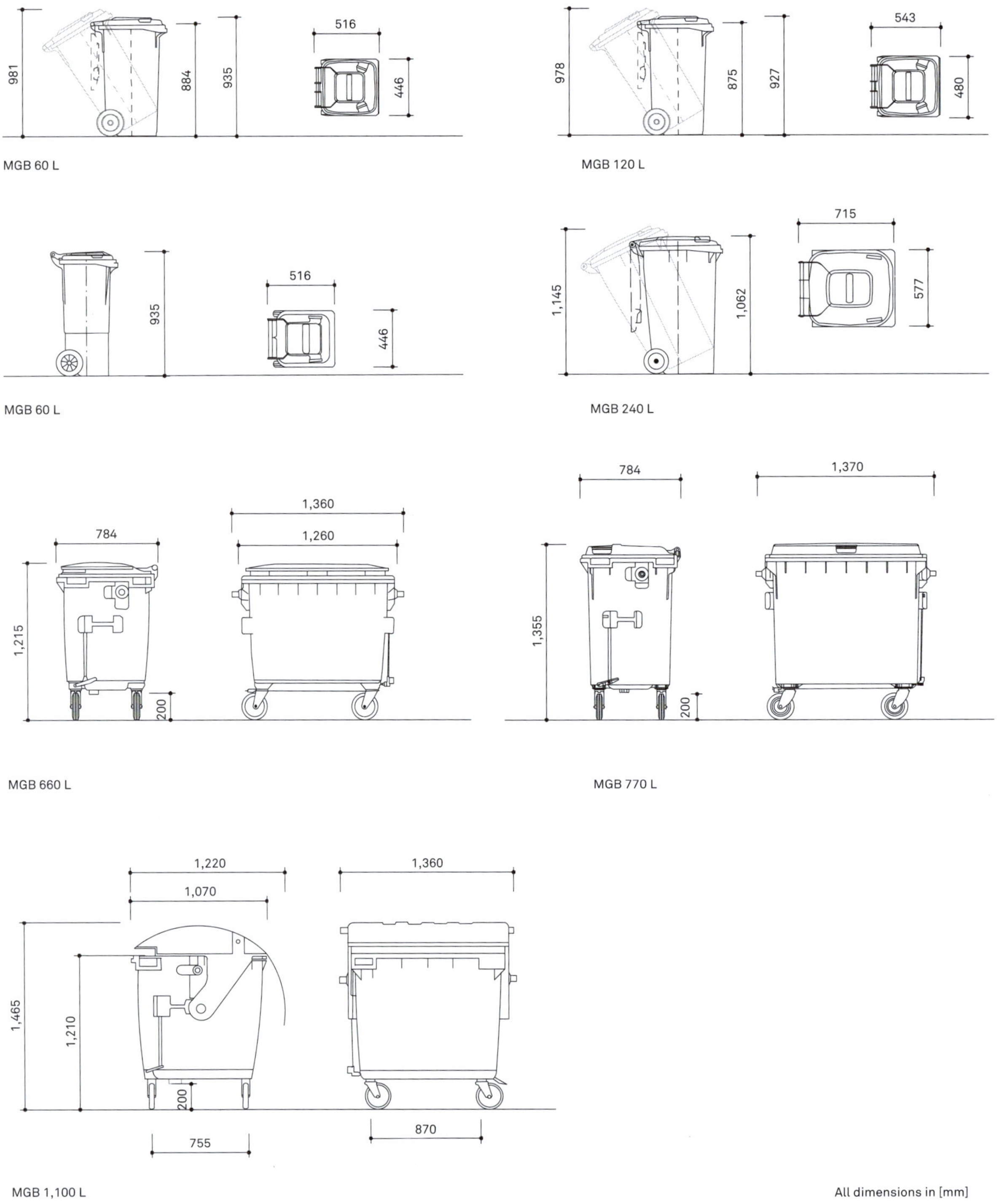

Figure 6.1 Common waste container sizes, in mm

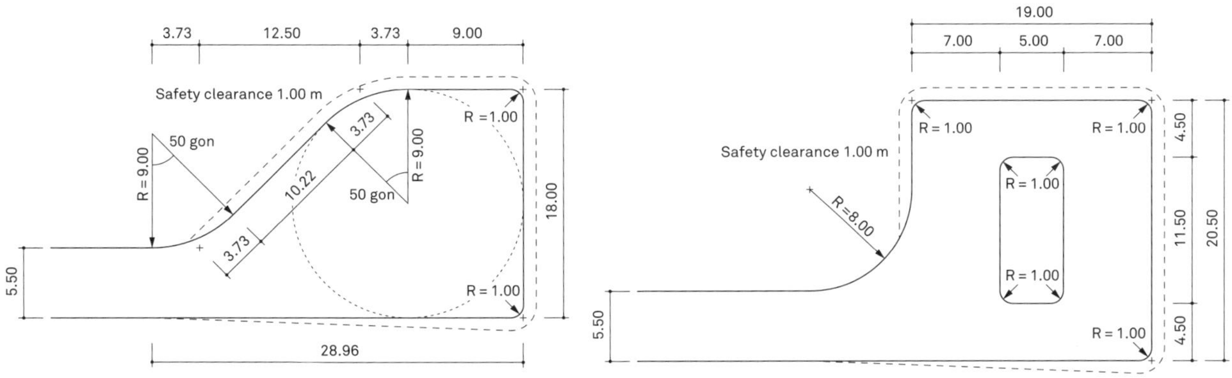

Turning circle for 2-axle garbage truck

Turning circle for 3-axle garbage truck

All dimensions in [m]

Figure 6.2 Space requirement for a turning circle for two- and three-axle garbage trucks (as per RASt 06)

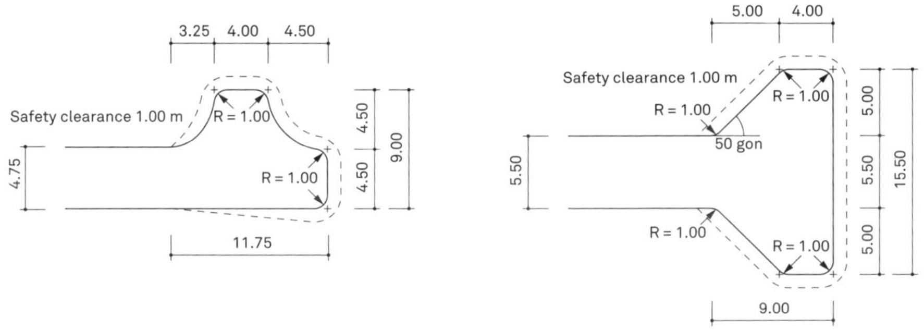

Car turnaround

Turnaround – 2-axle garbage truck (vehicles up to 9 m long)

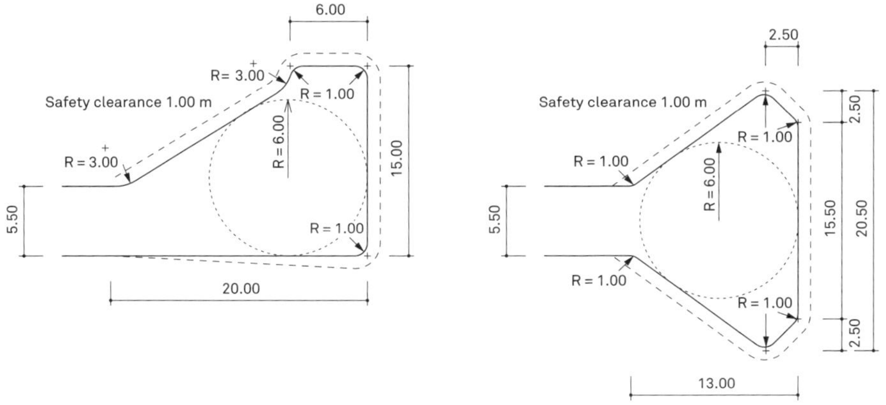

3-axle garbage truck – single-sided turnaround and 3-axle garbage truck – hammerhead turnaround (vehicles up to 10 m long)

All dimensions in [m]

Figure 6.3 Turnarounds for two- and three-axle waste collection vehicles

6.2 Seating

For adequate dimensioning of seating in outdoor facilities, the following dimensions of benches and seating groups can serve as guidelines. Because the designs of seating furniture, tables, and umbrellas are so highly diverse, manufacturer's data should be taken into account whenever appropriate.

For restaurant establishments, in addition to seating for the restaurant guests themselves, aisles between the seats and areas for storage and possibly for an outdoor counter should be taken into account as needed.

For terraces of a smaller size, too, however, the specifications pertaining to larger events can still be used to set out minimum distances between rows of seating and between table groups. As a general rule, each table must be located on an aisle that leads to an exit. The distance from each seat to an aisle is often assessed differently, but typically a maximum of 5–10 m is stipulated. Between rows of chairs – or to be precise, between occupied chairs – a clear width of at least 0.45 m should be available for passage, or alternatively, a distance of at least 1.5 m should be provided between the tables.

When dimensioning and laying out aisles, the space needed for maneuvering wheelchairs must always be taken into consideration. For seating areas in parks, too, spaces measuring 1.5 × 1.5 m (incl. movement area) should be incorporated for wheelchairs.

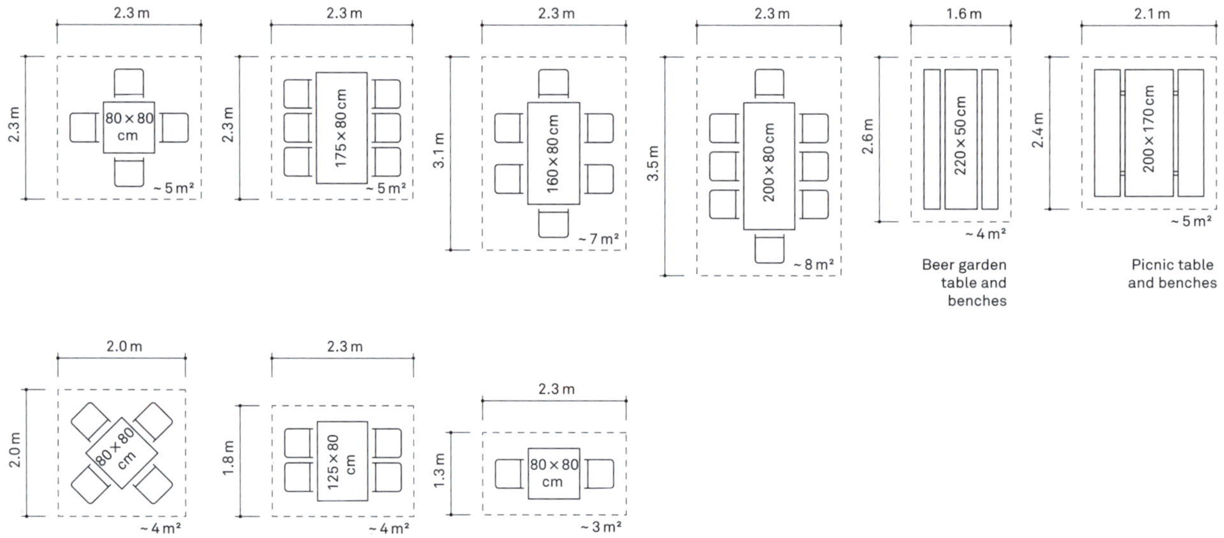

Figure 6.4 Space requirements for seating, including maneuvering space (minimum dimensions)

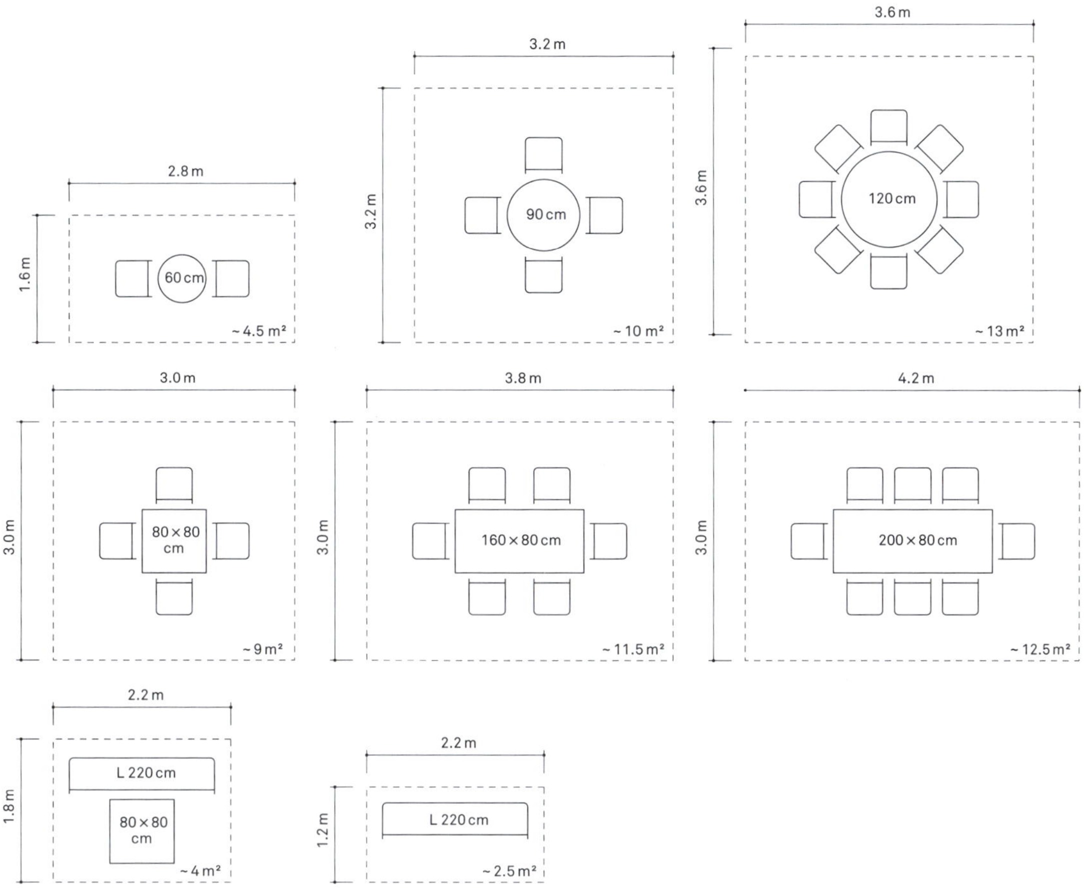

Figure 6.5 Space requirements for seating for solitary arrangement / on terraces

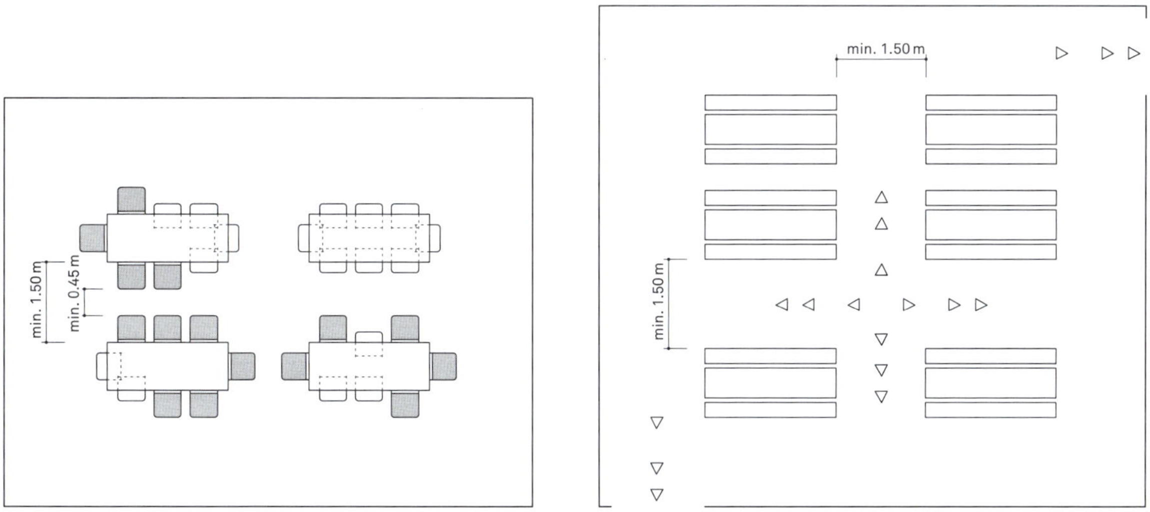

Figure 6.6 Aisle widths and clearances for groups of chairs and tables with no specific egress requirements

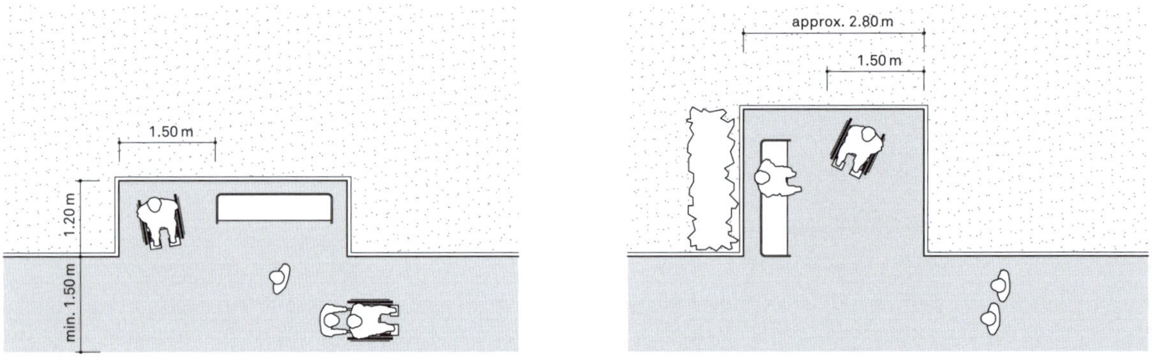

Figure 6.7 Space requirement for wheelchair spaces at benches in outdoor facilities

Type of umbrella	Length × width/diameter	Height when open	Clearance below	Height when closed
Small umbrella, round	Dia. = 2–3 m	2.60 m		
Large umbrellas, round	Dia. = 4 m	3.20 m		
	Dia. = 4.5 m	3.15 m	2.15–2.4 m	4.4 m
	Dia. = 5 m	3.15 m	2.15–2.4 m	4.3 m
	Dia. = 6 m	3.15 m	2.15–2.4 m	4.2 m
Large umbrellas, square	3 × 3 m	2.6 m		
	3.5 × 3.5 m	3.9 m		
	4 × 4 m			3.3 m
	5 × 5 m		2.15–2.4 m	3.35 m
	6 × 6 m	3.4 m	2.15–2.4 m	3.4 m
Large umbrellas, rectangular	6 × 4 m	3.4 m	2.15–2.4 m	3.4 m

Table 6.2 Exemplary dimensions of umbrellas

Type of seating	Space required	Total area
Individual dimensions		
Single chaise lounge	1.85 × 0.85 m	1.6 m²
Picnic table with benches (dimensions vary by manufacturer)	Length: approx. 2.00 m Width: approx. 1.70 m	3.4 m²
Beer garden table and benches	Large: table 2.20 × 0.50 m (0.80 m), bench 2.20 × 0.25 m Small: table 1.77 × 0.46 m, bench 1.77 × 0.23 m	2.2 m² (2.9 m²) 1.65 m²
Seating, including maneuvering space (minimum size)		
Seating with table (0.80 × 0.80 m) and 2 chairs	2.80 × 1.30 m	Approx. 3.7 m²
Seating with table (0.80 × 0.80 m) and 4 chairs	2.30 × 1.80 m to 2.30 × 2.30 m	Approx. 4 to 5 m²
Seating with table (1.60 × 0.80 m) and 6 chairs	2.30 × 2.30 m to 2.30 × 3.10 m	Approx. 5 to 7 m²
Seating with table (2.00 × 0.80 m) and 8 chairs	2.30 × 3.70 m	Approx. 8 m²
Picnic table with benches	2.40 × 2.10 m	Approx. 5 m²
Beer garden table and benches (2.2 m long)	2.60 × 1.6 m	Approx. 4 m²
Seating groups with tables, for solitary arrangements/on terraces		
Seating with round table (Ø 0.60 m) and 2 chairs	2.80 × 1.60 m	Approx. 4.5 m²
Seating with round table (Ø 0.90 m) and 4 chairs (+2)	3.20 × 3.20 m	Approx. 10 m²
Seating with table (0.80 × 0.80 m) and 4 chairs	3.00 × 3.00 m	Approx. 9 m²
Seating with table (1.60 × 0.80 m) and 6 chairs	3.00 × 3.80 m	Approx. 11.5 m²
Seating with table (2.00 × 0.80 m) and 8 chairs	4.00 × 3.00 m	Approx. 12.5 m²
Seating with round table (Ø 1.20 m) and 8 chairs	3.60 × 3.60 m	Approx. 13 m²
Seating with bench (length 1.80 m)	2.20 × 1.20 m	Approx. 2.6 m²
Seating with bench and table (0.80 × 0.80 m)	2.20 × 1.80 m	Approx. 4 m²
Seating with bench (length 1.80 m) and place for wheelchair	3.50 × 1.20 m	Approx. 4.2 m²
Recommended values for seating in restaurant facilities, per guest		
Fast food restaurant		1.2–1.5 m² per guest
System restaurant		1.3–1.6 m² per guest
Upscale restaurant		1.8–2.2 m² per guest

Table 6.3 Space requirements for seating

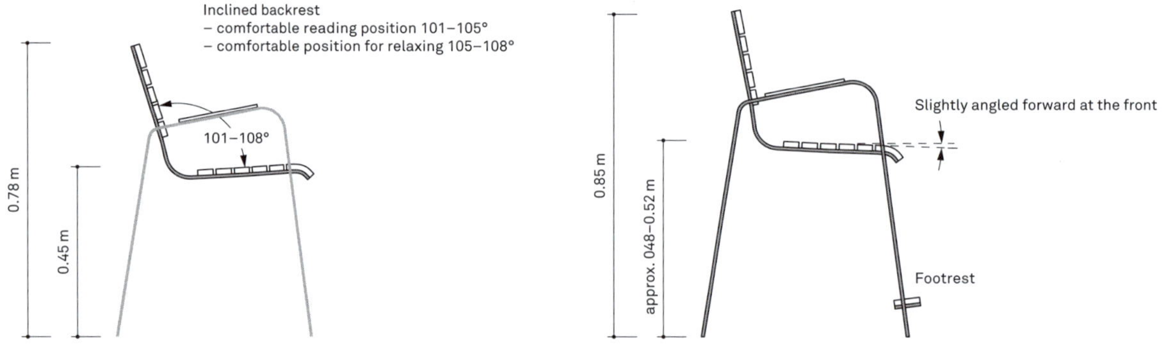

Standard seat height

Bench for seniors, with elevated seat

Figure 6.8 Seating comfort

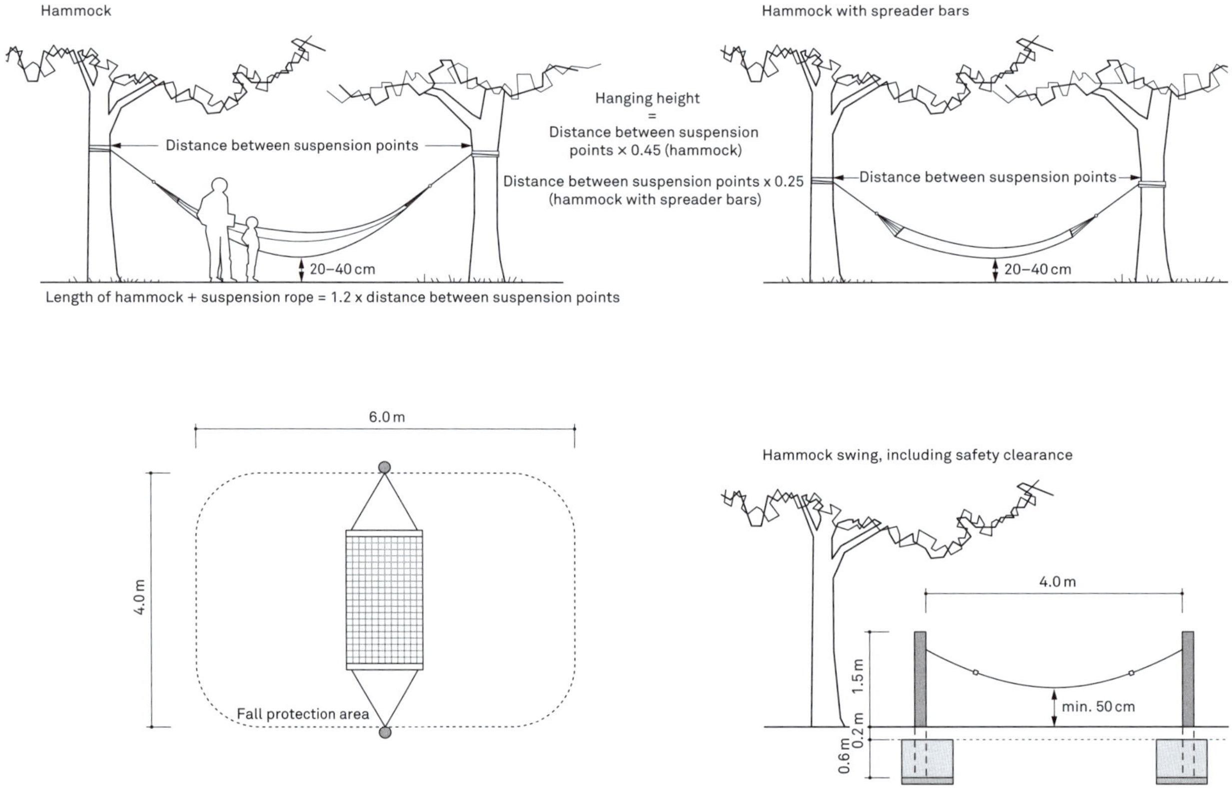

Figure 6.9 Dimensions and space requirements of hammocks, both portable and fixed in place

6.3 Lighting

Outdoors, lighting provides orientation, contributes to safety, and also defines space. Depending on the design intent and function, different types of luminaires are used.

Luminaire type	Image	Application
Floor lights		Orientation, building access
Bollard lights	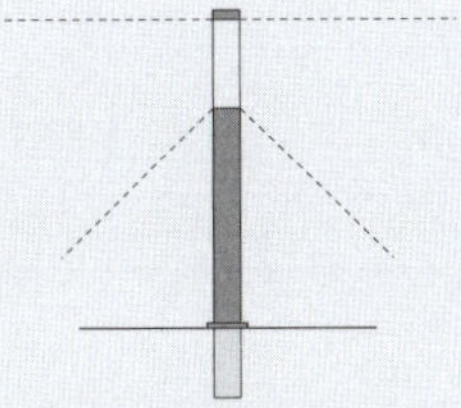	Orientation, building access, promenades
Floodlights	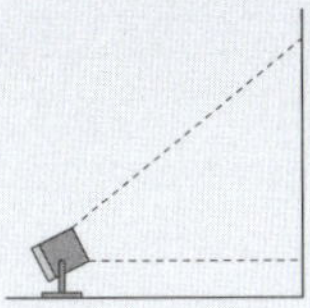	Lighting facades or objects, sports and area floodlighting
Wall-mounted luminaires Recessed wall luminaires	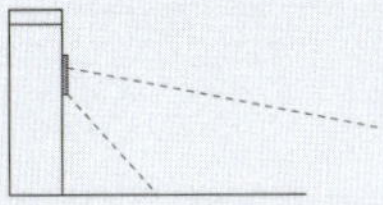	Stairs, building approach
Catenary suspended uminaires	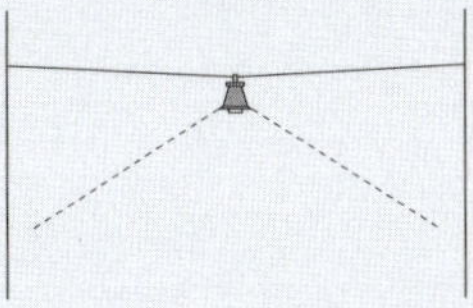	Streets and courtyards, especially between buildings
Mast lights with symmetric/ asymmetric light distribution	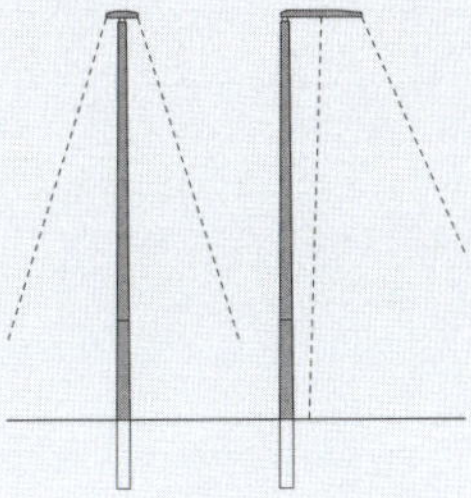	Road lighting, park paths, promenades

Table 6.4 Luminaire types and their applications

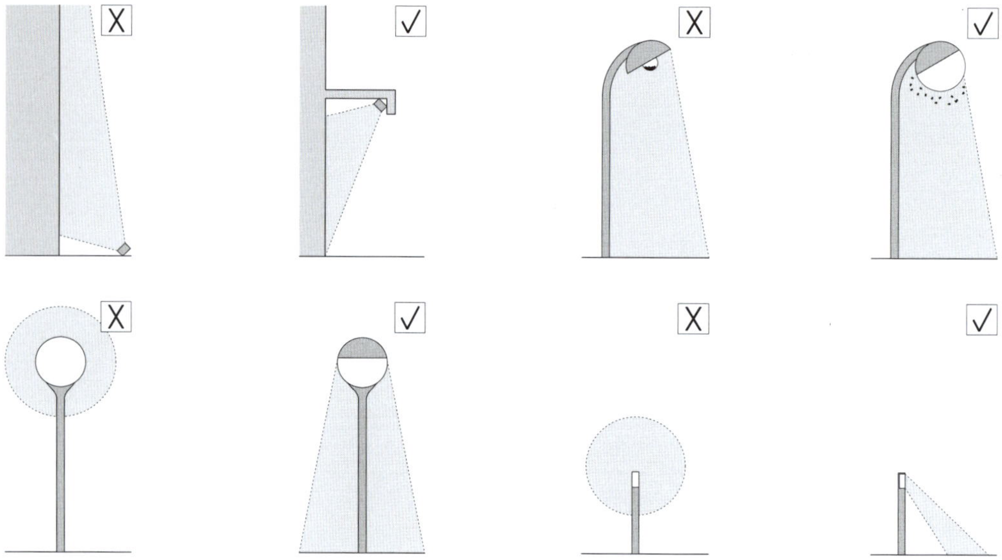

Figure 6.10 Sustainable use of luminaires outdoors: downward beam direction for general use and for illuminating facades, together with safeguards for nocturnal insects

Light source/lamp	Abbreviation	Luminous efficiency (approx.), in lumens/Watt	Life span (approx.), in hrs.	Light color	Negative effect on insects	Comments
Low-pressure sodium vapor lamps	SOX/LPS lamps	170–200	16,000	Orange-colored	< 10 %	Poor color fidelity, very insect-friendly, very efficient
High-pressure sodium vapor lamps	NA/HPS lamps	130–150	12,000–16,000	Warm white	10–20 %	Insect-friendly
Incandescent bulbs (general-service tungsten-filament lamps)	A lamps	12	1,000	Warm white	10–15 %	No longer state-of-the-art, inefficient
Halogen lamps	QT/QR lamps	25	5,000	Warm white	10–15 %	
Compact fluorescent lamps ("energy-saving lamps" with integrated ballast)	TC lamps	60	8,000–15,000	White	20–25 %	Only for low mounting heights
Linear fluorescent lamps (tubes)	T lamps	80	8,000–16,000	White	25–35 %	
High-pressure metal halide discharge lamps	HCI/HSI lamps	85	8,000–12,000	White	30–55 %	
High-pressure mercury vapor lamps	HPL/HPM lamps	50	12,000–16,000	White	100 %	Obsolete, soon no longer available
Light-emitting diodes, electroluminescent diodes	LED	90	50,000	Warm white to neutral white	10–15 %	Very efficient

Table 6.5 Characteristics of various lamps

	Illuminance	Uniformity	Standards, guidelines
Bikeways with pedestrians and high traffic flow, depending on crime rate and other criteria	3 to 15	E_{min} = 1 lx to 5 lx	EN 13202-2 lighting situation D4
Bikeways with pedestrians and normal traffic flow, depending on crime rate and other criteria	2 to 10	E_{min} = 0.6 lx to 3 lx	
Traffic areas for slow-moving vehicles (max. 10 km/h), e.g., bicycles, trucks, excavators	10	g_1 = 0.40	EN 12464-2
Paths for bicycles near roads for automobile traffic with fixed illumination	–	E_{min} = 3 lx g_2 = 0.15	FSGV values apply along the centerline of the bikeway
Paths for bicycles near roads for automobile traffic with no fixed illumination	–	E_{min} = 3 lx g_2 = 0.3	
Paths for bicycles farther away than 8 m from roads for automobile traffic with no fixed illumination	–	E_{min} = 1.5 lx g_2 = 0.15	

Table 6.6 Minimum requirements for lighting bikeways

	Illuminance in lux	Uniformity	Semicylindrical illuminance, in lux	Standards, guidelines
Pedestrian paths, high traffic flow, depending on crime rate and other criteria	7.5 to 20	–	1.5 to 5	EN 13201-2 lighting situation E1
Pedestrian paths, normal traffic flow, depending on crime rate and other criteria	2 to 15	–	0.5 to 3	EN 13201-2 lighting situation E1
Walkways solely for pedestrians	5	g_1 = 0.25	–	EN 12464-2
Traffic areas for slow-moving vehicles (max. 10 km/h), e.g., bicycles, trucks, excavators	10	g_1 = 0.40	–	EN 12464-2
Walkways on factory premises	3	g_1 = 0.08	–	EN 12464-2
Walkways in parks and housing complexes	–	E_{min} = 1 lx	≥ 1	FSGV
Walkways with steps, unevenness, and other safety hazards	–	E_{min} = 5 lx	≥ 1	FSGV
Squares and entries	5	g_2 = 0.1	≥ 1	FSGV
Squares and entries with occasional high crowd density	10	g_2 = 0.1	≥ 1	FSGV
Inner-city pedestrian areas	≥ 5	E_{min} = 1 lx g_2 = 0.08	≥ 1	FSGV
Stairs, exterior	15	g_2 = 0.3	-	FSGV

Table 6.7 Minimum requirements for lighting pedestrian areas

7 Water

Water always flows to the lowest point and accumulates as soon as it reaches a depression. Thus natural ponds and lakes always fill an appropriate concave area, and the water surface traces the changing course along its edge, where it intersects the undulating terrain at a constant elevation. An artificially created pond seems most natural when it is sited to fit within the existing topography and is located at a low point in the terrain. If it is built using nonrigid construction – with membrane or clay seals, for example – not only is a seminatural character created that way, but the structural stability of the natural soil mass can be optimally utilized. No additional means of support are needed.

While still in the planning stage, choices should be made between nonrigid and rigid construction (concrete basin, masonry, prefabricated plastic basins), between a planted and an unplanted basin, and between facilities with standing or moving water (fountains, streams, etc.), in order to make allowances for the requirements that emerge regarding the site, the dimensions, and the technical equipment. This is important not in the least because these factors can significantly influence the functionality of a facility and the intensity of maintenance it requires.

7.1 Water Features and Basins

Once it is intended to include plants, certain minimum dimensions should not be exceeded. The water depth depends on the type of planting and can therefore vary.

Terraced steps on the bottom of the pool or pond allow for different water zones in a relatively small space. If a lasting ecological balance is sought, however, the depth should be no less than 80 cm and preferably 100–120 cm. To enable aquatic life to survive in the water over the winter, the pond should not freeze fully and, depending on the region, the water depth that is required can vary accordingly; it is roughly 100 cm in Central Europe.

For seminatural designs and the creation of a peripheral flat shore or terracing, a minimum size of 10 m² should be expected. The larger the facility, the more likely it is that a stable ecosystem will develop.

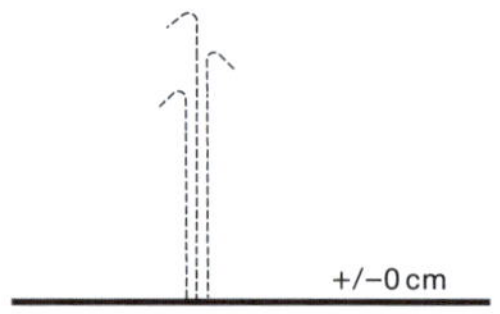

Water feature

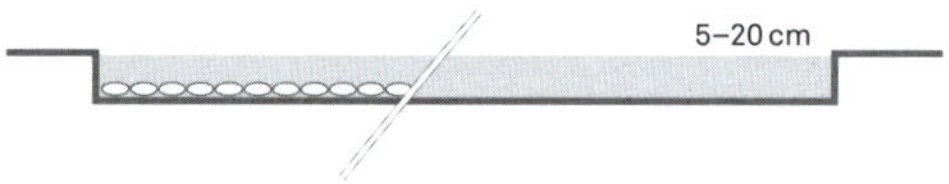

Reflecting pool and water feature

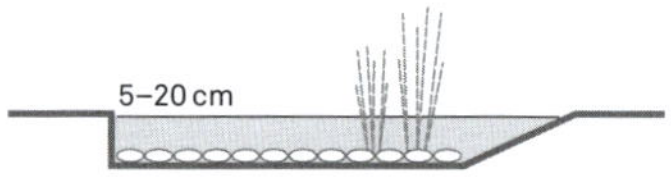

Pool with planting in the marsh and bank zones

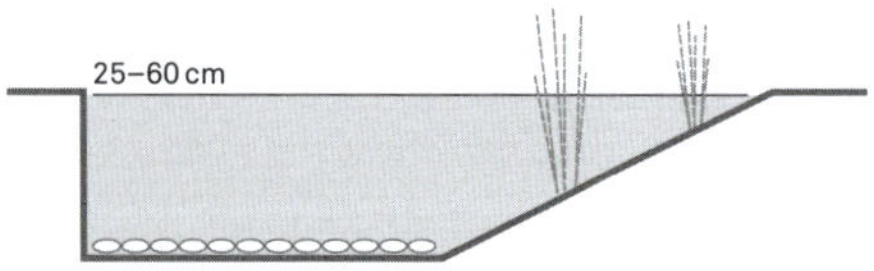

Pools and ponds with planting in the shallow water zone

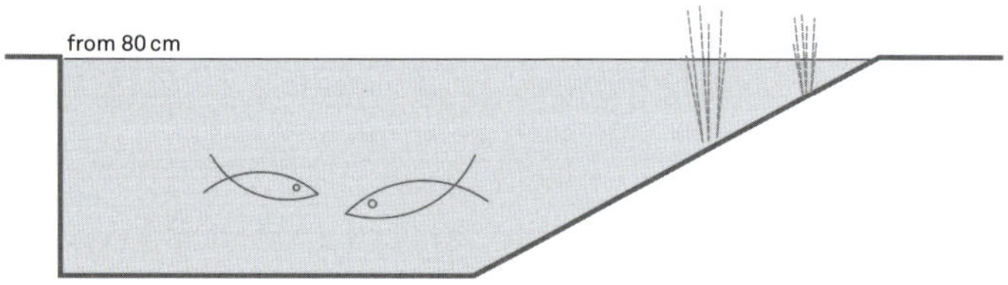

Pools and ponds with planting in the deepwater zone (and possibly the bank and shallow-water zone) and fish stock

Figure 7.1 Water depths for different uses and plant zones

	Planted pools	Seminatural ponds
Site		
Location	Freely selectable	At a low point in the natural terrain
Exposure to sunlight	Optimal: 6–7 hours, more for lily hybrids	
	Alternative: Use of floating-leaved plants, as long as they do not take up more than 50 % of the water surface	
	Avoid direct proximity to deciduous trees	
Dimensions		
Minimum size	None	Minimum 6–10 m²
Minimum size with fish stock	6 m²	
Minimum size for swimming ponds	35–60 m²	
Minimum depth	None	80 cm, preferably 100–120 cm
Minimum depth with fish stock	Depending on the freezing depth: 80 cm in Central Europe, preferably 100–120 cm	
Minimum depth for swimming ponds	1.35 cm	

Table 7.1 Local conditions and minimum sizes of pools and ponds

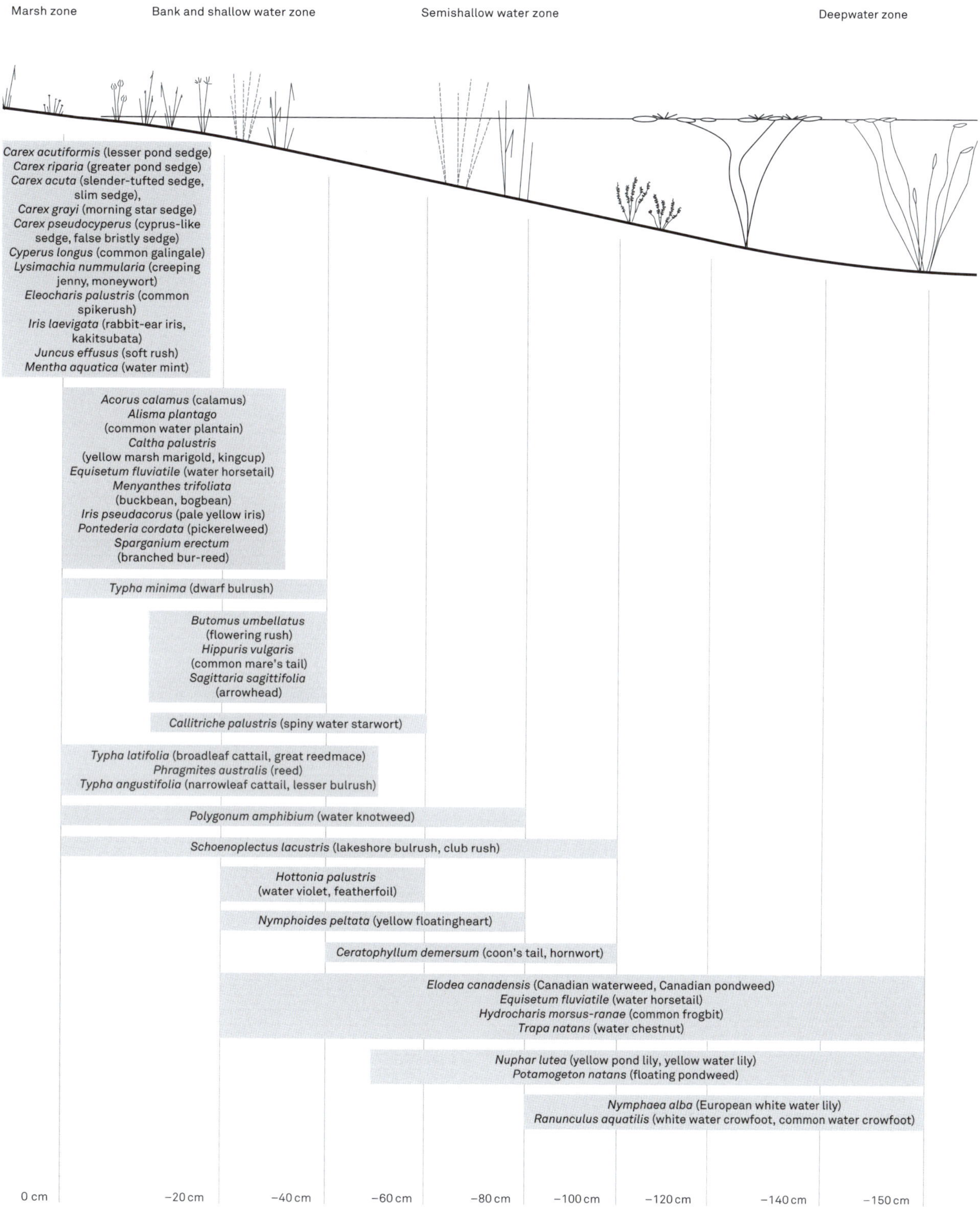

Figure 7.2 Habitats of aquatic plants

7.2 Stormwater Infiltration

The infiltration of stormwater is only an option if the pollution level of the surface runoff does not give reason to expect it would cause significant contamination of the soil and the groundwater. For certain special areas, such as truck parking lots, yards, and streets in commercial and industrial areas, as well as unroofed storage areas for recyclable materials (organic compost, paper, refuse), stormwater infiltration is fundamentally not an option or may only be considered in exceptional cases. Rainwater draining from metal roofs made of uncoated copper, zinc, or lead and the runoff from car parking spaces are not suitable for all types of infiltration, because the harmful substances occurring there could contaminate the soil and the groundwater. Uncontaminated water can percolate through every system.

The following minimum distances from infiltration facilities should be maintained:

- 3 m to property lines
- 1.5 m between decentralized infiltration systems and buildings without waterproofing resistant to hydrostatic pressure (DWA)
- 6 m to buildings (or 1.5 m × basement depth), 10 m to other infiltration systems

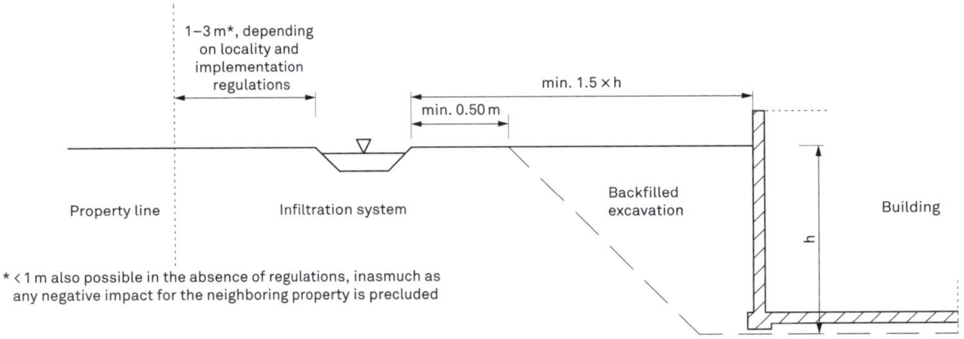

Figure 7.3 Minimum distance between decentralized infiltration systems and buildings without hydrostatic pressure resistant waterproofing

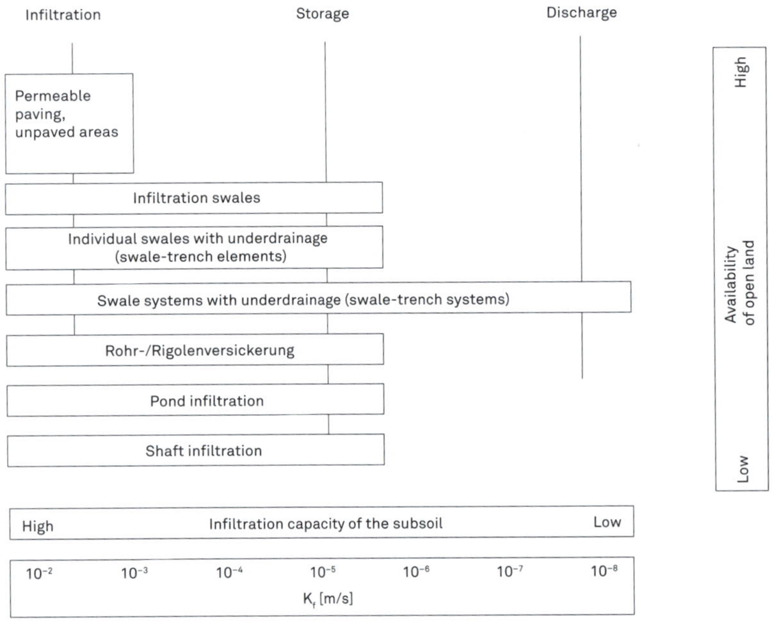

Figure 7.4 Selection of the infiltration system depends on subsoil and land availability

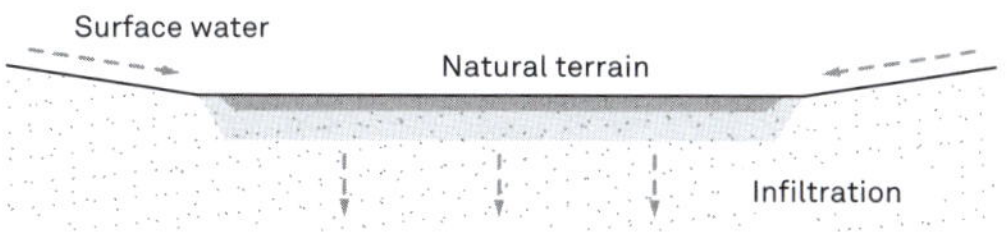

Infiltration field

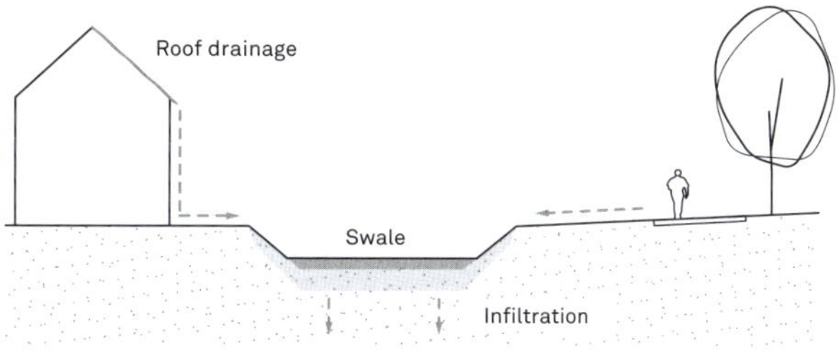

Infiltration swale

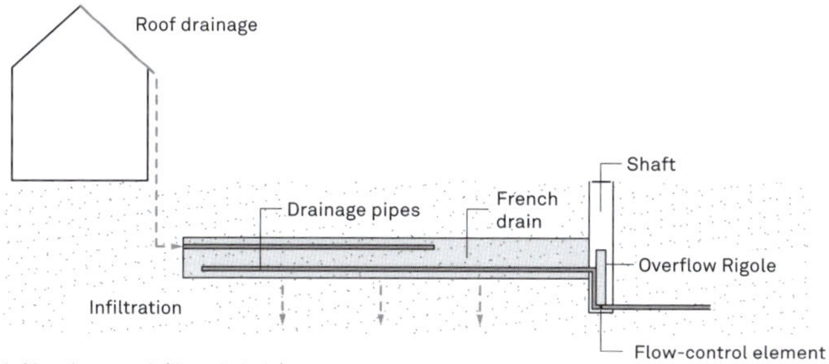

Infiltration trench (French drain)

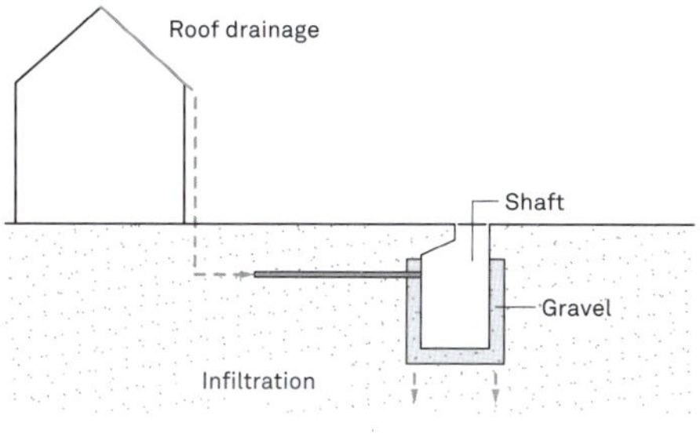

Infiltration shaft

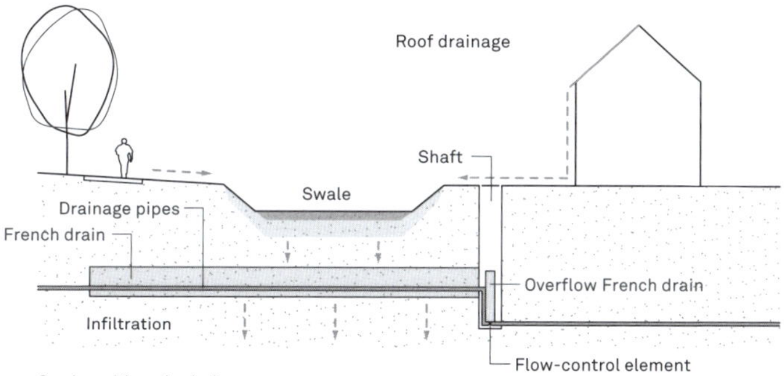

Swales with underdrainage

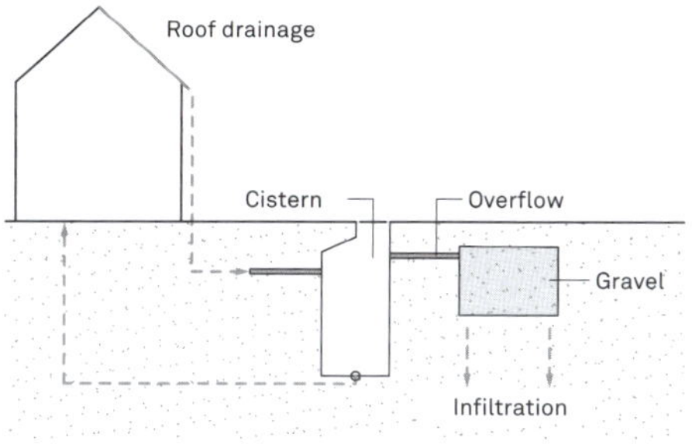

Rainwater harvesting with infiltration

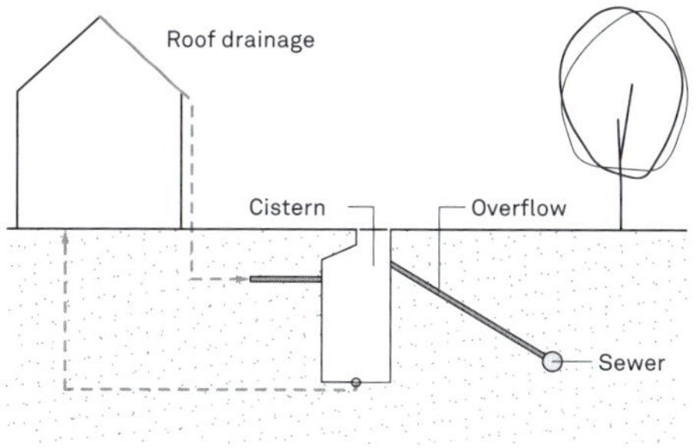

Rainwater harvesting with discharge

Figure 7.5 Schematic representations of various infiltration systems

7.3 Swimming Pools and Bathing Ponds

Outdoor swimming pools can be built either as conventional (chlorinated) pools or in the form of swimming and bathing ponds – commonly known as natural swimming pools (NSPs).

The size needed for a public outdoor swimming pool is determined by the municipality's analysis of requirements, the quantity and size of any nearby existing (outdoor) pools, the way the pool will primarily be used (e.g., recreational swimming or waterpark or nature adventure pool), and the partially resultant catchment area. As a basis for calculation, the required water surface area can be taken to be 0.05–0.15 m² per inhabitant, depending on the population of the catchment area.

As a rule of thumb, the site must have roughly 10–16 m² for each square meter of usable water surface area. An area of 5–15 m² is also considered sufficient for swimming and bathing pond facilities.

Public swimming ponds should not be less than 500 m² in size. The minimum size for a private natural swimming pool depends on the swimming pond type.

Function	Area/portion
Areas for sunbathing, children's play, and recreational sports	50 % of the site area
Ratio between sunbathing and play areas	2:1 to 3:1
	Per 1,000 m² utilization area
Entry court	100 m²
Covered entry zone, including ticket desk and entry control	50 m²
Sand play / sandbox	≥ 100 m²
Play area	≥ 300 m²
Water play area	≥ 100 m²

Table 7.2 Area requirements for outdoor facilities – reference values (based on German KOK guidelines)

Function	Area
Management office (if needed)	≥ 10 m²
First-aid room	≥ 8 m²
Or: Pool supervisor and first-aid room	≥ 14 m²
Storage and equipment rooms (as needed)	20–30 m² (50–80 m² recommended)

Table 7.3 Area requirements inside building

Total water surface	Site area without parking spaces	Pool types	Examples of pool sizes	Water surface areas	Diving facilities
Maximum 1,500 m²	15,000–24,000 m²	Swimmer pool Diving pool Nonswimmer pool Wading pool	16.66 × 25 m 12.5 × 11.75 m 750 m² Approximately 100 m²	417 m² 147 m² 750 m² 100 m²	1 m board + 1 m platform + 3 m platform + 5 m platform
Maximum 3,000 m²	30,000–48,000 m²	Swimmer pool Diving pool Nonswimmer pool Wading pool	25 × 50 m 18.35 × 15 m 1,500 m² Approximately 200 m²	1,250 m² 275 m² 1,500 m² 200 m²	1 m board + 3 m board + 1 m, 3 m, 5 m, 7.5 m, and 10 m platforms

Table 7.4 Exemplary division of the water surface area into separate areas of use

	Per 1,000 m² utilization area	
Changing places (cubicles)	≥5, of which 4 are to be changing cubicles, including 1 cubicle for families and people with disabilities, plus 1 screened changing place near the sunbathing area	±20%
Changing places in communal changing rooms	Minimum 2, each with 10 m bench length	
Clothing lockers	50	
Lockers for valuables	10	
Foot-washing stations	2 spigots	
Warm-up space and lounge	30–100 m²	
Toilets	Women: 3 toilets Men: 1 toilet and 3 urinals, of which 1 is to be suitable for use by children	
Showers	Minimum 2 hot water showers each for men and women	

Table 7.5 Infrastructural amenities for swimming pond facilities (Source: FLL, 2003)

Area	Required minimum width/clearance
General circulation areas	Width ≥ 2.5 m
Pools with foot baths	
at access points	Width ≥ 3 m
at the starting block side	Width ≥ 3 m
behind pool steps to the nonswimmer area / water slides	Width ≥ 3 m
at the diving facilities	Width ≥ 5 m
Between two pool sections	Sum of the individual dimensions
Pools without foot baths, showers at the entrance (variant for bathing ponds)	
Location of showers	Distance from access to pond ≤ 2 m Hard-surfaced area surrounding the showers ≥ 2 m in all directions
Entries	Fan-like widening toward the adjoining functional areas

Table 7.6 Requirements for entrances and circulation areas

Dimensions of diving pools		
Width × Length	Water Depth	Diving Facilities (boards/platforms)
10.6 × 12.5 m	3.8 m	1 m and 3 m boards; 5 m platform
12.5 × 11.75 m	3.8 m	1 m and 3 m boards; 1 m, 3 m, and 5 m platforms
16.9 × 11.75 m	3.8 m	2 × 1 m and close up space: 2 × 3 m boards; 1 m, 3 m, and 5 m platforms
18.35 × 15 m	4.5–5 m	1 m and 3 m boards; 1 m, 3 m, 5 m, 7.5 m, and 10 m platforms
22,40 × 15 m	4.5–5 m	2 × 1 m and 2 × 3 m boards; 1 m, 3 m, 5 m, 7.5 m, and 10 m platforms

Table 7.7 Dimensions of diving pools

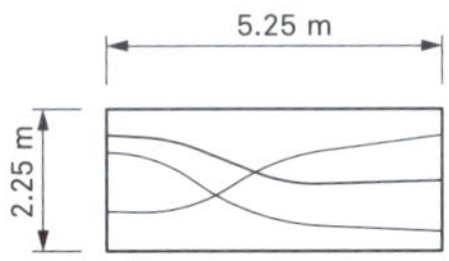

One-lane swimming pool for 1–2 people, 2 strokes possible

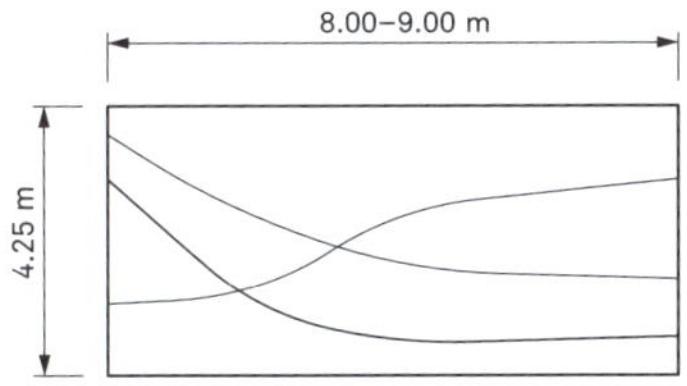

Two-lane swimming pool for 4–5 people, 3–4 strokes and starting dive from the end possible

Figure 7.6 Space required for private swimming pool facilities

Pool type	Size Length × width	Water depth	Swimming lanes: quantity and misc.	Water temperature in °C*	Remarks
Swimmer pool	25 × 12.5 m 25 × 16.66 m 50 × 16.66 m 50 × 21 m 50 × 25 m	Minimum 1.80 m (per DIN 19643, pools with water depths > 1.35 m are considered swimmer pools)	5 6 6 8 10	23°–25°	Pool rest ledge 0.1–0.15 m wide, at 1.2–1.35 m below the highest possible water level
Nonswimmer pool	Shape as desired 600–1,500 m²	0.5/0.6–1.35 m 0.5–1.1 m 0.9–1.35 m Maximum floor slope: 10 %	For school swimming: 2 m wide with two parallel sides	23°–25°	
Wading pool	Shape as desired 80–200 m²	0–0.3/0.5/0.6 m or 0.1/0.2/0.3–0.6 m	Floor slope: 5 %–10 %	24°–26°	
Wave pool	As desired, but minimum 12.5 × 33 m or 16.66 × 33 m 21 × 33 m	Tapers out toward the end: 0 or 0.15/0.3 m in the deep area: 2 m or dependent on use: 1.8 m; 1.35 m	Wave height: 0.6–1 m	23°–25°	
Diving pool	Dependent on diving facilities provided	3.4–5 m	Training possible with 20 or 25 m width	23°–25°	
Teaching pool (special type of nonswimmer pool)	12.5 × 8 m 16.66 × 10 m	0.5/0.6–1.35 m Recommended: 0.8–1.2 m	Maximum floor slope: 10 %	23°–25°	
Foot bath	6 × 3–4 m approximately 3 × 3 m	0.15 at the center, 0.1 at entry/exit	Trough shape, box shape	–	For swimming ponds, can be replaced by showers when located less than 2 m from the access point
Minimum sizes for private swimming pool facilities	2.25 × 5.25 m 4.25 × 8–9 m	–	–	–	Smallest one-lane swimming pool (2 strokes, 1–2 people) Mid-sized two-lane swimming pool (3–4 strokes) shortest pool for starting dive from the end

* Water temperature: for swimming ponds, the maximum temperature is 23°C.

Table 7.8 Reference values for pools according to type of use

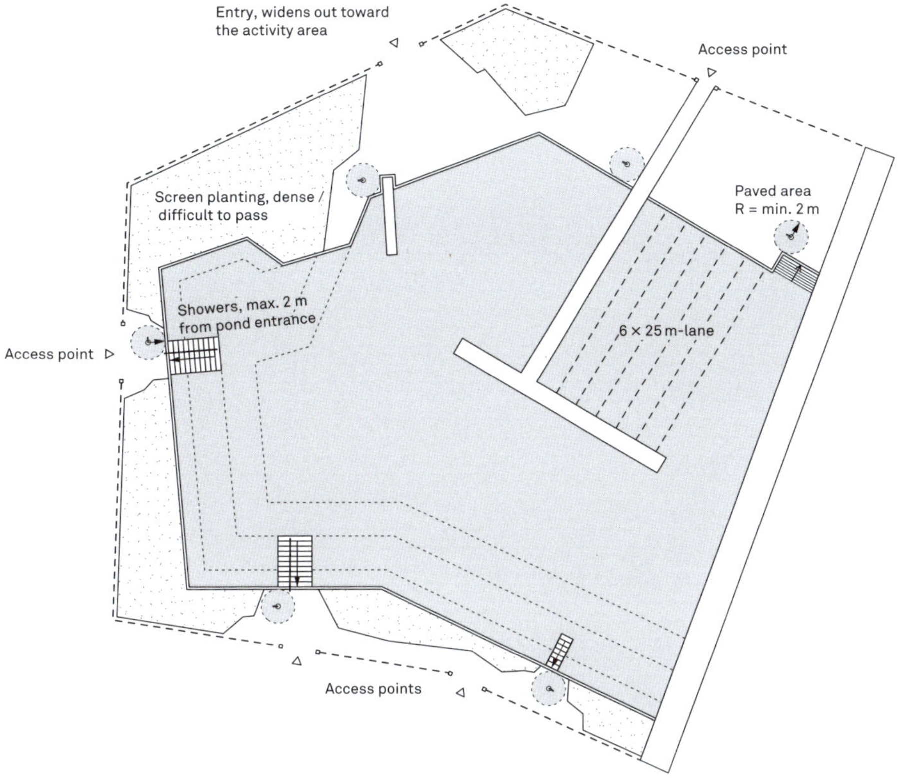

Figure 7.7 Dimensions for ponds, including circulation areas – example with 25 m lane (dimensions based on German KOK guidelines)

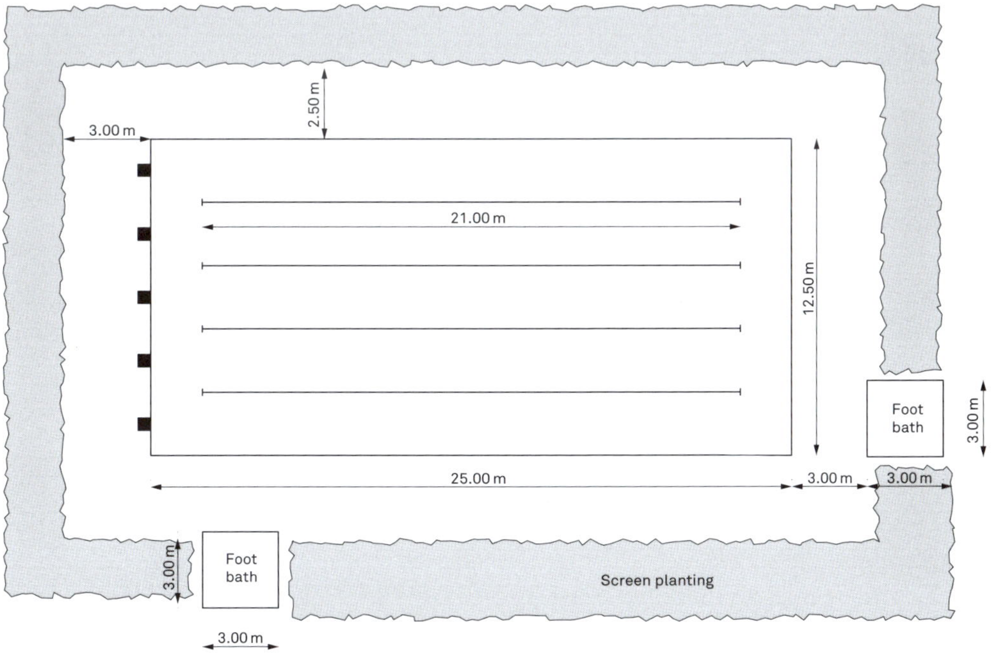

Figure 7.8 Dimensions for swimming pools and ponds, including circulation areas – example with 25 m lane (dimensions based on German KOK guidelines)

	Dimensions of diving facilities	1-meter board 4.8 × 0.5 m	3-meter board 4.8 × 0.5 m	1-meter platform 4.5 × 0.6 m	3-meter platform 5 × 0.6 m	5-meter platform 6 × 1.5 m	7.50-meter platform 6 × 1.5 m	10-meter platform 6 × 2 m
A	6 m	5 m	6 m	6 m	8 m	12 m	1.5 m	1.5 m
A-A	From front edge of plat-form back to front edge of platform directly below	–	–	–	–	1.25 m	1.25 m	1.25 m
B	From plummet to pool wall at the side	2.5 m	3.5 m	2.3 m	2.8 m	4.25 m	4.5 m	5.25 m
C	From plummet to adjacent plummet	1.9 m	1.9 m	–	–	2.1 m	2.1 m or 2.45 m	3.13 m or 2.65 m
D	From front edge of board/ platform to pool wall ahead	9 m	10.25 m	8 m	9.5 m	10.25 m	11 m	13.5 m
E	From board/platform to bottom of ceiling above	5 m	5 m	3 m	3 m	3 m	3.2 m	3.4 m
F	Clear overhead space behind and to each side of plummet ("E" dimension maintained)	3.4 m	3.8 m	3.4 m	3.4 m	3.8 m	4.1 m	4.5 m
G	Clear overhead space ahead of plummet ("E" dimension maintained)	5 m	5 m	5 m	5 m	5 m	5 m	6 m
H	Depth of water at plummet	3.4 m	3.8 m	3.4 m	3.4 m	3.8 m	4.1 m	4.5 m
J	Clearance ahead of front edge of board/platform	6 m	6 m	5 m	6 m	6 m	8 m	12 m
K	Water depth up to distance "J"	3.3 m	3.7 m	3.3 m	3.3 m	3.7 m	4 m	4.25 m
L	Clearance to each side of plummet	2.25 m	3.25 m	2.05 m	2.55 m	3.75 m	3.75 m	4.5 m
M	Water depth up to distance "L"	3.3 m	3.7 m	3.3 m	3.3 m	3.7 m	4 m	4.25 m

Table 7.9 Minimum dimensions of springboard facilities and platforms

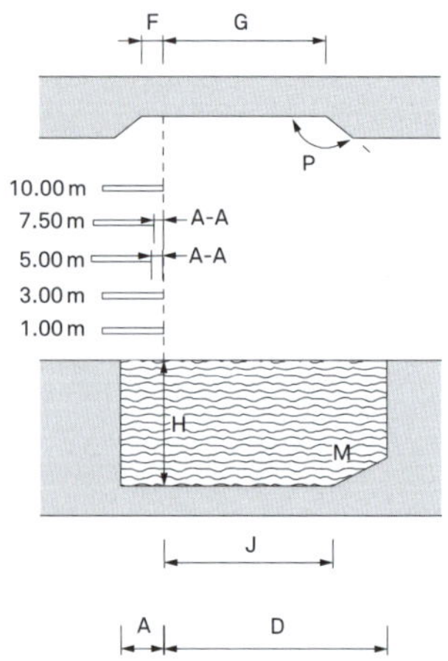

Figure 7.9 Safety clearances for diving facilities, key to dimensioning

Attribute	Swimming pond type* Type I	Type II	Type III	Type IV	Type V
Aim of the technique	–	Ease of maintenance	Improve conditioning, optimize water quality, and stabilize its functional behavior, ease of maintenance		
Treatment area – standard design	• No controlled flow through plant zone • Open water		• (Planted) controlled flow through filter zone • Open water, possibly without controlled flow through plant zone		• (Planted) controlled flow through filter zone • open water • and possibly without controlled flow through plant zone
Operation of technical equipment					
Flow	Natural circulation	Surface flow	Surface flow and forced flow through treatment area		
Water purification	Plants Zooplankton Microorganisms	Plants, zooplankton, microorganisms. Increasing support by means of hydraulic/technical devices			
Recommended standard values for minimum sizes, according to use					
Private swimming ponds (3–4 people)	≥120 m²	≥100 m²	≥80 m²	≥60 m²	≥50 m²
Public swimming ponds	Unsuitable				≥500 m² (Size in accord with nominal number of visitors)
Portion reserved for regeneration	≥60 %	≥50 %	≥40 %	≥40 %	≥40 % (with optimized treatment, ≥30 %)
Water depth in utilization area	≥65 % with a minimum 2 m depth		≥60 % with a minimum 2 m depth (can be reduced to ≥40 % with appropriate technical effort)	≥40 % with a minimum 2 m depth	Depending on the situation; for public pools: ≥40 % with a minimum 2 m depth
Care and maintenance expenditures					
Maintenance of structural and technical facilities	Low ⟶				High
Care of vegetation and water areas	High ⟵				Low

Table 7.10 Attributes of swimming pond types illustrated in Figure 7.9
(Source: FLL 2006, amended and supplemented)

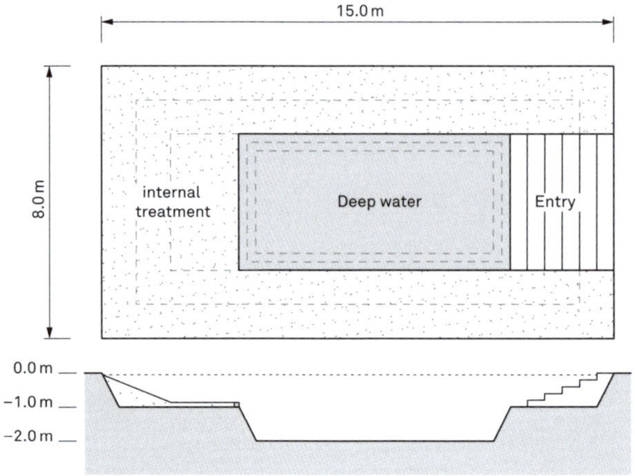

Type I: Total required water surface min. 120 m²
portion reserved for regeneration min. 60 %

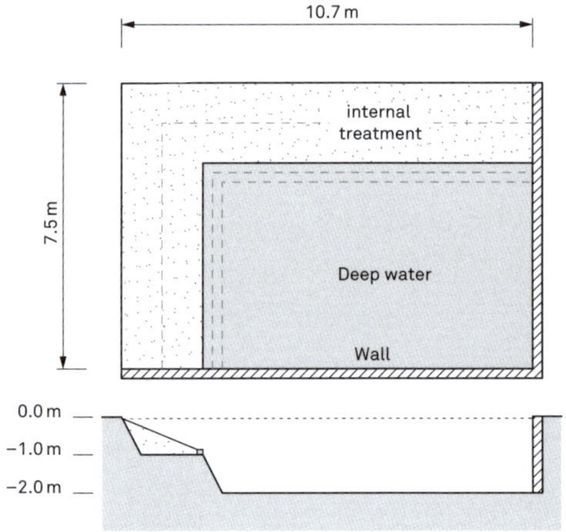

Type II: Total required water surface min. 80 m²
portion reserved for regeneration min. 40 %

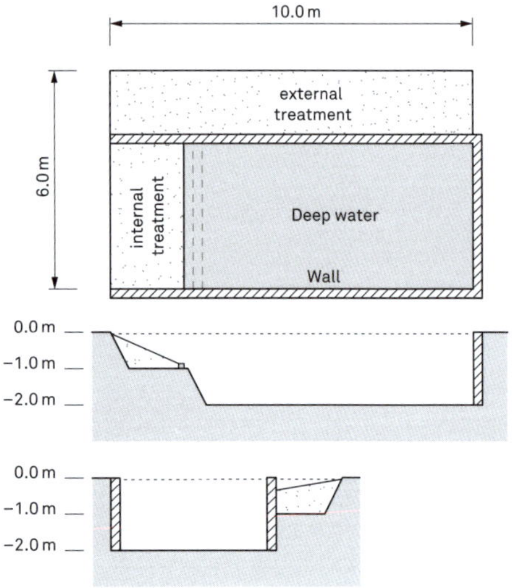

Type III: Total required water surface min. 60 m²
portion reserved for regeneration min. 40 %

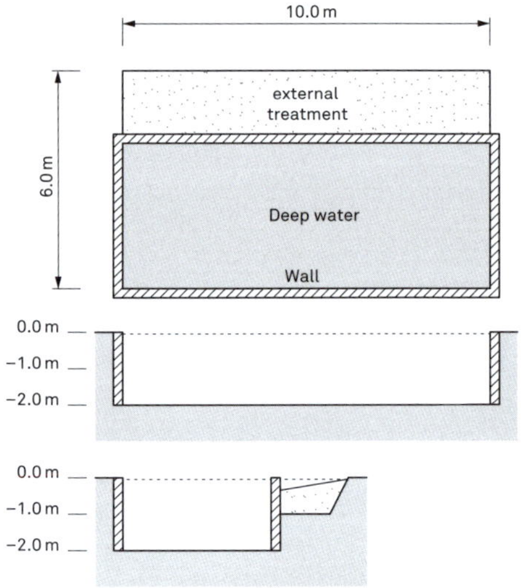

Type IV: Total required water surface min. 50 m²
portion reserved for regeneration min. 30 %

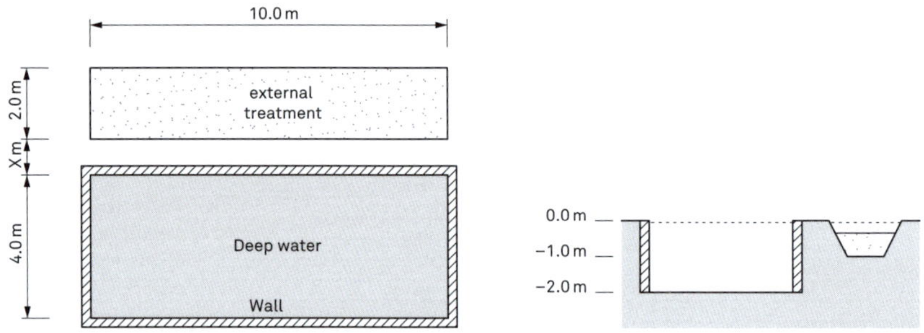

Type V: Total required water surface min. 50 m²
portion reserved for regeneration min. 30 %

Figure 7.10 Principle of swimming and bathing ponds with integrated/separate regeneration area (based on FLL 2003, amended)

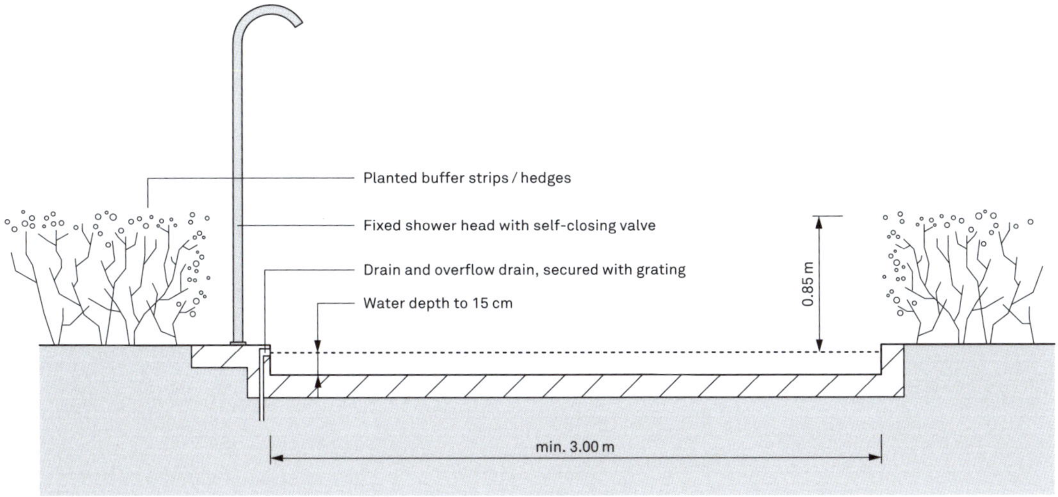

Figure 7.11 Dimensions of a foot bath

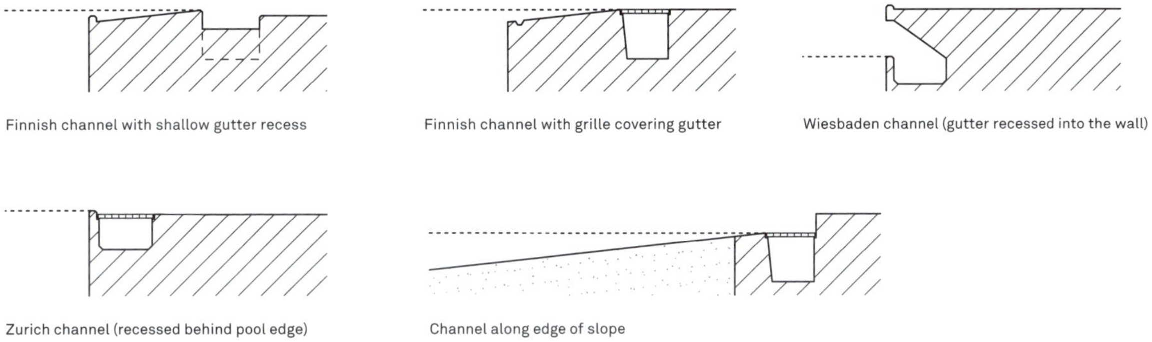

Figure 7.12 Pool edges with perimeter overflow channels

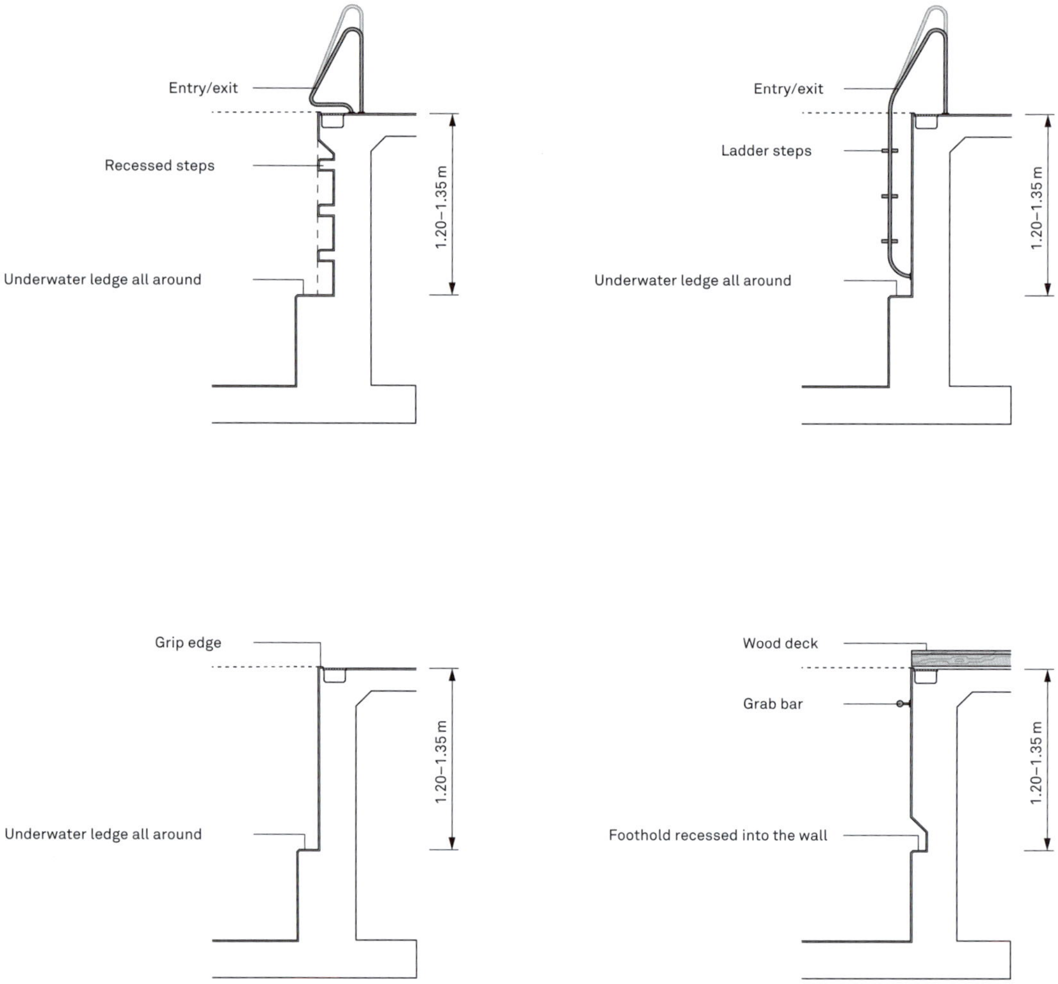

Figure 7.13 Pool ledge with and without entry/exit

7.4 Water-Treading Pools

Water-treading pools, as a form of Kneipp (naturopathic) hydrotherapy treatment, are found in spa parks as well as along natural stream courses beside the edges of hiking paths. They have an average volume of 7 m³. The minimum dimensions in plan are 1.3 × 3.6 meters with a depth of 0.6 meter. The actual water depth should be 0.4–0.45 meter. The average area required for the pool itself is approximately 20–60 m². With ancillary areas, such as an access path, benches, temporary storage surfaces, a relaxation area, and planted areas for spatially integrating the facility into the landscape, 300 m² or more should be available.

Pools on private property or pools that make use of existing underground springs or natural stream courses, for example along a hiking path, will need less area.

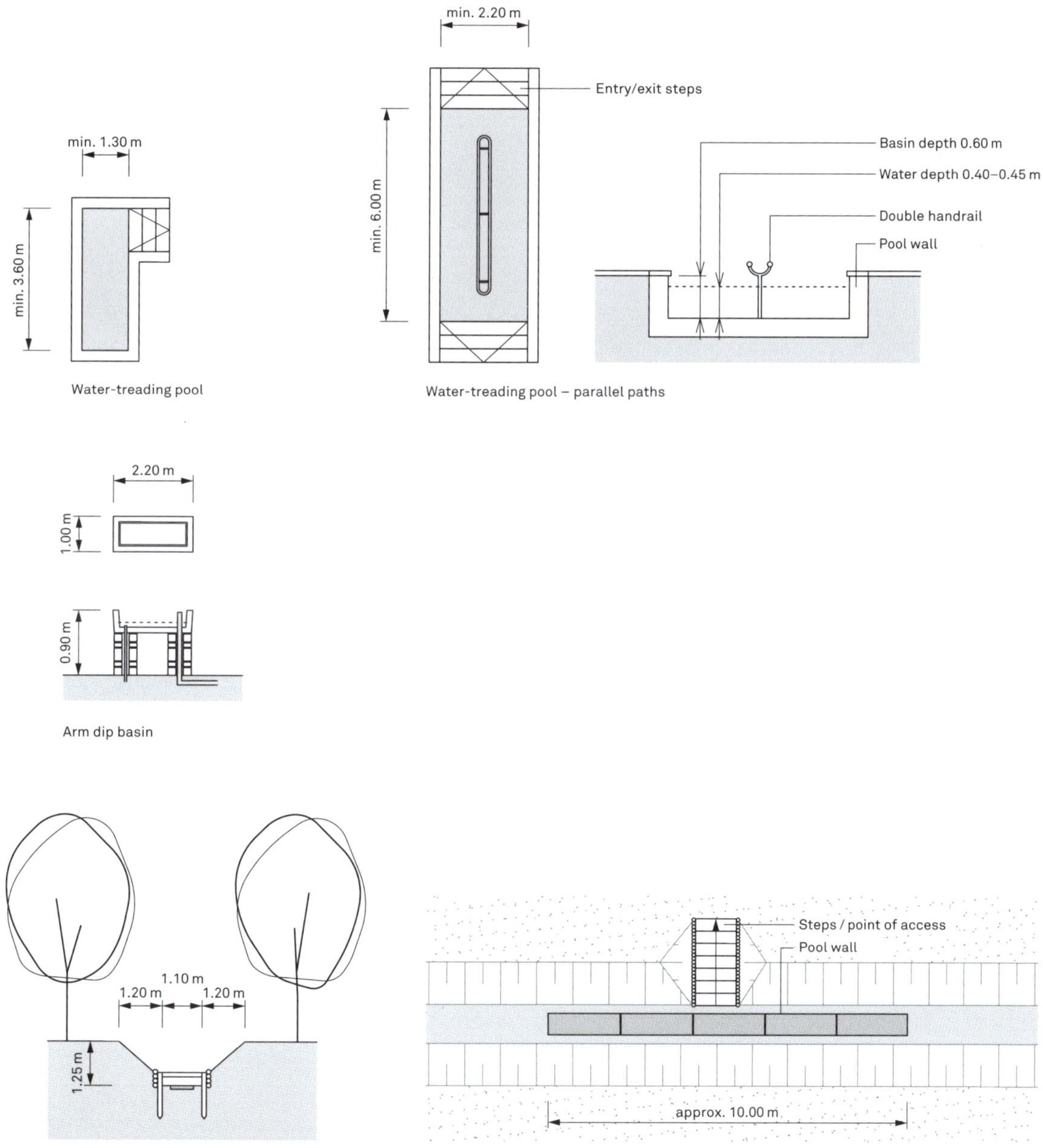

Figure 7.14 Dimensions of water-treading pools and arm dip basins

8 Plants

Temperature equalization, shading, dust control, oxygen production, and carbon dioxide reduction are some of the positive benefits for the surroundings that can be expected from plants. They also increase humidity and can provide protection from the wind, and hence they play an important role in designs for open spaces.

8.1 Trees

In its natural habitat, a tree develops a root zone whose volume amounts to as much as 0.75 m^3 per square meter of crown projection surface (see Bakker and Kopinga).

Whether the integration of existing trees into a new installation is functionally necessary or desired from a design standpoint, the objective is to provide optimum protection for the tree's habitat. In so doing, the utmost attention must be given to the tree's root zone. As a rule, the following measures must be taken into account:

- It is essential to maintain the original ground level within the area beneath the tree canopy. Neither the filling nor the removal of soil is permitted in this area, as most woody plants react very sensitively and their long-term existence would thereby be endangered.
- The area beneath the tree canopy plus 1.5 m (5 m for columnar-shaped trees) must be kept free of built structures and surfacing.

The various species of both deciduous and coniferous trees have different characteristics with regard to the growth of their crowns. These are important aspects of design and relevant characteristics for spatial planning.

However, the crown shape of every tree only takes on its characteristic form over the course of time. This aspect illustrates once more the process-like aspect of planning with vegetation, which rarely or only after years reaches a lasting state.

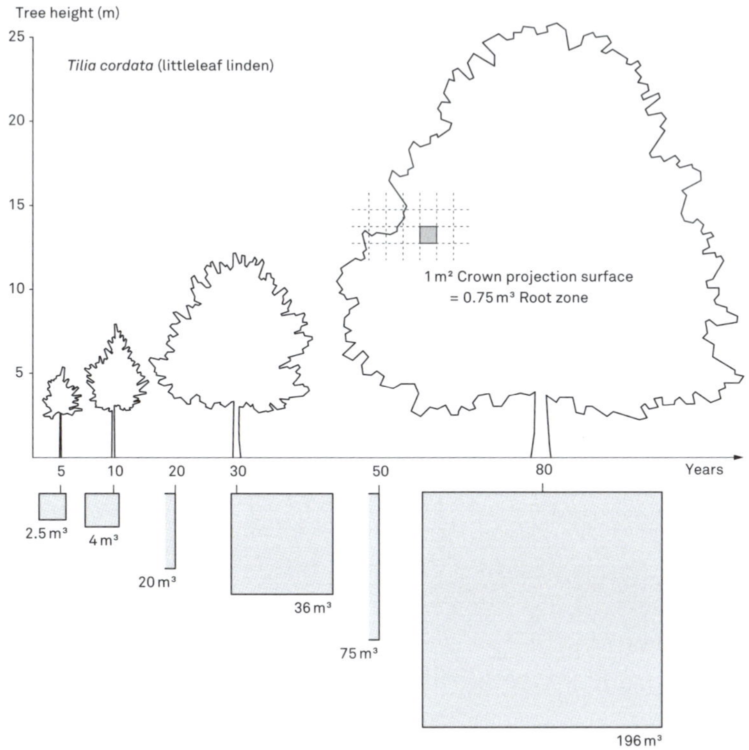

Figure 8.1 Relationship between crown projection surface and the root-permeable space of trees under natural conditions, as exemplified by *Tilia cordata*

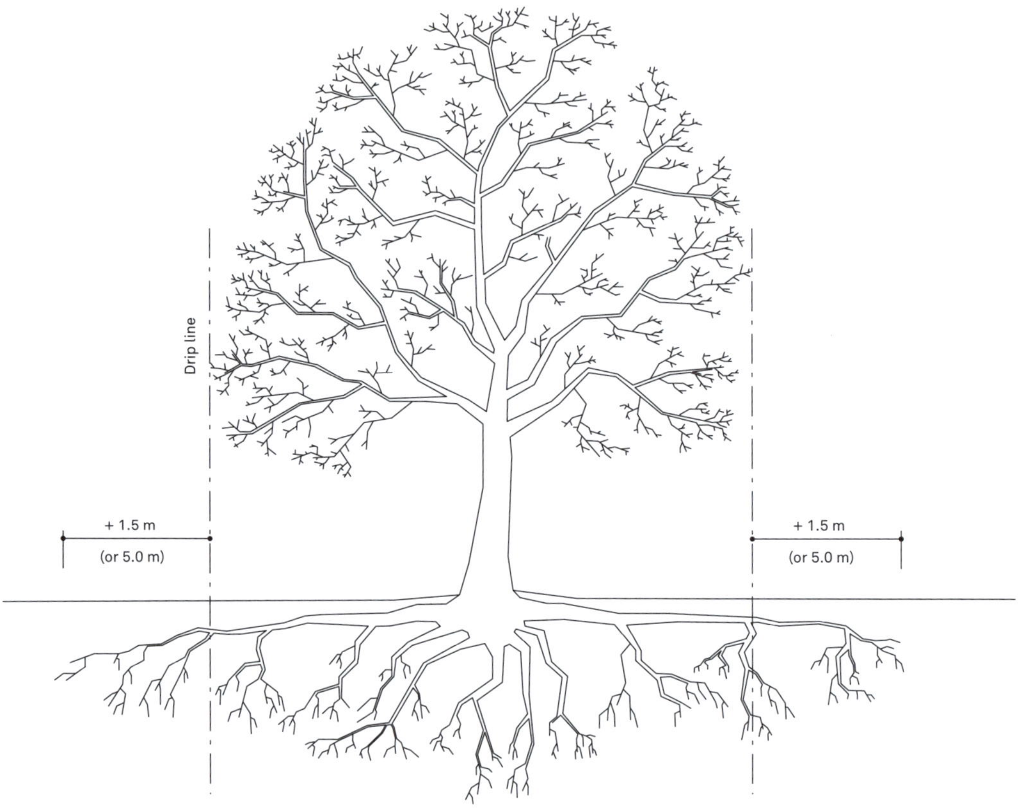

Figure 8.2 Protection for the root zone of existing trees (tree protection zone)

Traffic areas, buildings, and technical equipment and facilities (as per RASt 06)	Clearance
Traffic space for bicycle traffic	≥0.75 m
Traffic space for motorized traffic	≥1 m
Traffic space for rail transport	≥2 m
Buildings, for trees with small crowns	≥3 m
Buildings, for trees with large crowns	≥7 m
Cable tunnel with internal access	≥1.5 m
Underground piping and cable routes (minimum clearance of up to 5 m, depending on the type and size of utility lines)	≥2 m
Luminaires	≥3 m

Table 8.1 Minimum clearance distances for tree plantings

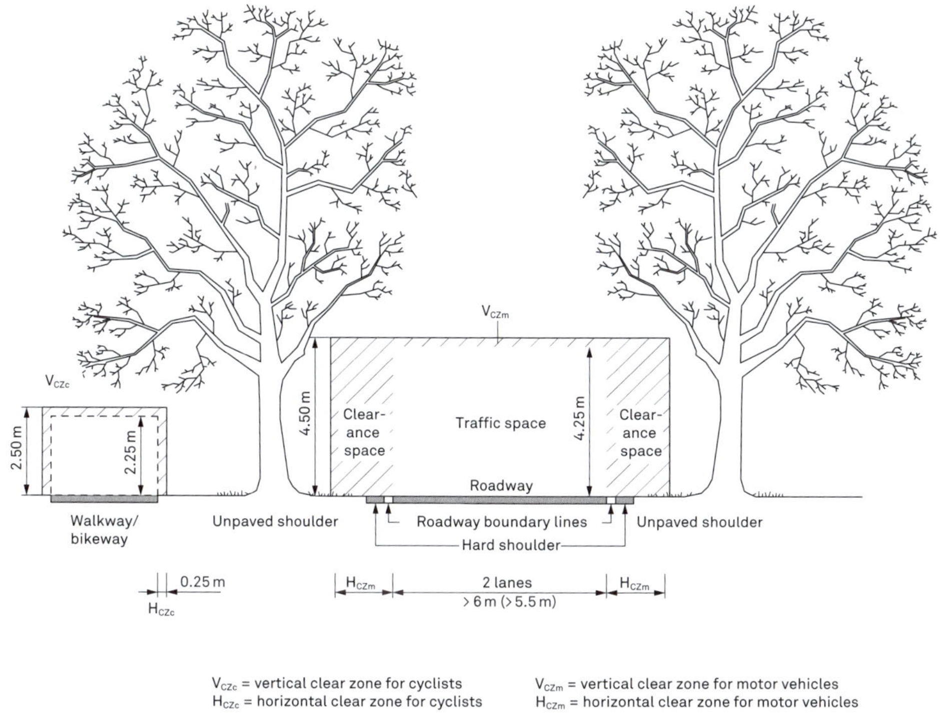

Figure 8.3 Clearances along roads

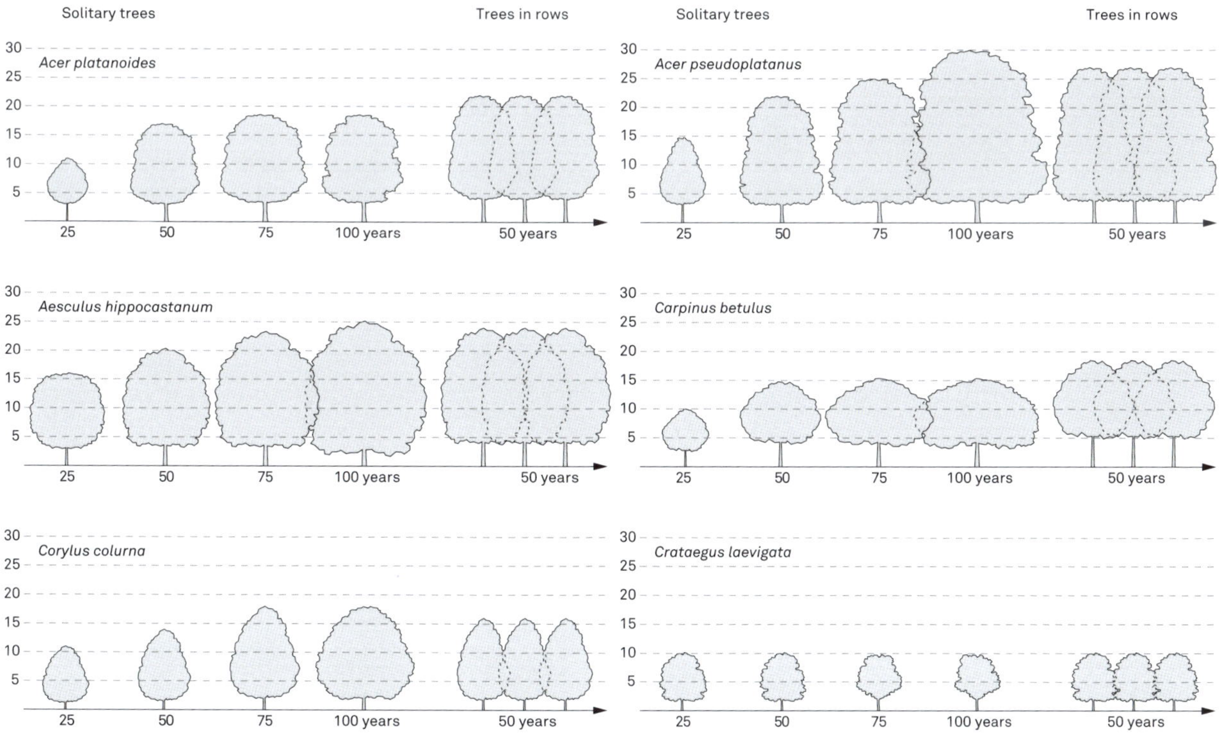

Figure 8.4 Typical development of various tree species from juvenile to mature form as solitary trees and in rows

Botanical and common names	Height in m	Width in m	Permeability to light	Light requirements	Suitability for city streetscapes	Drough tolerance (according to KLAM)	Winter hardiness (Winter hardiness zoness) (according to KLAM)	Comments
Acer campestre (field maple, hedge maple)	10–15 (20)	10–15	Medium	○–◗	R	VG	VG	Ovoid and irregular crown, becoming more rounded with age; tolerates dry soils and high degree of surface sealing, good for holding topsoil on banks and on slopes
Acer campestre 'Elsrijk' (field maple)	6–12 (15)	4–6	Medium	○–◗	R	–	–	Like the species but with straight central leader, narrower and more uniform growth, localized frost damage in the crown, mildew-free
Acer platanoides (Norway maple)	20–30	15–22	Low	○–◗	R	S	VG (4)	Rounded, densely closed crown, blooms before leaves sprout; very frost-hardy, sensitive to soil compaction, honeydew secretion
Acer platanoides, 'Allershausen' (Norway maple)	15–20	up to 10	Low	○–◗	S	–	–	Highly branched, dense crown, well suited for locations susceptible to frost, honeydew secretion, included in Straßenbaumtest [street tree test] 2 since 2005
Acer platanoides 'Apollo' (tapered Norway maple)	14–18	10–15	Low	○–◗	R	–	–	Like the species but grows faster and more upright, frost-resistant, honeydew secretion, included in Straßenbaumtest 2 since 2005
Acer platanoides 'Cleveland' (tapered Norway maple)	10–15	7–9	Low	○–◗	S	–	–	Oval crown, broadly ovoid and regular with age; bright red shoots, good for urban environments, honeydew secretion
Acer platanoides 'Columnare' Types 1, 2, 3 (columnar Norway maple)	up to 10 (16)	2–7	Low	○–◗	S	–	–	Narrow, columnar growth, very frost-hardy, heat-tolerant, drought-tolerant, wind- and shade-tolerant, honeydew secretion, good compartmentalization of decay
Acer platanoides 'Deborah' (Norway maple)	15–20	10–15	Low	○–◗	R	–	–	Rounded to broadly rounded, straight central leader, honeydew secretion, heed results of Straßenbaumtest 1
Acer platanoides 'Emerald Queen' (Norway maple)	up to 15	8–10	Low	○–◗	R	NA	NA	Oval crown, markedly upright when young, heat- and drought-tolerant, wind-tolerant, suitable for narrow streets, honeydew secretion
Acer platanoides 'Farlake's Green' (Norway maple)	15–20	10–15	Low	○–◗	R	–	–	Symmetrical habit, heat- and drought-tolerant, wind-tolerant, scarcely susceptible to mildew, sensitive to road salt (experience from NL), heed results of Straßenbaumtest 1
Acer platanoides 'Globosum', (globe Norway maple)	up to 6	5–8	Low	○–◗	S	–	–	Densely branched, compact round crown, give regard to clearance profile, frost-hardy, heat- and drought-tolerant, wind and shade-tolerant, honeydew secretion, suitable for tubs and containers
Acer platanoides 'Olmsted' (Norway maple)	10–12 (15)	2–3	Low	○–◗	S	–	–	Narrow, columnar; suitable for restricted spaces in exposed urban locations with dry air; presumably equivalent to type 1 of *Acerplatanoides* 'Columnare,' honeydew secretion
Acer platanoides 'Royal Red' (red-leafed Norway maple)	up to 15 (20)	8–10	Low	○–◗	R	–	–	Leaves are bright red as buds, then consistently deep crimson and glossy until autumn, very frost-hardy, heat-tolerant, wind-tolerant, honeydew secretion

NA = not available; R = with restrictions; VG = very good; WS = well-suited; S = suitable; P = problematic; VL = very limited suitability

Table 8.2 Suitability of trees for streets and inner-city locations, per GALK and KLAM

Botanical and common names	Height in m	Width in m	Permeability to light	Light requirements	Suitability for city streetscapes	Drough tolerance (according to KLAM)	Winter hardiness (Winter hardiness zoness) (according to KLAM)	Comments
Acer platanoides 'Summershade', (Norway maple)	20–25	15–20	Low	○–◗	R	–	–	Expansive hanging branches, forms whorls, susceptible to wind breakage, good for urban environments, honeydew secretion
Acer rubrum (red maple)	10–15 (20)	6–10 (14)	Low	○–◗	R	VG	S	Deep red blossoms in advance of leaf shoots, frost-hardy, somewhat sensitive to heat, conditionally good for urban environments, shallow roots, risk of chlorosis in chalky soil
Aesculus hippo-castanum (horse chestnut)	up to 25 (30)	15–20 (25)	Low	○	R	VL	S	Sensitive to soil compaction and road salt, be mind-ful of fruit fall, strong crown and root pressure
Aesculus hippo-castanum 'Baumannii' (double-flowering horse chestnut)	up to 25 (30)	15–20 (25)	Low	○	R	–	–	Like the species, but blooms longer and has filled blossoms, no fruit production
Aesculus × carnea (red horse chestnut)	10–15 (20)	8–12 (16)	Low	○–◗	R	S	VG	Difficult to cut away branches, unsuitable for com-pact soils and high degree of surface sealing, minor infestation by leaf-mining moths, negligible fruit fall
Aesculus × carnea 'Briotii' (ruby red horse chestnut)	10–15	8–12	Low	○–◗	R	–	–	Like the species but more deeply colored blossoms, available in different varieties
Alnus cordata (Italian alder)	10–15 (20)	8–10	Medium	○	R	S	S	Shoots form early, so occasionally subject to frost in late spring, good for urban and industrial envi-ronments, very wind-tolerant, risk of breakage from snow due to long-lasting foliage
Alnus × spaethii (Spaeth's alder)	12–15	8–10	Medium	○	WS	S	VG	Frost-hardy, wind-tolerant, vigorous growth, straight central leader, risk of breakage from snow due to long-lasting foliage, heed results of Straßenbaum-test 1
Amelanchier arborea 'Robin Hill' (downy serviceberry)	6–8	3–5	Medium	○–◗	S	–	–	Broadly ovoid crown, blossoms early and has pleasant fragrance, suitable for tubs and containers, included in Straßenbaumtest 2 since 2005
Betula papyrifera (paper birch)	18–25	7–12	High	○	R	–	–	Pyramidal crown, short-lived, not good for urban environments, do not use within paved areas, observe proper planting times
Betula pendula, syn. B. verrucosa (silver birch, European white birch)	18–25 (30)	10–15 (18)	High	○	R	S	VG	Loose, high domed crown; side branches often hang down far, frost-hardy, not good for urban environ-ments, tends to lift up pavements; do not use within paved areas, observe proper planting times
Betula utilis, syn. B. jacquemontii (Himalayan birch)	8–10 (15)	5–7	High	○	R	VL	P	Grows upright, shallow spreading roots, large per-centage of fine roots in the upper soil zone, observe proper planting times
Carpinus betulus (European, or common hornbeam)	10–20 (25)	7–12 (15)	Low	◗	R	S	VG	Conical; high domed crown with age; not good for urban environments, so do not use within paved areas

NA = not available; R = with restrictions; VG = very good; WS = well-suited; S = suitable; P = problematic; VL = very limited suitability

Table 8.2 (continuation) Suitability of trees for streets and inner-city locations, per GALK and KLAM

Botanical and common names	Height in m	Width in m	Permeability to light	Light requirements	Suitability for city streetscapes	Drought tolerance (according to KLAM)	Winter hardiness (Winter hardiness zoness) (according to KLAM)	Comments
Carpinus betulus 'Fastigiata' (fastigiate hornbeam)	15–20	4–6 (10)	Low	◗	S	–	–	Columnar to conical crown, spreads apart with age, less sensitive to heat and radiation than the species, suitable for tubs and containers
Carpinus betulus 'Frans Fontaine' (columnar European hornbeam)	10–15	4–5	Low	○–◗	R	–	–	Like *Carpinus betulus* 'Fastigiata', but columnar even in maturity, crown not entirely closed when young, very wind-tolerant, increased late frost damage to the trunks of young trees, suitable for tubs and containers
Catalpa bignonioides (Southern catalpa, Indian bean tree)	8–10 (15)	6–10	Medium	○–◗	R	P	P	Rounded crown and broadly spreading side branches, species-specific characteristic is no central leader; striking flowers, leaves, and fruits; heed clearance profile
Celtis australis (European hackberry or nettle tree)	10–20	10–15	Medium	○	R	VG	P	Expansive, round, umbrella-shaped crown; trunk formation better than *Celtis occidentalis*; loves warmth and suitable for dry sites (viticulture climate)
Cercis siliquastrum (Judas tree, lovetree)	4–6	4–6	Low	○	R	VG	VL	Round, wide-growing crown, loves warmth (viticulture climate), suitable for dry sites, watch for straight leading shoots
Cornus mas (Cornelian cherry, cornejo macho, cornel)	5–6 (8)	3–5	Medium	○–◗	WS	VG	VG	Small crowned, very early blooming trees for narrow streets, trunks with peeling bark, undemanding, not sensitive to frost, good for urban environments, be mindful of fruit fall, heed clearance profile
Corylus colurna (Turkish hazelnut)	15–18 (23)	8–12 (16)	Low	○–◗	S	S	S	Regular, widely conical crown; undemanding, good for urban environments, severe fruit fall in some years
Crataegus crus-galli syn. C. prunifolia 'Splendens' (cockspur hawthorn)	5–7 (9)	5–7 (9)	Medium	○–◗	R	–	–	Broadly rounded crown, especially long thorns, frost-hardy, wind-tolerant, heed clearance profile, suitable for tubs and containers
Crataegus laevigata 'Paul's Scarlet' syn. C. monogyna 'Kermesina Plena' (English or common hawthorn)	4–6 (8)	4–6 (8)	Medium	○	R	–	–	Regular, widely conical crown, has filled blossoms, undemanding, not too dry, suitable for tubs and containers
Crataegus lavallei 'Carrierei' syn. C. carrierei (Carrière's hawthorn)	5–7	5–7	Medium	○	S	VG	VG	Widely conical crown; shoots with strong thorns; long-lasting, leathery, shiny dark green foliage; suitable for tubs and containers
Crataegus monogyna 'Stricta' (upright hawthorn)	5–7 (10)	2–3	Medium	○–◗	R	–	–	Stiffly upright to columnar, spreads apart with age, shoots covered with thorns, suitable for tubs and containers
Crataegus × prunifolia syn. C. × persimilus (plumleaf hawthorn)	6–7	5–6	Medium	○	R	–	–	Like *Crataegus crus-gallii*, glossy, dark green foliage, frost-hardy, good for urban environments

NA = not available; R = with restrictions; VG = very good; WS = well-suited; S = suitable; P = problematic; VL = very limited suitability

Table 8.2 (continuation) Suitability of trees for streets and inner-city locations, per GALK and KLAM

Botanical and common names	Height in m	Width in m	Permeability to light	Light requirements	Suitability for city streetscapes	Drough tolerance (according to KLAM)	Winter hardiness (Winter harding zoness) (according to KLAM)	Comments
Fraxinus angustifolia 'Raywood' syn. F. oxyacarpa 'Flame', F. oxyacarpa 'Raywood' (narrow-leafed ash)	10–15 (20)	10–15	High	○–◗	R	–	–	Heat-tolerant and loves warmth, sensitive to frost in some areas, good for urban environments, without fruits, striking fall foliage
Fraxinus excelsior (European or common ash)	25–35 (40)	20–25 (30)	High	○–◗	R	S	S	Rounded, light crown, widely spreading; late shoots, early leaf fall, sensitive to surface compaction
Fraxinus excelsior 'Altena' syn. F. excelsior 'Monarch' (ash)	15–20	10–12	High	○–◗	R	–	–	Like the species but more slender and regular, ascending twigs, straight central leader, sensitive to surface compaction and dryness
Fraxinus excelsior 'Atlas' (ash)	15–20	10–15	High	○–◗	S	–	–	Like the species but compacter and narrower crown, loves warmth, heat-tolerant, heed results of Straßenbaumtest 1
Fraxinus excelsior 'Diversifolia' syn. F. excelsior 'Monophylla' (single-leaved ash)	10–18	6–12	High	○–◗	S	–	–	Like the species but smaller and more narrow growth, good for urban environments, loose crown, upright growth, wind-tolerant, heed results of Straßenbaumtest 1
Fraxinus excelsior 'Geessink' (ash)	15–20	10–12	High	○–◗	S	–	–	Like the species but narrower and weaker growing, very wind-resistant, hardly subject to late freezing
Fraxinus excelsior 'Globosa' syn. F. excelsior 'Nana' (European Globehead ash)	3–5	3–5	Medium	○–◗	S	–	–	Like the species, but small and spherical, with densely branched crown, slow-growing, heed clearance profile, suitable for tubs and containers
Fraxinus excelsior 'Westhof's Glorie' (non-fruiting ash)	20–25 (30)	12–15	High	○–◗	S	–	–	Like the species but leaves shoot very late, thus hardly subject to late freezing; straight central leader
Fraxinus ornus (flowering ash, manna ash)	8–12 (15)	6–8 (10)	High	○	S	VG	VL	Slow growing, good for urban environments, seldom with straight leading shoots, give regard to clearance profile, do not use within paved areas, attractive blossoms
Fraxinus ornus 'Rotterdam' (flowering ash, manna ash)	8–12	6–8	Medium	○	S	–	–	Like the species but with a regular and conical crown, leading shoots, tolerant of dryness and heat, suitable for tubs and containers, attractive blossoms
Ginkgo biloba (ginkgo, maidenhair tree)	15–30 (35)	10–15 (20)	High	○	WS	VG	S	Undemanding, good for urban environments, free of pests, needs plentiful light, attractive fall foliage, diocious, draw on male selections
Gleditsia triacanthos (thornless honey locust)	10–25	8–15 (20)	High	○	S	–	–	Like the species but thornless variety in which thorns can subsequently form in individual cases; sensitive to frost as young tree

NA = not available; R = with restrictions; VG = very good; WS = well-suited; S = suitable; P = problematic; VL = very limited suitability

Table 8.2 (continuation) Suitability of trees for streets and inner-city locations, per GALK and KLAM

Botanical and common names	Height in m	Width in m	Permeability to light	Light requirements	Suitability for city streetscapes	Drough tolerance (according to KLAM)	Winter hardiness (Winter hardiness zoness) (according to KLAM)	Comments
Gleditsia triacanthos 'Shademaster' (thornless honey locust)	10–15 (20)	10–15	High	○	S	–	–	Like the species but thornless variety in which thorns can subsequently form in individual cases, later leaf fall
Gleditsia triacanthos 'Skyline' (thornless honey locust)	10–15 (20)	10–15	High	○	WS	–	–	Like the species but regular closed crown with ascending branches, thornless variety in which thorns can subsequently form in individual cases, forms no fruits
Gleditsia triacanthos 'Sunburst' (honey locust)	8–10	6–8	High	○	R	–	–	Like the species but thornless, light yellow shoots, later yellow-green, give regard to clearance profile
Koelreuteria paniculata (goldenrain tree, pride of India, varnish tree)	6–8	6–8	High	○	R	VG	VL	Small, slow-growing, very wide crown, striking flowers and seedpods, included in Straßenbaumtest 2 since 2005
Liquidambar styraciflua (sweetgum)	10–20 (30)	6–12	Medium	○	R	S	P	Varies significantly, open crown with age, lime-sensitive, long-lasting fall foliage if in a sunny location and exposed to cold nights
Liquidambar styraciflua 'Moraine' (sweetgum)	10–20	6–12	Medium	○–◗	R	–	–	Like the species but smaller, with more uniform crown and faster growth, attractive fall foliage
Liquidambar styraciflua 'Paarl' (sweetgum)	15–25	3–4	Medium	○	R	–	–	Like the species but with slim and pointed-conical crown, average growth vigor, early and long-lasting fall foliage, included in Straßenbaumtest 2 since 2005
Liriodendron tulipifera (tulip tree)	25–35	15–20	Medium	○	R	P	S	Broadly conical crown, straight central leader, loves warmth but also frost-hardy, rapid-growing, older specimens are susceptible to wind breakage, attractive fall foliage
Liriodendron tulipifera 'Fastigiata' (columnar tulip tree)	15–18	4–6	Low	○	R	–	–	Like the species but with narrow crown, grows stiffly upright, attractive fall foliage
Malus spec, (crab apple varieties)	4–12	2–6	Medium	○–◗	R	–	–	Richly flowering and fruit-bearing varieties, sometimes fruits remain hanging into the winter, heed clearance profile, suitable for tubs and containers
Malus tschonoskii (Chonosuki crab, pillar apple)	8–12	2–4	Medium	○–◗	S	S	VG	Narrow conical crown, becomes wider with age, straight and continuous leading shoots; fruits yellow to red, minor susceptibility to scab, included in Straßenbaumtest 2 since 2005
Malus hybrid 'Evereste' (crab apple)	4–6	3–5	Medium	○–◗	R	–	–	Broadly upright crown, overhanging side branches with age, heed clearance profile, small orange-red fruits, minor susceptibility to scab, suitable for tubs and containers

NA = not available; R = with restrictions; VG = very good; WS = well-suited; S = suitable; P = problematic; VL = very limited suitability

Table 8.2 (continuation) Suitability of trees for streets and inner-city locations, per GALK and KLAM

Botanical and common names	Height in m	Width in m	Permeability to light	Light requirements	Suitability for city streetscapes	Drough tolerance (according to KLAM)	Winter hardiness (Winter hardiness zoness) (according to KLAM)	Comments
Malus hybrid 'Red Sentinel' (crab apple)	4–5	3–4	Medium	○–◗	R	–	–	Slender crown, deeply overhanging side branches, heed clearance profile, dark red fruits, minor susceptibility to scab, suitable for tubs and containers
Malus hybrid 'Rudolph' (crab apple)	5–6	4–5	Medium	○–◗	R	–	–	Upright crown, later broadly ovoid to rounded, heed clearance profile, orange-yellow fruits; minor susceptibility to scab, tends to develop superficial cracks in the bark, suitable for tubs and containers
Malus hybrid 'Street Parade' (Siberian crabapple)	4–6	2–3	Medium	○–◗	R	–	–	Narrow ovoid crown, heed clearance profile, minor susceptibility to mildew and scab, small purple fruits; suitable for tubs and containers
Metasequoia glyptostroboides (dawn redwood)	25–35 (40)	7–10	High	○	R	P	VG	Pointedly conical crown with dense branches, straight central leader, bases of roots become wide, expansive root system, ensure sufficient distance to edges of streets, etc.
Ostrya carpinifolia (hop hornbeam)	10–15 (20)	8–12	Medium	○–◗	S	VG	VG	Conical, later rounded crown, appearance similar to common hornbeam; Fruits similar to hops, decorative, included in Straßenbaumtest 2 since 2005
Platanus acerifolia syn. P. × hybrida, P. hispanica (London plane)	20–30 (40)	15–25	Low	○	R	–	–	Broadly extended crown, striking trunks due to peeling bark, undemanding, not sensitive to frost, good for urban environments, often causes root heave, foliage rots poorly, infestation by harmful organisms has increased in recent years
Populus berolinensis (Berlin poplar)	18–25	8–10	Medium	○	R	S	VG	Broadly columnar, branches ascend diagonally upward, conical when young, irregular with age, straight central leader, forms suckering shoots
Populus simonii syn. P. brevifolia (Simon poplar)	12–15	6–8 (10)	Medium	○	R	P	S	Narrow and conical, wide and round with age, short-lived, early shoots at risk of breakage from snow
Populus simonii 'Fastigiata' (balsam poplar)	7–10	4–6	Medium	○	R	–	–	Like the species but initially narrow and columnar, later broadly conical, tolerates road salt
Prunus avium 'Plena' (double-flowering sweet cherry)	10–15	8–10	Low	○	R	–	–	Like the species but with a regularly pyramidal, dense and closed crown; has filled blossoms, no fruits; good for urban environments
Prunus padus 'Schloss Tiefurt' (bird cherry, hackberry)	9–12	–8	Medium	○–◗	S	–	–	Like the species but smaller and with regular, closed crown; forms strikingly beautiful and straight stems; striking, strongly fragrant blossoms; included in Straßenbaumtest 2 since 2005
Prunus sargentii (Sargent's cherry, hill cherry)	8–12	5–8	Medium	○–◗	R	P	S	Broad fan-shaped crown, funnel-shaped branches, crown spreads broadly with age, sparse fruit-bearing, striking fall foliage

NA = not available; R = with restrictions; VG = very good; WS = well-suited; S = suitable; P = problematic; VL = very limited suitability

Table 8.2 (continuation) Suitability of trees for streets and inner-city locations, per GALK and KLAM

Botanical and common names	Height in m	Width in m	Permeability to light	Light requirements	Suitability for city streetscapes	Drough tolerance (according to KLAM)	Winter hardiness (Winter hardiness zoness) (according to KLAM)	Comments
Prunus sargentii 'Accolade' syn. Pr. 'Accolade' (flowering cherry)	5–8	3–5 (7)	Medium	○–◗	R	–	–	Rounded to slightly funnel-shaped crown, give regard to clearance profile, striking blossoms and fall foliage
Prunus sargentii 'Rancho' (flowering cherry)	6–8	3–4	Medium	○–◗	R	–	–	Like the species but with narrow and columnar crown and stronger coloration of blossoms, does not bear fruit
Prunus serrulata 'Kanzan' syn. Pr. 'Hisakura', Pr. 'Kwanzan' (Japanese or Oriental cherry)	7–10 (12)	5–8	Medium	○–◗	R	–	–	Wide funnel-shaped, later overhanging crown, give regard to clearance profile, striking blossoms and fall foliage, seldom bears fruit
Prunus spec. (Japanese cherry species and varietals)	3–15	1–10	Low	○	R	–	–	Different crown shapes, highly ornamental owing to blossoms; trunk or root suckers, depending on grafting method; suitable for tubs and containers
Prunus subhirtella 'Autumnalis' (winter-flowering cherry, rosebud cherry)	5–8	3–5	Medium	○	R	–	–	Small tree with striking blossoms and fall foliage, give regard to clearance profile, suitable for tubs and containers
Prunus × schmittii (flowering cherry)	8–10	3–5	Medium	○–◗	S	–	–	Closed, narrow conical crown, branches grow upright, straight central leader, only flowers for a short time
Pyrus calleryana 'Chanticleer' (flowering pear, callery pear)	8–12 (15)	4–5	Medium	○	R	–	–	Narrow conical crown, later loose and broadly pyramidal, leaf fall not until after a strong frost (risk of breakage from snow), infrequent fruit production, early aging
Pyrus caucasica (Caucasian wild pear)	8–12	3–4	Medium	○–◗	R	–	–	Columnar to conical crown, grows stiffly upright, straight central leader; very adaptable, tolerates dryness, fruit production, heed results of Straßenbaumtest 1
Pyrus communis 'Beech Hill' (common pear)	8–12	5–7	Medium	○–◗	R	–	–	Initially grows stiffly upright, later spreads apart; vulnerable to fire risk; pear trellis rust in some areas; fruit production; heed results of Straßenbaumtest 1
Pyrus regelii (wild pear, Regel's pear)	8–10	7–9	Low	○–◗	R	–	–	Ovoid to rounded loose, ungainly branching, vulnerable to fire risk, pear trellis rust in some areas, occasionally strong fruit production, heed results of Straßenbaumtest 1
Quercus cerris (European Turkey oak)	20–30	10–15 (25)	Medium	○	S	–	–	Bluntly conical, broad central leader, spreads with age; long-lasting and slowly rotting foliage; also thrives in dry soils, good for urban environments
Quercus frainetto (Hungarian, or Italian oak)	10–20 (25)	10–15	Low	○–◗	R	–	–	Regular and closed crown, oval to rounded, looser with age, good for urban environments, foliage rots slowly, included in Straßenbaumtest 2 since 2005

NA = not available; R = with restrictions; VG = very good; WS = well-suited; S = suitable; P = problematic; VL = very limited suitability

Table 8.2 (continuation) Suitability of trees for streets and inner-city locations, per GALK and KLAM

Botanical and common names	Height in m	Width in m	Permeability to light	Light requirements	Suitability for city streetscapes	Drough tolerance (according to KLAM)	Winter hardiness (Winter hardiness zoness) (according to KLAM)	Comments
Quercus palustris (pin oak)	15–20 (25)	8–15 (20)	Medium	○	S	S	S	Regular conical crown, straight central leader, also thrives in moderately dry soils, risk of chlorosis in chalky soil, foliage often long-lasting, striking fall colors
Quercus petraea (durmast or sessile oak)	20–30 (40)	15–20 (25)	Medium	○	S	S	S	Regular ovoid crown, glossy deep green leaves, better for urban environments than *Quercus robur*
Quercus robur syn. Quercus pedunculata (pedunculate, or English oak)	25–35 (40)	15–20 (25)	High	○	S	P	VG	Broad conical crown, widely spreading, long-lasting and slowly rotting foliage, may not be planted prior to December, tolerates flooding, reacts to reduced groundwater table with treetop drought; frost-hardy
Quercus robur 'Fastigiata' syn. Quercus pedunculata 'Fastigiata' (pedunculate oak, pyramid-shaped oak)	15–20	5–7	Low	○	S	–	–	Like the species but columnar crown, spreads apart with age, sowing often yields atypical growth form, long-lasting foliage; frost-hardy, undemanding
Quercus robur 'Fastigiata Koster' syn. Quercus robusta 'Koster' (upright English oak)	15–20	3–5	Medium	○–◗	S	–	–	Like *Quercus robur* 'Fastigiata' but has slender and compact growth also with age, long-lasting foliage often remains until spring; frost-hardy, undemanding
Quercus rubra syn. Quercus borealis (northern red oak)	20–25	12–18 (20)	Medium	○	R	S	S	Rounded crown, continuous central leader, less demanding than *Quercus robur*; risk of chlorosis in chalky soil, good for urban environments, long-lasting foliage, striking fall foliage
Robinia pseudoacacia (black locust, false acacia)	20–25	12–18 (22)	High	○	S	VG	VG	Loose irregular crown, rapid-growing when young, umbrella-shaped with age; undemanding, susceptible to wind breakage in nutrient-rich soils, formation of deadwood with age; flowers very fragrant
Robinia pseudoacacia 'Bessoniana' (black locust)	20–25	10–12 (15)	High	○	S	–	–	Broad, rounded, and densely branched crown with age; usually straight and continuous leading shoots, few and only small thorns, seldom flowering
Robinia pseudoacacia 'Monophylla' (syn. Robinia pseudoacacia 'Unifolia' (single-leaf black locust)	15–20 (25)	8–10	Medium	○	S	–	–	Irregular conical crown, upright growth, main branches are slender and upright,straight and continuous leading shoots, only a few small thorns
Robinia pseudoacacia 'Nyirsegi' (black locust, false acacia)	25–30	10–15	Medium	○	S	–	–	Upright and rounded ovoid, densely branched crown; straight central leader extends into the crown, few thorns, lower risk of breakage than the species

NA = not available; R = with restrictions; VG = very good; WS = well-suited; S = suitable; P = problematic; VL = very limited suitability

Table 8.2 (continuation) Suitability of trees for streets and inner-city locations, per GALK and KLAM

Botanical and common names	Height in m	Width in m	Permeability to light	Light requirements	Suitability for city streetscapes	Drough tolerance (according to KLAM)	Winter hardiness (Winter hardiness zoness) (according to KLAM)	Comments
Robinia pseudoacacia 'Sandraudiga' (black locust, false acacia)	20–25	12–18 (22)	High	○	S	–	–	Widely pyramidal, strikingly loose crown, straight central leader, pink blossoms, heed results of Straßenbaumtest 1
Robinia pseudoacacia 'Semperflorens' (black locust, false acacia)	15–20	10–15 (18)	High	○	S	–	–	Upright and loose crown, broadly oval with age; few thorns, often has blossoms continuously from June to September owing to second flowering
Robinia pseudoacacia 'Umbraculifera' (umbrella black locust)	4–6	4–6	Low	○	S	–	–	Dense and spherical crown with fine shoots; more broadly oval with age, heed clearance profile, tolerates radical pruning, no blossoms, suitable for tubs and containers
Sophora japonica (Japanese pagoda tree)	15–20 (25)	12–18 (20)	High	○	R	VG	S	Broad and rounded, very loose and light crown spreads with age; pay heed to obtaining a straight central leader; summer pruning; young trees susceptible to frost in some areas; striking blossoms
Sophora japonica 'Regent' (Japanese pagoda tree)	15–20 (25)	10–15	High	○	R	–	–	Like the species, broad and rounded crown, spreads with age, superfluous variety since it does not represent an improvement to the species, heed results of Straßenbaumtest 1
Sorbus aria (chess-apple, whitebeam)	6–12 (18)	4–7 (12)	Medium	○	R	VG	VG	Regularly structured conical crown, wider and looser with age, slow-growing, heed clearance profile
Sorbus aria 'Magnifica' (chess-apple, hitebeam)	6–12 (18)	4–7 (12)	Medium	○	S	–	–	Like the species but smaller and narrower, with regularly structured crown, wider with age
Sorbus aria 'Majestica' syn. S. aria decaisneana (chess-apple, whitebeam)	8–10 (12)	4–7	Medium	○	R	–	–	Like the species but with narrow conical crown, umbrella-shaped with age, fruits and leaves larger
Sorbus intermedia syn. Sorbus suecica (Swedish whitebeam)	10–15 (20)	5–7	Medium	○	R	S	VG	Conical crown, round with age, heed clearance profile
Sorbus intermedia 'Brouwers' (Swedish whitebeam)	9–12	4–7	Low	○	S	–	–	Like the species but with compact pyramidal crown, straight central leader, good for urban environments, wind-tolerant, frost-hardy
Sorbus × thuringiaca 'Fastigiata' (Thuringian hybrid ash)	5–7	4–5	Medium	○	S	–	–	Narrow, conical, and compact crown; good for urban environments, wind-tolerant, frost-hardy, drought-tolerant, slow-growing

NA = not available; R = with restrictions; VG = very good; WS = well-suited; S = suitable; P = problematic; VL = very limited suitability

Table 8.2 (continuation) Suitability of trees for streets and inner-city locations, per GALK and KLAM

Botanical and common names	Height in m	Width in m	Permeability to light	Light requirements	Suitability for city streetscapes	Drough tolerance (according to KLAM)	Winter hardiness (Winter hardiness zoness) (according to KLAM)	Comments
Tilia americana 'Nova' syn. T. flaccida 'Nova' (American lime, American basswood)	25–30	15–20	Low	○–◗	S	–	–	Broadly conical crown, round with age, straight central leader, comparatively large leaves, honeydew secretion, frost-hardy, heat-tolerant
Tilia cordata (littleleaf linden, small-leaved lime)	18–20 (30)	12–15 (20)	Low	○–◗	R	S	VG	Very strongly fragrant, outstanding pollen source; habits can be highly variable, resulting in a difficult crown structure, difficult to cut away branches; honeydew secretion
Tilia cordata 'Erecta' syn. T. cordata 'Böhlje' (densely crowned littleleaf linden)	15–20	10–12 (14)	Low	○–◗	S	–	–	Like the species but with smaller and more regular crown, small leaves, slow-growing as young tree, less honeydew secretion
Tilia cordata 'Greenspire' (American linden)	18–20	10–12	Low	○–◗	WS	–	–	Narrow, regular, and dense crown, wider with age; ascending branches; good for urban environments; honeydew secretion
Tilia cordata 'Rancho' (American linden)	8–12 (15)	4–6 (8)	Low	○–◗	S	–	–	Like the species but with narrow ovoid crown that becomes broadly rounder and more regular with age; slow and compact growth; less honeydew secretion, heed results of Straßenbaumtest 1
Tilia cordata 'Roelvo' (littleleaf linden, linden)	10–15	7–10	Low	○–◗	S	–	–	Like the species but with broadly conical to rounded crown, longer shoots and growth not as compact as `Rancho,' less honeydew secretion, heed results of Straßenbaumtest 1
Tilia tomentosa (silver linden)	25–30	15–20	Low	○	R	VG	S	Regular and broadly conical closed crown, tendency to forked growth; late profusion of flowers, not hazardous to bees or bumblebees, no honeydew secretion, the use of varieties is recommended
Tilia tomentosa 'Brabant' (Brabant silver linden)	20–25 (30)	12–18 (20)	Low	○	WS	–	–	Broad and conical, dense and regularly structured crown; selection with straight central leader, better formation of leading shoots than the species, no honeydew secretion
Tilia × euchlora syn. Tilia × europaea 'Euchlora' (Caucasian lime)	15–20 (25)	10–12	Medium	○	S	S	VG	Bluntly conical crown, straight central leader, heavily hanging branches, give regard to clearance profile, fast-growing, wind-tolerant, frost-hardy, honeydew secretion
Tilia × europaea syn. T. × intermedia, T. × vulgaris, T. × hollandica (Dutch linden)	25–35 (40)	15–20	Low	○	S	P	VG	Regularly structured conical crown, good for urban environments, drought-tolerant and loves warmth, bee pasture, honeydew secretion

NA = not available; R = with restrictions; VG = very good; WS = well-suited; S = suitable; P = problematic; VL = very limited suitability

Table 8.2 (continuation) Suitability of trees for streets and inner-city locations, per GALK and KLAM

Botanical and common names	Height in m	Width in m	Permeability to light	Light requirements	Suitability for city streetscapes	Drough tolerance (according to KLAM)	Winter hardiness (Winter hardiness zoness) (according to KLAM)	Comments
Tilia × europaea 'Pallida' syn. T. × intermedia 'Pallida', T. × vulgaris 'Pallida' (Emperor's lime)	30–35 (40)	12–18 (20)	Low	○	WS	–	–	Like the species but regular conical crown, spreads widely with age; leaves remain in autumn longer than for the species, various selections available commercially; honeydew secretion
Tilia × flavescens 'Glenleven' (Glenleven linden)	15–20 (25)	12–15	Low	○	R	–	–	Closed, broadly conical crown, spreads and becomes rounder with age, straight central leader, fast-growing, good for urban environments, honeydew secretion, heed results of Straßenbaumtest 1
Ulmus × hollandica 'Lobel' (Lobel elm)	12–15	4–5	Low	○	R	–	–	Initially narrow- and upright-growing columnar crown, later becomes more conical and broader, vigorous growth, less susceptibility to Dutch elm disease
Ulmus hybrid 'Dodoens' (elm)	12–15	5–6	Low	○–◗	R	–	–	Loose and slender upright crown, broadly conical with age, less susceptibility to Dutch elm disease
Ulmus 'New Horizon' (elm)	20–25	5–6	Low	○–◗	m-E.	–	–	Columnar to conical and dense crown, slim and conical when young, later wider, presumably highly resistant to Dutch elm disease, included in Straßenbaumtest 2 since 2007/08
Ulmus hybrid 'Rebona' (Rebona elm)	15–20	10–15	Low	○–◗	R	–	–	Broadly conical crown, branches protrude horizontally, presumably resistant to Dutch elm disease
Ulmus hybrid 'Regal' (elm)	15–20	6–8	Medium	○	R	–	–	Initially slim and conical, wide and columnar with age, fast-growing, presumably resistant to Dutch elm disease, included in Straßenbaumtest 2 since 2007/08
Zelkova serrata syn. Z. acuminata, Z. keaki (Japanese zelkova)	20–25	15–25	Low	○–◗	R	S	S	Wide, round crown with broadly extended growth, watch for straight leading shoots, good for urban environments, included in Straßenbaumtest 2 since 2005

NA = not available; R = with restrictions; VG = very good; WS = well-suited; S = suitable; P = problematic; VL = very limited suitability

Table 8.2 (continuation) Suitability of trees for streets and inner-city locations, per GALK and KLAM

8.2 Hedges

According to their structure, the intensity of care, and their application, hedges can be divided into three main groups: seminatural hedges in the open landscape, free-growing hedges, and trimmed (topiary) hedges.

Seminatural hedges are distinguished by the use of native woody plants. They were and are today sometimes still planted as windbreaks for shielding fields, as enclosures, and for marking boundaries.

Free-growing hedges provide decorative or functional enclosure of a property or they structure an open space as linear elements. They can be planted as flowering hedges, evergreen hedges, as mixed plantings, or as homogeneous hedgerows. Since these hedges only receive occasional maintenance pruning, their growth is more consistent with natural conditions, generally making their space requirements relatively large.

Trimmed hedges are given shape through regular and repeated pruning, so the plants which are used must be accordingly tolerant of pruning. They are more laborious to care for than free-growing hedges.

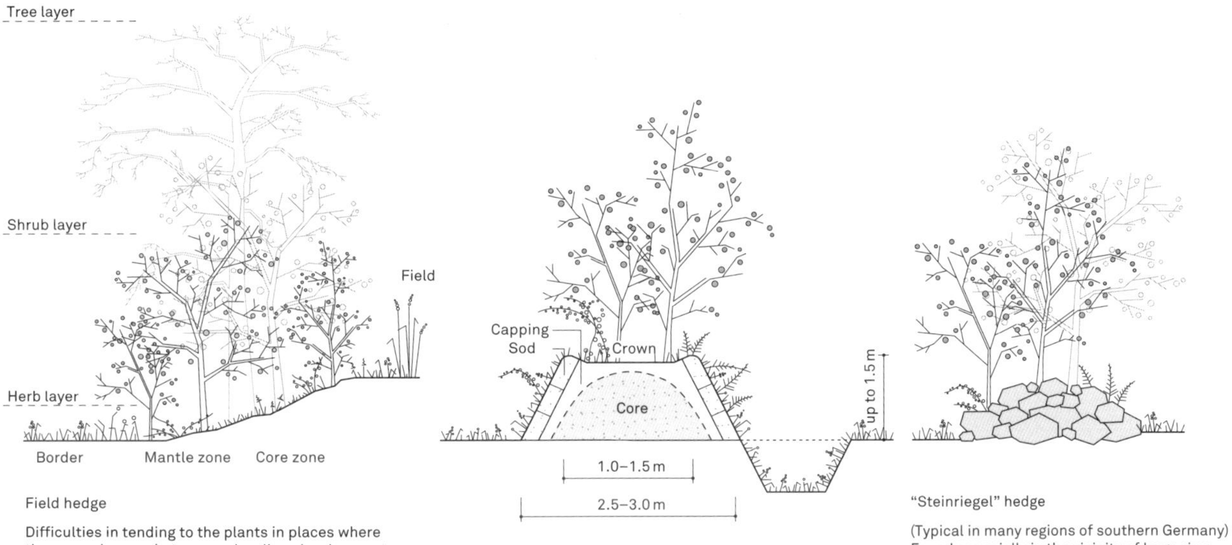

Field hedge

Difficulties in tending to the plants in places where there are changes in topography allow development of a double woodland margin

Hedgebank without/with trench

(Typical in many regions of northern Germany)
Woody plants are (traditionally) cut back to the trunk every 7–10 years; Berm form restricts spread of the root system

"Steinriegel" hedge

(Typical in many regions of southern Germany)
Found especially in the vicinity of large river valleys / where fieldstones are prevalent

Figure 8.5 Various types of seminatural hedges

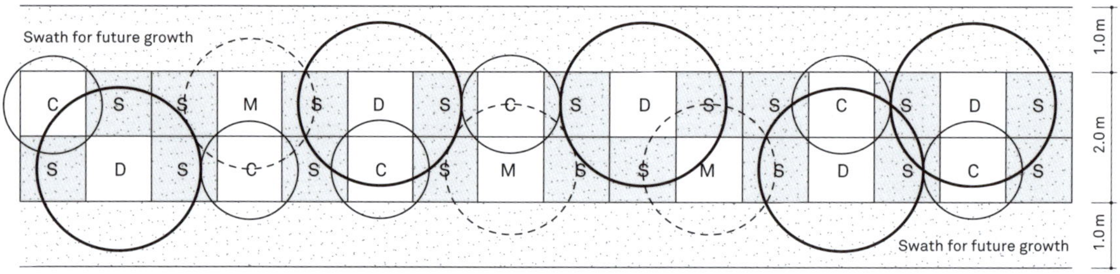

Trees and shrubs planted in two rows on a 1 × 1 m grid, with underplanting

D Dominant
M Mantle shrubs
C Companion trees and shrubs
S Perennials, herbs, and secondary woody plants

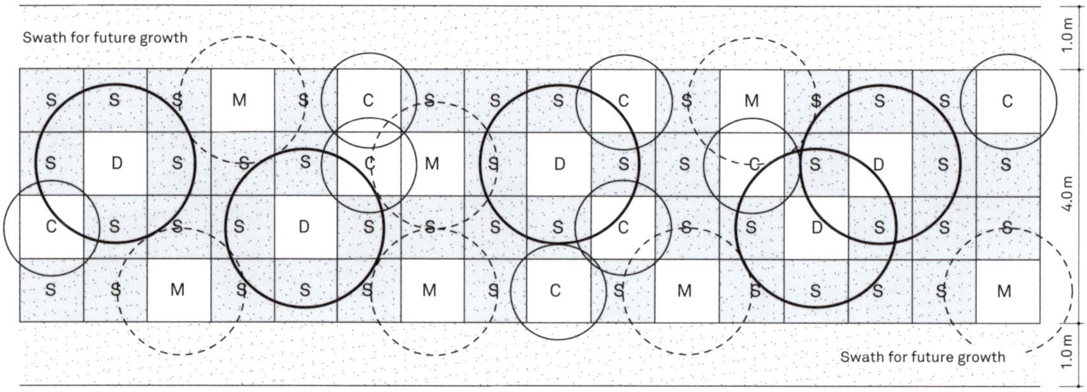

Trees and shrubs planted in four rows on a 1 × 1 m grid, with underplanting

Figure 8.6 Planting scheme for free-growing hedges

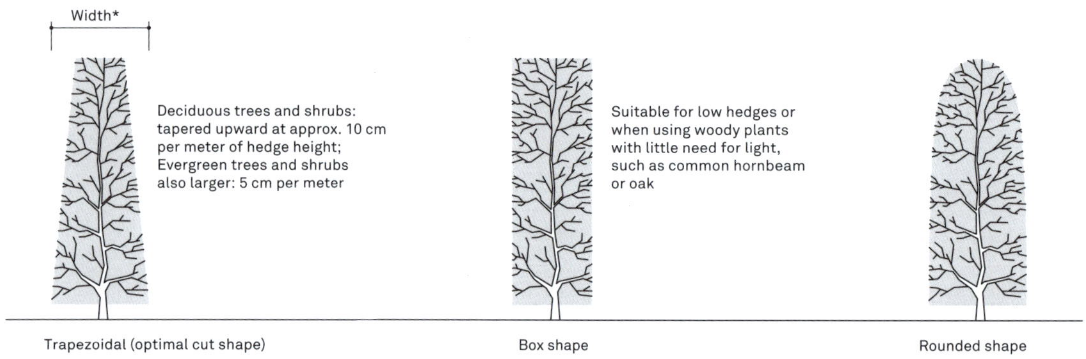

* Minimum width = planned height × approx. 0.4 (high hedges) to 0.6 (low hedges)

Figure 8.7 Trimmed hedge profiles

Species	Max. growth height	Suitable for hedge height, in m			Suitable for hedge height, in m	Plants per m, depending on initial height	Light needs	Comments
		up to 1	1–2	2–4				
Acer campestre (field maple, hedge maple)	15 m		x	x	35–40	2–3	FSu–PSh	Yellow fall foliage; bee pasture; also for hedge gateways and hedge arbors; susceptible to mildew
Berberis vulgaris (barberry)	3 m	x	x		20–50	3–4	FSu–PSh	Thorns, bright red fall foliage; insect food
Berberis thunbergii 'Atropurpurea' (Japanese, or red barberry)	1.5–2 m	x			20–40	2–4	FSu–PSh	Dark red foliage, yellow flowers; undemanding
Buxus sempervirens (common box)	2–6 m	x	x	x	10	4–5	FSu–FSh	Infestation with the fungus Cylindrocladium buxicola possible
Carpinus betulus (European, or common, hornbeam)	25 m		x	x	25–35	2,5–4	FSu–FSh	Undemanding, heat- and drought-tolerant, dry foliage persistent through winter
Cornus mas (Cornelian cherry)	3–7 m		x	x	20–40	3–4	FSu–PSh	Deciduous; yellowish-red-orange (variable) fall foliage; bee pasture; protective planting for birds
Crataegus monogyna (one-seed or common hawthorn)	up to 8 m		x	x	20–25	3–4	FSu–FSh	Protective planting for birds; also tolerates being pruned back completely; can succomb to fire blight
Crataegus prunifolia (plum-leaved thorn)	up to 7 m		x	x	20–25	2–3	FSu–PSh	Bark is very thorny
Fagus sylvatica (common beech)	up to 30 m			x	20–50	2–3	FSu–PSh	Prefers loose soil; retains dry leaves for long time
Ilex aquifolium (English holly)	4–7 m		x	x	15–40	2–4	PSh–FSh	
Juniperus communis (common juniper)	up to 10 m		x	x	10–15	1–2	FSu–PSh	Undemanding; can prune from spring to mid-September; intermediate host for pear trellis rust
Ligustrum vulgare 'Atrovirens' (privet)	2–4 m	x	x		20–50	3–4	FSu–PSh	Undemanding; tolerates heat
Ligustrum vulgare 'Lodense' (dwarf privet)	up to 0.7 m	x			5–8	3–4	FSu–PSh	
Prunus laurocerasus 'Herbergii' (cherry laurel)	2–3 m		x		20–45	2–3	FSu–FSh	Evergreen; tolerates much shade and root pressure
Pyracantha coccinea 'Red Column' (firethorn, pyracantha)	1.5–2.5 m	x	x		10–20	2–3	FSu–PSh	Evergreen; thorns; conspicuous berries
Ribes alpinum (Alpine currant)	1.5–2 m	x	x		15–25	2–3	FSu–FSh	Food source for birds and insects
Spirea japonica 'Froebeli' (Japanese spirea)	0.8–1.2 m	x	x		10–20	3–4	FSu–PSh	Deciduous; spring pruning encourages blossoms
Taxus baccata (common or European yew)	12–15 m		x	x	20–40	3–4	FSu–PSh	Very resilient; also nutrient-poor soils; tolerates radical rejuvenation pruning
Thuja occidentalis (arborvitae)	15–20 m		x	x	20–25	2–5	FSu–PSh	Very hardy, wind-resistent, high sprouting and regeneration capacity

Table 8.3 Woody plants for trimmed hedges: standard values for plant spacing, plant size/height, and annual growth

8.3 Vegetated Roofs

Vegetated roofs, also known commonly as green roofs or living roofs, constitute a broad category that encompasses the landscaped roofs of conventional buildings as well as any landscape situated on a built structure, be it a courtyard above an underground parking garage or a park running directly over a subterranean structure or even set atop a bridge. Their positive effect on the (local) climate and their abilities to trap dust and pollutants, retain stormwater, create habitats for flora and fauna, and protect the roof as well as an increase in the quality of any usable open spaces all represent good arguments for green roofs.

With regard to the composition of layers and their thicknesses, distinctions are made between extensive, semiintensive, and intensive forms of landscaping.

All types of green roofs are feasible on flat roof slopes, but only the extensive system is feasible for roof slopes greater than 5 °. Because positions of these landscapes and their exposure to the elements are generally predetermined by the building's configuration, the potential planting is sometimes subjected to extreme site-specific differences. The prevailing wind conditions on roofs are often much more harsh than on the ground or within courtyards. The exposure on the roof or location within a courtyard often yield extreme situations with intense solar radiation or complete shade.

Especially on steeply sloped roofs, the conditions can become extremely dry because precipitation can barely be held in the thin substrate layers and quickly drains away.

The thickness of the root-permeable layers determines the fundamentally different types of planting. The range of these planting forms is shown in **Table 8.4**.

Both walkable and trafficable areas can be constructed with either bound or unbound material. The details and layer thicknesses are dependent on the anticipated loading from vehicles.

Root-permeable layer thickness, in cm		4	6	8	10	12	15	18	20	25	30	35	40	45	50	60	70	80	90	100	125	150	200
Extensive landscaping (≥45 Vol. %)*	Moss/sedum mix	◀	■	■																			
	Sedum/moss/herb mix		■	■	■																		
	Sedum/grass/herb mix				■	■	■																
	Grass/herb mix						■	■	■														
Semi-intensive landscaping (≥50 Vol. %)*	Grass/herb mix					■	■	■	■	■	■	■	▶										
	Wildflowers/woody plants mix					■	■	■	■	■	■	■	■	■	■	▶							
	Woody plants/perennials mix						■	■	■	■	■	■	■	■	■	▶							
	Woody plants								■	■	■	■	■	■	■	■	■	■	▶				
Intensive landscaping (≥55 Vol. %)*	Grass						■	■	■	■	■	▶											
	Low perennials and woody plants						■	■	■	■	■	■	■	■	▶								
	Medium-height perennials and woody plants								■	■	■	■	■	■	▶								
	High perennials and woody plants											■	■	■	■	■	▶						
	Large shrubs and small trees															■	■	■	■	■	▶		
	Tall and medium-height trees																			■	■	■	▶
	Tall trees																					■	▶

* maximum water capacity of the vegetation substrate and drainage layer

Table 8.4 Possible types of vegetation as a function of vegetation layer thickness

	Type of planting		
	Extensive landscaping	Semi-intensive landscaping	Intensive landscaping
Layers 1 Extensive substrate 2 Intensive substrate 3 Inorganic substrate (growth medium) 4 Filter layer 5 Rigid drainage board 6 Drainage layer 7 Protection layer 8 Roof waterproofing (root-resistant)	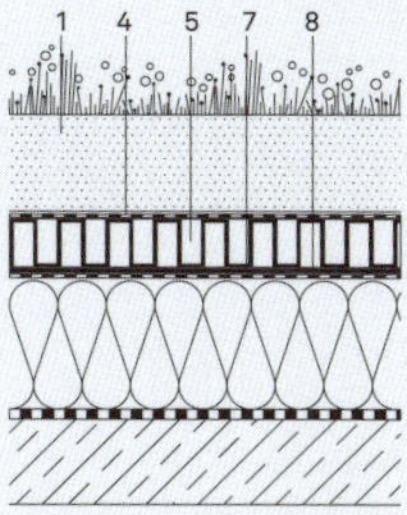	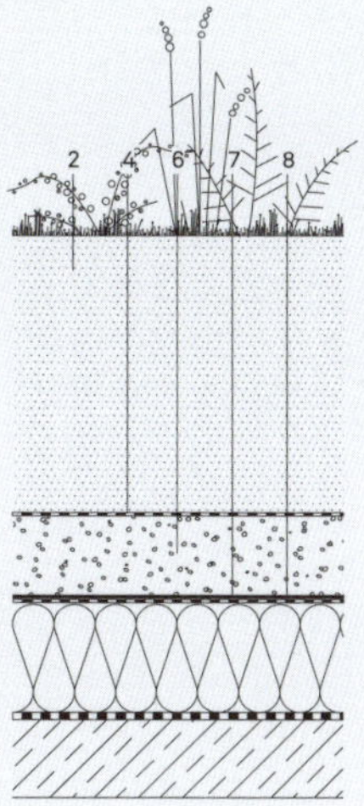	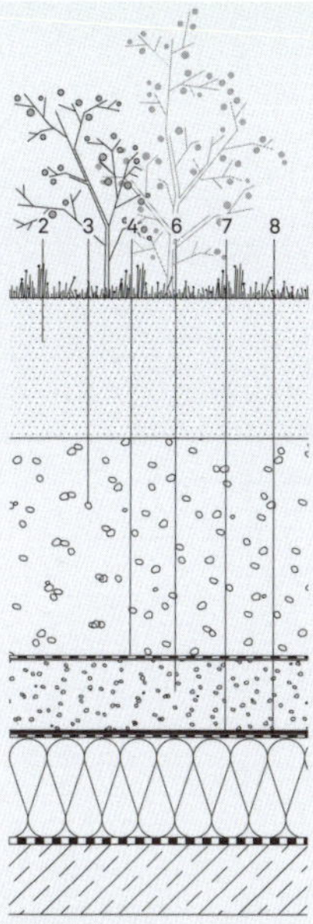
Drainage layer	Approx. 3 cm (omitted for single-layer system)	3–5 cm	>10 cm
Vegetation layer	5–15 cm	10–25 cm	>25 cm
Roof load	50–150 kg/m²	150–350 kg/m²	>350 kg/m²
Type of vegetation	Mosses, some drought-tolerant grasses and perennial flowers, particularly mixtures of moss/sedum, sedum/moss/herbs, sedum/grass/herbs, and grass/herbs	Drought-tolerant perennial flowers, grasses, and woody plants	Nearly unrestricted use of plants, depending on local conditions; no wind-sensitive plants and no large woody plants
	No strongly growing climbing plants or plants with aggressive root growth, e.g., some bamboo species, which could damage the root barrier or roof waterproofing		
Maintenance	Low: no irrigation ordinarily required	Moderate: occasional irrigation when needed (dry periods); pruning back and fertilizing as required, depending on plant species	High: regular irrigation; pruning back and fertilizing as required, depending on plant species
	Inspection of the roof drains and, if necessary, removal of foreign growth – particularly from protective strips		
Roof pitch	(0) 1°–35° (up to 45° in exceptional cases) 20° pitch or greater only with protection against shear forces and slippage in order to prevent erosion due to the runoff velocity of precipitation.	(0) 1°–5° (approx. 8 %)	(0) 1°–5° (approx. 8 %)
Suitable roof types	• Simple structures such as carports, pavilions, garden sheds, etc. • Ventilated (cold) roofs	• Simple structures only after verifying specific conditions	
	• Inverted roof with thermal insulation • Nonventilated (warm) roofs, when pressure-resistant insulation is used • Watertight concrete roof with thermal insulation • Roofs without thermal insulation (e.g., underground garages, bridges, outbuildings, etc.)		

Table 8.5 Characteristics of the different types of green roofs
(Source: State Research Institute for Horticulture Weihenstephan, amended and supplemented)

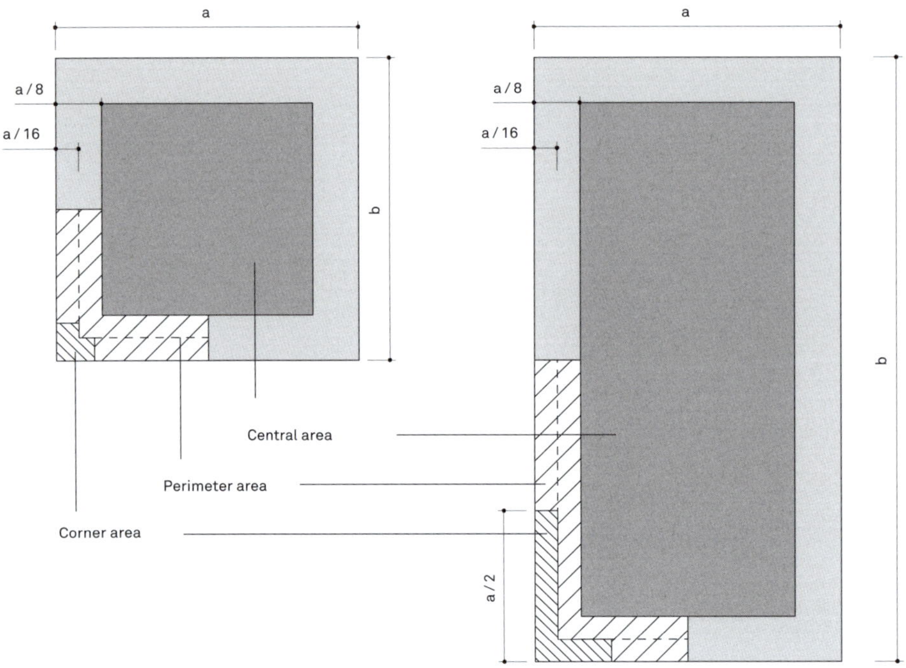

Area distribution for flat roofs with a nearly square plan square plan (b / a ≤ 1.5)

Area distribution for flat roofs with a rectangular plan (b / a > 1.5)

Figure 8.8 Area distribution for flat roofs with a maximum 8° slope for determining the required ballast

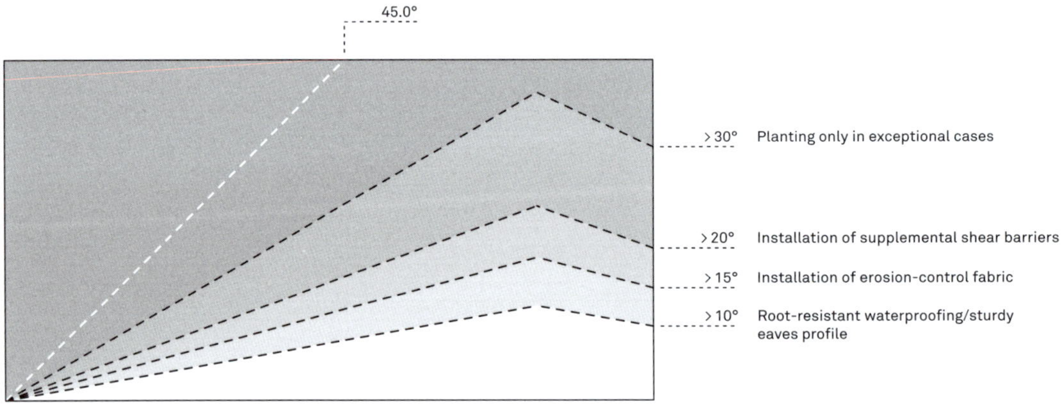

Figure 8.9 Safeguards needed as roof slope increases

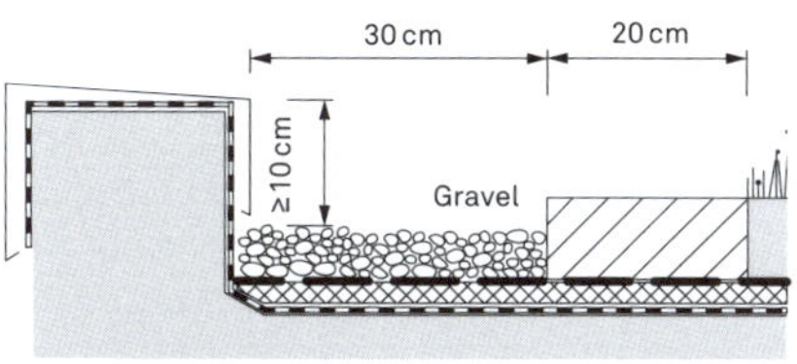

Clearance strip along roof edge

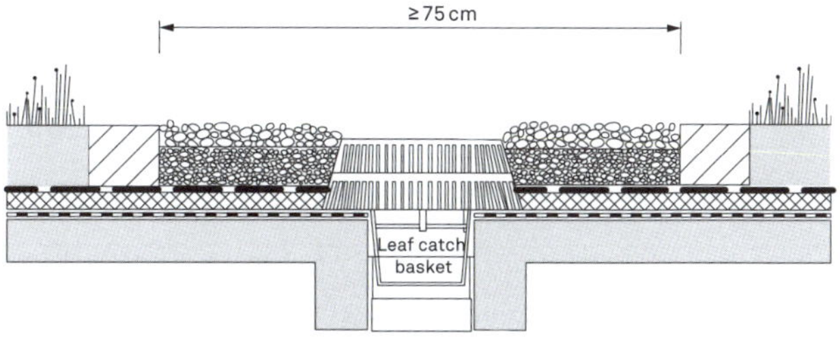

Vegetation-free zone around a roof drain

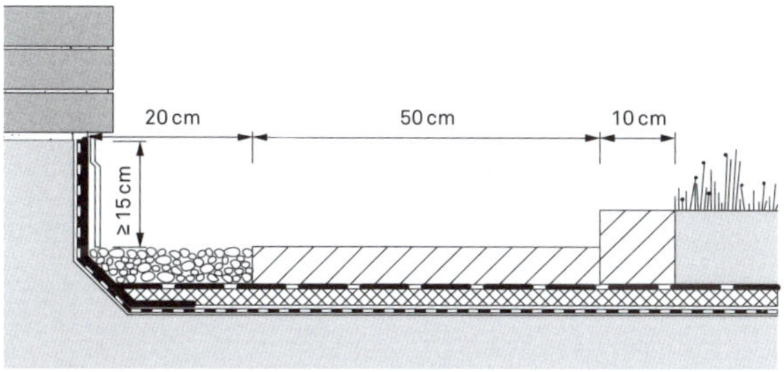

Protective strip along a masonry wall

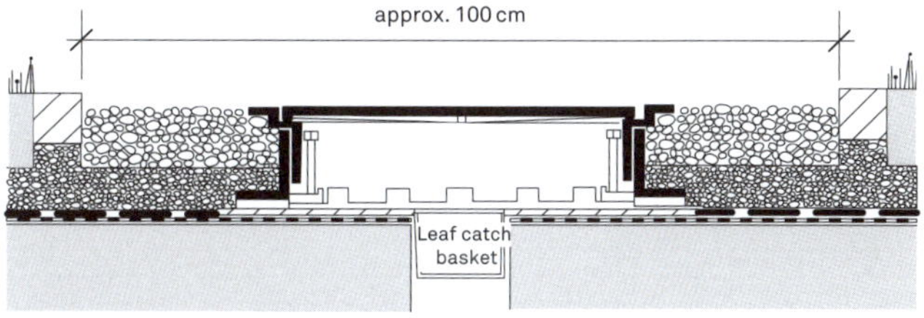

Roof drain

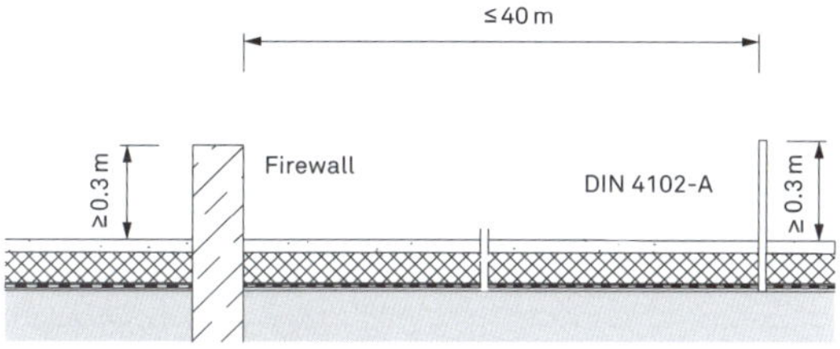

Fire compartment wall extending above roof as per DIN 4102-A

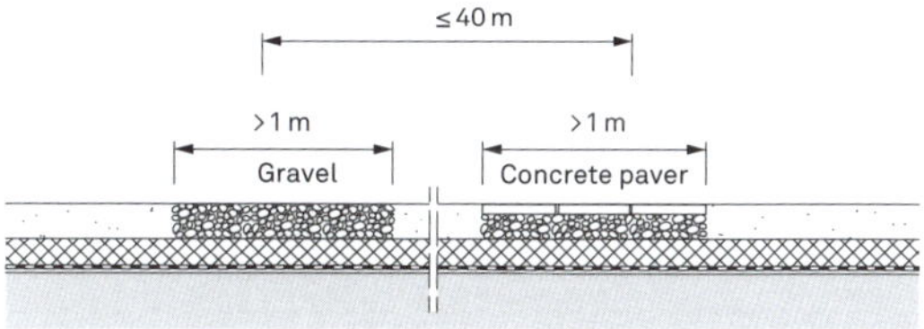

or bands of gravel or concrete pavers at a spacing of ≤40 m

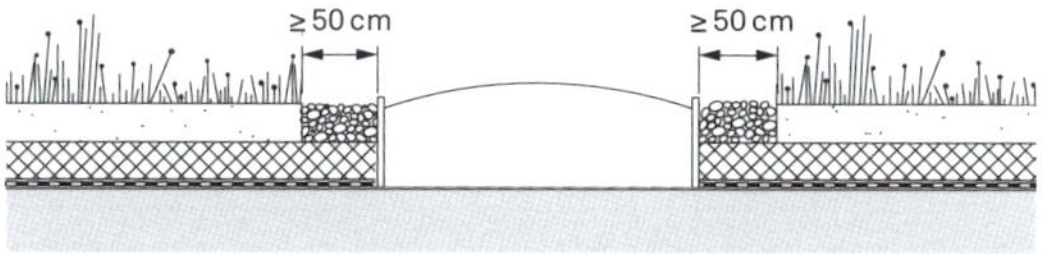

Bands of gravel or concrete pavers surrounding roof openings (e.g. domed skylights)

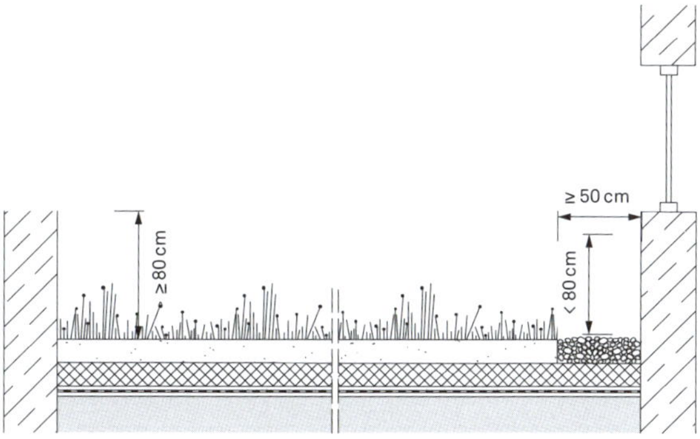

Bands of gravel or concrete pavers in front of walls with window sill height < 80 cm.

Figure 8.10 Minimum clearances to vertical building components and edge conditions

8.4 Vertical Planting

Vertical planting embraces the cultivation of climbing plants that grow along a climbing aid, such as a trellis panel or espalier, as well as self-climbing plants that can grow directly on a building or a thicket. Vegetated pots or trough systems can also be arranged along a facade. A sort of further development and synthesis of these systems is represented by facade greening systems (also called "living walls") in which plants grow on substrate mats or within bags, thus making it possible to have a landscape that grows across the entire surface of a building wall.

A distinction can be made among the following plant groups used for vertical planting, based on their application and the corresponding properties: annual and perennial climbing plants, trained woody plants, plants for facade greening systems (perennials, herbs, and dwarf shrubs), and trimmed shrubs.

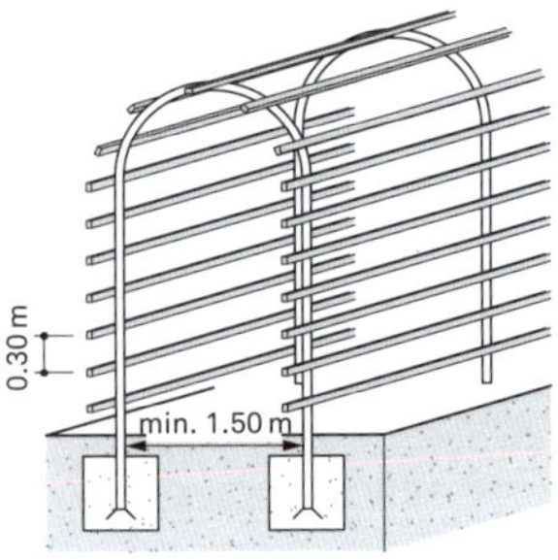

Pergola

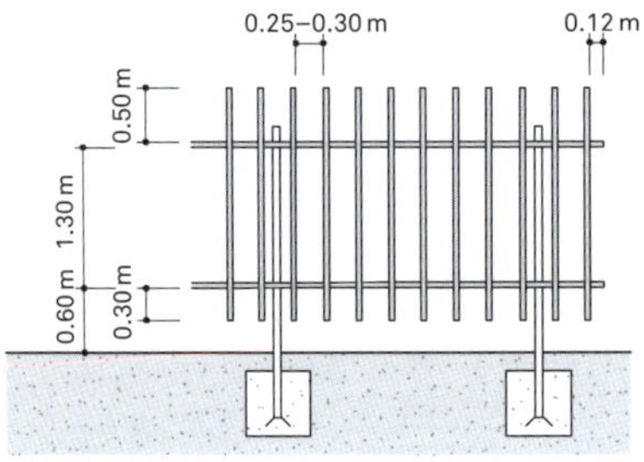

Freestanding espalier constructed of slats

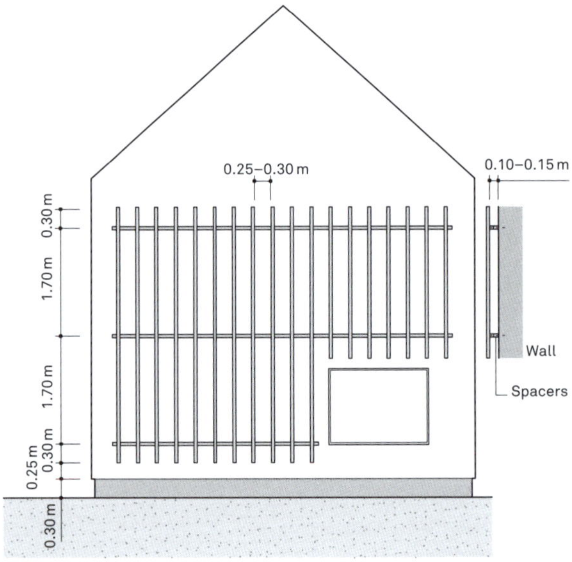

Wall trellis

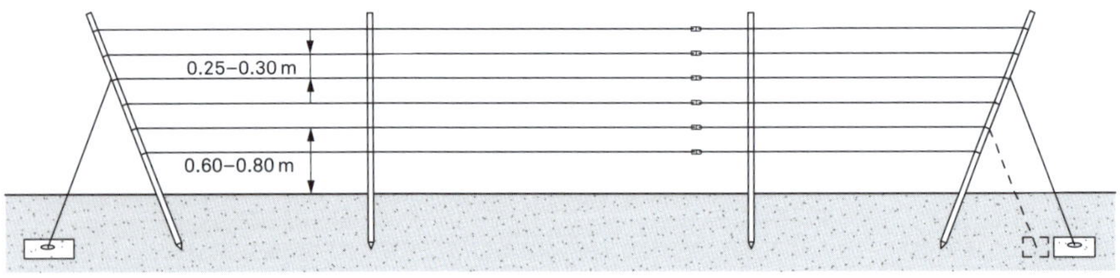

Archetypal espalier for wine growing

Figure 8.11 Wall trellises and freestanding espaliers

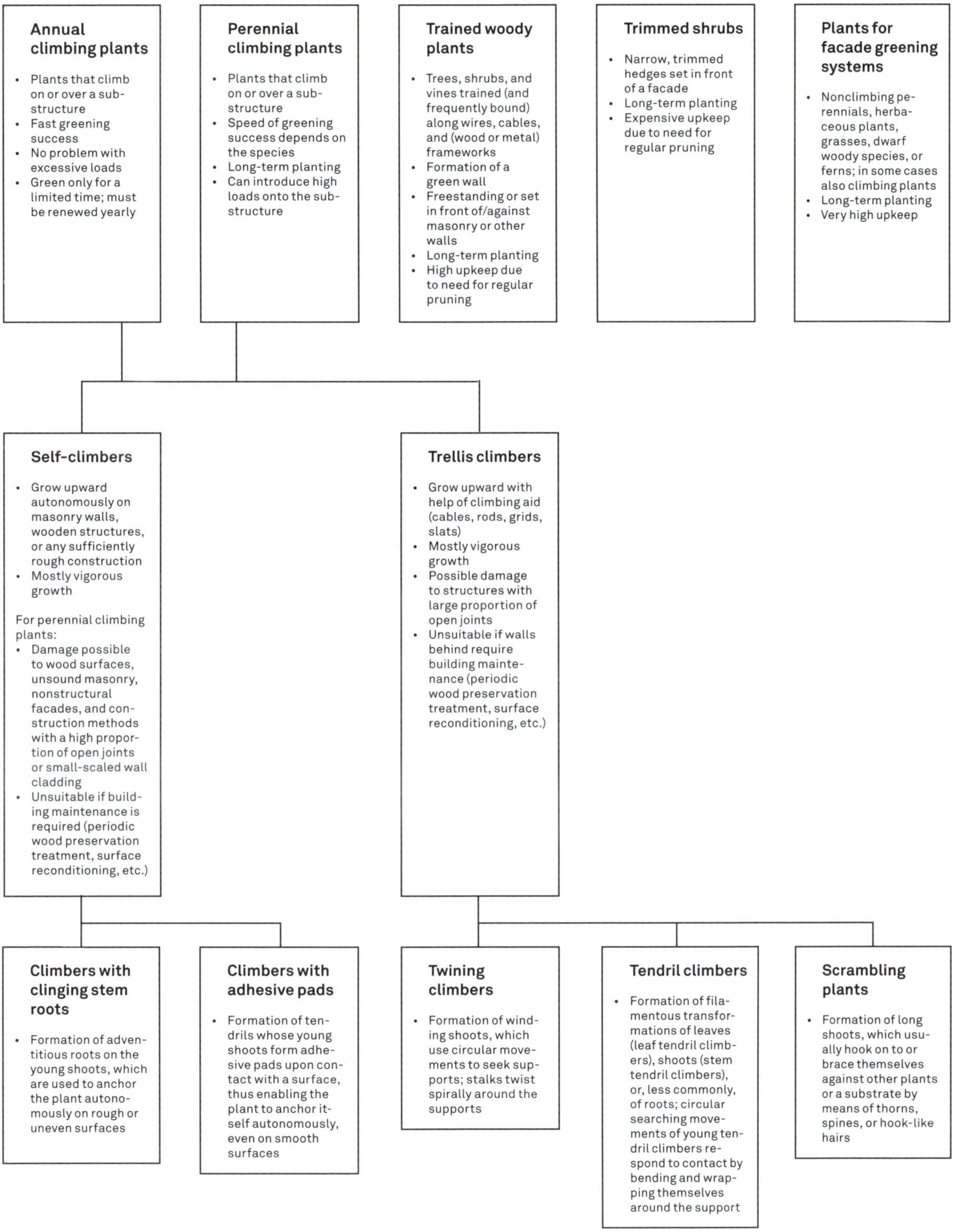

Figure 8.12 Categories of plants used for vertical planting

Botanical and common name	Average growth height (climbing)	Width of growth (= sensible width of climbing aid if needed)	Growth (annual increase in height under typical conditions)				Max. shoot diameter at root collar /clearance between wall and climbing aid	Section thickness of climbing aid	Light requirement	Foliage	Special characteristics
			>200 cm	100–200 cm	50–100 cm	<50 cm			FSu = Full sun PSh = Partial shade FSh = Full shade	Deciduous (D) Evergreen (E)	
Self-climbers											
Climbers with clinging stem roots											
Campsis radicans (trumpet creeper or trumpet vine)	6–12 m	6–10 m	x	x			up to 20 cm	–	FSu	D	Initially slow-growing, fast-growing after 3–5 years; light-shunning shoots, protected location
Campsis radicans 'Flava' (yellow trumpet creeper)	4–5 m, in favorable locations up to 8 m	4 m		x			–	–	FSu	D	Dense, with overhanging branches
Campsis × tagliabuana 'Madame Galen' (Madame Galen trumpet creeper)	3–5 m	5–6 m	x		x	x	up to 10 cm	–	FSu	D	Slow-growing, shoots overhang far, clings weakly, climbing aids that let the long shoots cling to them are recommended, light-shunning shoots, protected location
Euonymus fortunei var. *radicans* (winter creeper or spindle)	0.5–0.8 m 4–6 m	0.8–1.2 m				x	up to 10 cm	–	PSh	E	
Euonymus fortunei var. *vegetus* (winter creeper or spindle)	4–6 m	1–4 m 1–1,5 m				x	up to 10 cm	–	FSu–PSh	E	
Euonymus fortunei varieties (winter creeper or spindle)	3–5 m					x	up to 10 cm	–	PSh–FSh	E	
Hedera colchica (Persian ivy)	6–8 m in favorable locations 10–20 cm	up to 10 cm		x	x		up to 15 cm	–	PSh–FSh	E	
Hedera helix (common ivy)	10–20 m (–30 m)	2–15 m		x	x			–	FSu–FSh	E	Clinging stem roots on the shaded side infiltrate even the finest cracks and pores (0.2 mm) and anchor themselves there

Table 8.6 Characteristics of perennial climbing plants

Botanical and common name	Average growth height (climbing)	Width of growth (= sensible width of climbing aid if needed)	Growth (annual increase in height under typical conditions)				Max. shoot diameter at root collar /clearance between wall and climbing aid	Section thickness of climbing aid	Light requirement	Foliage	Special characteristics
			>200 cm	100–200 cm	50–100 cm	<50 cm			FSu = Full sun PSh = Partial shade FSh = Full shade	Deciduous (D) Evergreen (E)	
Hedera helix 'Woerner' (common ivy)	10–15 m	5 m and more		x				–	FSu–FSh	E	
Hedera helix 'Hibernica' (Irish ivy)	5–20 m	>5 m 4–10 m		x				–	FSu–FSh	E	Strong-growing, but prefers creeping and mat-like growth
Hydrangea petiolaris (climbing hydrangea)	10–12 m 10–20 m	2–6 m 8–12m				x		–	FSu–FSh	D	Loosely flung, overhanging branches; older plants show some twining tendencies, very slow-growing for the first three to five years; annual growth: 5–10 cm
Climbers with adhesive pads											
Parthenocissus quinquefolia 'Engelmannii' (Engelmann's ivy)	15–18 m 10–15 m	3–4 m		x	x		up to 20 cm		FSu–FSh	D	Strong-growing, also overhangs droopily
Parthenocissus tricuspidata 'Veitchii' (Virginia creeper 'Veitchii')	15–18 m 20–25 m			x					FSu–PSh	D	Very strong-growing, mat-like and dense
Trellis climbers											
Twining climbers											
Actinidia arguta (hardy kiwi)	5–12 m	5–6 m	x	x	x		up to 15 cm	up to 3.5 cm	FSu–PSh	D	Anchors very solidly
Actinidia chinensis (kiwi)	8–10 m	6–8 m	x	x	x		up to 20 cm	up to 4 cm	FSu–PSh	D	
Actinidia kolomikta (kolomikta)	2–(6) m	3–5 m		x	x		up to 3 cm	up to 3.5 cm	FSu	D	Slow-growing
Akebia quinata (chocolate vine or five-leaf akebia)	4–(10) m	2–4 m 6–8 m		x			up to 3 cm	up to 3 cm	FSu–PSh	D	Also overhangs droopily (approx. 2 m long)

Table 8.6 (Continuation) Characteristics of perennial climbing plants

Botanical and common name	Average growth height (climbing)	Width of growth (= sensible width of climbing aid if needed)	Growth (annual increase in height under typical conditions)				Max. shoot diameter at root collar /clearance between wall and climbing aid	Section thickness of climbing aid	Light requirement FSu = Full sun PSh = Partial shade FSh = Full shade	Foliage Deciduous (D) Evergreen (E)	Special characteristics
			>200 cm	100–200 cm	50–100 cm	<50 cm					
Aristolochia macrophylla (Dutchman's pipe or pipevine)	8–10 m	1–8 m 4–6 m	x	x			up to 10 cm	2 (3) cm	FSu–PSh	D	Very slow-growing at the outset, strong-growing from the 3rd to 5th year onward
Celastrus orbiculatus (Oriental bittersweet)	8–12 m (15 m)	2–6 m 8–10 m	x	x			up to 16 cm	Young plants: 1–2 cm; for older plants: up to 7.5 cm	FSu–PSh	D	Entwined trees up to 20 cm in diameter can be strangled by strong growth in thickness; pendent with loosely flung branches reaching out up to 2 m, also overhangs droopily (2–3 m long)
Humulus lupulus (common hop)	3–6 m 5–6 cm	8–12 m 1–2 m	x				up to 2 cm	up to 2 cm	FSu–PSh	D	Perennial, dies back after each growing season, losing the superficial parts of the plant; growth performance during the vegetation period 0.5–1 m per week, strong tendency to spread
Lonicera japonica var. *repens* (creeping Japanese honeysuckle)	up to 3 m (10) m					x	up to 2 cm	up to 2 cm	FSu–PSh	D	
Lonicera × *brownii* 'Dropmore Scarlet' (Dropmore Scarlet honeysuckle)	2–5 m	0.5–1 m			x	x	up to 2 cm	0.5–1.5 cm	FSu	D	
Lonicera caprifolium (Italian or goat-leaf honeysuckle)	2–5 (8) m	0.5–2 m			x		up to 2 cm	0.5–3 cm	FSu–PSh	D	
Lonicera × *heckrottii* 'Gold Flame' (Gold Flame honeysuckle)	2–6 m	2–3 m branches, reaching out up to 1.5 m			x	x	up to 2 cm	0.2–1 cm	PSh	D	Only weakly twining, tends to grow loose and shrubby
Lonicera henryi (evergreen honeysuckle)	5–8 m	1–2 m		x			up to 4 cm	1–3 cm	PSh–FSh FSu–PSh	E	Also overhangs droopily (2–3 m long)

Table 8.6 (Continuation) Characteristics of perennial climbing plants

Botanical and common name	Average growth height (climbing)	Width of growth (= sensible width of climbing aid if needed)	Growth (annual increase in height under typical conditions)				Max. shoot diameter at root collar /clearance between wall and climbing aid	Section thickness of climbing aid	Light requirement FSu = Full sun PSh = Partial shade FSh = Full shade	Foliage Deciduous (D) Evergreen (E)	Special characteristics
			>200 cm	100–200 cm	50–100 cm	<50 cm					
Lonicera periclymenum (common or European honeysuckle or woodbine)	1–3 (6) m				x		up to 2 cm	up to 2 cm	FSu–PSh	D	Strong-growing, strangling
Lonicera × tellmanniana (Tellmann's honeysuckle)	4–6 m	1–4 m		x			up to 3 cm	0.5–3 cm	PSh–FSh FSu–PSh		Side branches stand away horizontally
Polygonum aubertii (silver lace vine)	8–15 m (20) m	5–10 m	x					1–5 cm	FSu–PSh	D	Dense and mat-like, can strangle itself on supports that are too thin
Wisteria floribunda (Japanese wisteria)	6–8 m high and more		x	x			up to 25 cm	up to 7.5 cm	FSu–PSh	D	Powerful twiners with extremely strong growth in thickness; can crush fragile supports and tear out anchorages
Wisteria sinensis (Chinese wisteria)	6–15 m	2–10 m 8–30 m	x				up to 50 cm	2–10 cm	FSu	D	Can strangle itself on supports that are too thin; strangles small trees, crimps rainwater downspouts
Tendril climbers											
Clematis alpina varieties (alpine clematis)	1.5–2 m	1–3 m				x	up to 3 cm	0.2–0.5 cm	PSh–FSh	D	Thin, cobweb-like shoots
Clematis hybrid varieties (clematis hybrids)	Depending on the variety: 2–3 m or 3–4 m	1–2 m						0.2–0.5 cm		D	Only the upper third is tightly branched and has blossoms if left untrimmed; overhangs droopily
Clematis macropetala varieties (downy clematis)	2–3 m	2–2.5 m			x			up to 0.7 cm	FSu–PSh	D	Partly dense and mat-like; thin, bowed, occasionally overhanging shoots
Clematis montana varieties (anemone clematis)	3–6 m (–11 cm)	2–4 m			x			0.2–1 cm			

Table 8.6 (Continuation) Characteristics of perennial climbing plants

Botanical and common name	Average growth height (climbing)	Width of growth (= sensible width of climbing aid if needed)	Growth (annual increase in height under typical conditions)				Max. shoot diameter at root collar/clear-ance between wall and climbing aid	Section thickness of climbing aid	Light requirement	Foliage	Special characteristics
			>200 cm	100–200 cm	50–100 cm	<50 cm			FSu = Full sun PSh = Partial shade FSh = Full shade	Deciduous (D) Evergreen (E)	
Clematis montana 'Rubens' (clematis 'Rubens')	3–6 (10) m	2–4 m					up to 5 cm	0.2–1 cm	FSu–PSh	D	
Clematis orientalis 'Orange Peel' (orange peel clematis)	4–6 m (occasionally to 8 m),				x		up to 5 cm		FSu	D	Dense, mat-like growth; strong-growing in treetops
Clematis tangutica (golden clematis)	4–6 m	2–4 m		x	x		up to 5 cm	0.2–0.5 cm	FSu–FSh	D	Branched tightly and cobweb-like
Clematis texensis varieties (crimson or scarlet clematis)	1–1.5 (2.5) m									D	Tendril climbing subshrub, climbs cobweb-like over other plants
Clematis vitalba (old man's beard or traveler's joy)	5–15 (30) m	2–8 m	x				up to 15 cm	0.2–1 cm	FSu–PSh	D	Impenetrable mat-like growth, in isolation up to 500 cm
Clematis viticella varieties (virgin's bower)	2–5 m	2–3 m			x			0.2–0.5 cm	FSu–PSh	D	Also overhangs droopily (up to 2 m long)
Cobaea scandens (cathedral bells or cup-and-saucer vine)										D	
Parthenocissus quinquefolia (inserta) (Northern creeper)	6–10 (15) m	1–4 m	x		x		up to 20 cm	up to 1.3 cm	FSu–PSh	D	Also overhangs droopily, also forms adhesive pads
Vitis coignetiae (crimson glory vine)	6–8 m, climbs up to 25 m high in trees	10–12 m			x			3 cm	FSu–PSh	D	Covers up to 30 m² with no gaps; fast-growing, tendrils up to 25 cm long, clasps around supports
Scrambling plants											
Jasminum nudiflorum (winter jasmine)	2–3 (5) m	2–3 m			x		up to 3 cm	–	FSu–PSh	D	Also overhangs droopily, then 2–5 m long, 2–3 m wide; tolerates pruning into hedge shape

Table 8.6 (Continuation) Characteristics of perennial climbing plants

Botanical and common name	Average growth height (climbing)	Width of growth (= sensible width of climbing aid if needed)	Growth (annual increase in height under typical conditions)				Max. shoot diameter at root collar /clearance between wall and climbing aid	Section thickness of climbing aid	Light requirement	Foliage	Special characteristics
			>200 cm	100–200 cm	50–100 cm	<50 cm			FSu = Full sun PSh = Partial shade FSh = Full shade	Deciduous (D) Evergreen (E)	
Rosa arvensis (field rose)	0.5–2 m	1–2 m			x			–	FSu–PSh	D	Partly with thin, creeping, rooted shoots and partly climbing
Climbing roses	2–3 (6) m 2–6 m				x		up to 20 cm	–	FSu–PSh	D	Usually grows upright
Rubus fruticosus (blackberry)	0.5–3 (4) m	2–3 m		x	x		up to 4 cm	–	FSu–FSh	D	
Rubus henryi (climbing evergreen blackberry)	2–4 cm			x			up to 2 cm	–	PSh–FSh	D	Shoots tend to exhibit twining

Table 8.6 (Continuation) Characteristics of perennial climbing plants

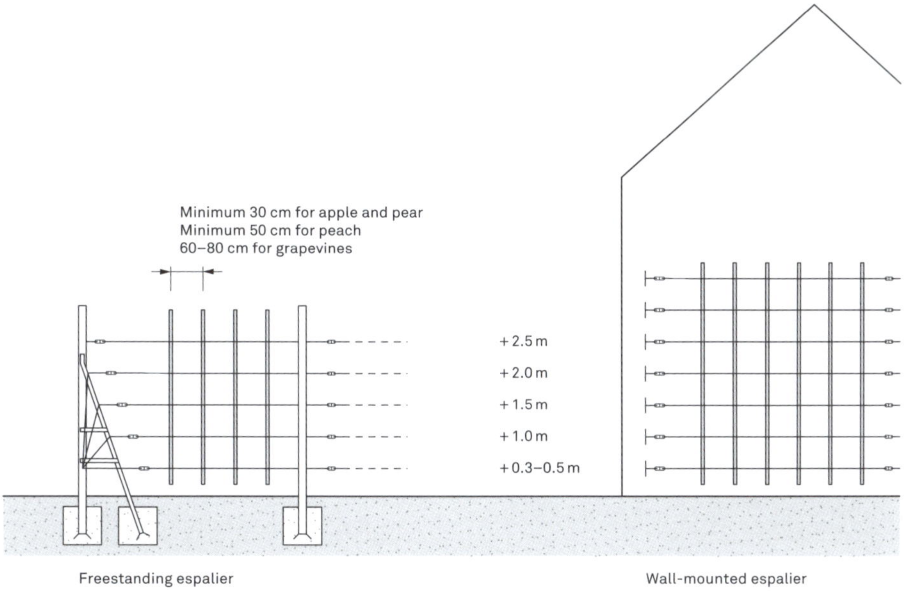

Figure 8.13 Freestanding and wall-mounted espaliers for fruit

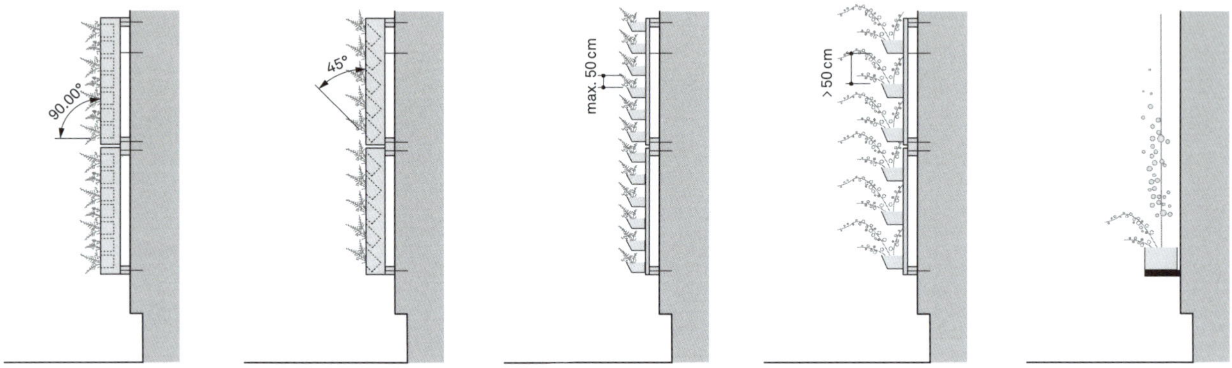

Full-surface vegetation carrier, plants oriented at 90°

Full-surface vegetation carrier, plants oriented at < 90° (e.g., 45°)

Partial-surface vegetation carrier, linear, ≤ 50 cm between plant levels

Partial-surface vegetation carrier, linear, > 50 cm between plant levels

Partial-surface vegetation carrier, solitary elements

Figure 8.14 Components of facade greening systems

Type	Material/type of construction			Upkeep			
	Support systems	Suitable facades	Plant species	Servicing	Irrigation	Maintenance actions	Establishment phase
Ground-based vertical planting systems							
Rigid climbing aid, planar	Framework and grating: e.g., steel frame with steel bars, steel rod grids, wood latticework and wall trellises	Well suited: • Masonry and concrete construction • Exterior insulation and finish systems (structural suitability must be confirmed, poor workmanship can yield thermal bridges) Unsuitable: • Rear-ventilated (rainscreen) facades not suitable for plants with negative phototropism (e.g., clinging stem roots of ivy)	Trellis climbers	Average, every 5–10 years	As needed	As needed	> 3 years
Rigid climbing aid, linear	Rod-like/linear elements: e.g., steel tubes or steel rods		Trellis climbers	Average, every 5–10 years	As needed	As needed	1–2 years
Flexible climbing aid, planar	(Stainless steel wire) nets and stretched cables		Trellis climbers	Average, every 5–10 years	As needed	As needed	> 3 years
Flexible climbing aid, linear	(Stainless steel wire) nets and stretched cables		Trellis climbers	Average, every 5–10 years	As needed	As needed	> 3 years
Without climbing aid	Building and garden walls		Self-climbers	Average, every 5–10 years	As needed	As needed	> 3 years

Table 8.7 Overview of ground-based and facade-bound vertical planting systems with regard to use of materials and need for maintenance

Type	Material/type of construction			Upkeep			
	Support systems	Suitable facades	Plant species	Servicing	Irrigation	Maintenance actions	Establishment phase
Facade-bound vertical planting systems							
Full-surface vegetation carrier, 90° orientation	Vegetation carrier on mounting plate, visible surface material: Metal, non-woven fabric, geotextile and/or synthetic	Well suited: • Rear-ventilated (rainscreen) facade • With masonry and concrete walls, rear-ventilation should be retroactively installed • Exterior insulation and finish systems when structural suitability is confirmed (poor workmanship can yield thermal bridges)	Well suited: • Grasses, perennials, herbs Moderately suited: Climbing plants • (tendency to overgrow) • Woody plants (restricted root zone)	Very high, <3 years	High, daily	High, 1–2/year	Full coverage attained immediately or near-term
Full-surface vegetation carrier, <90° orientation (e.g., 45°)			Well suited: • Grasses, perennials, herbs, and sedum Moderately suited: • Climbing plants (tendency to overgrow) • Woody plants (restricted root zone)	Very high, <3 years	High-very high, daily to several times daily	Very high, >2/year	1–2 years
Partial-surface vegetation carrier, linear, ≤50 cm between plant levels			Well suited: • Grasses, perennials, herbs, and sedum Moderately suited: • Climbing plants (tendency to overgrow) • Woody plants (restricted root zone)	High, every 3–5 years	Average, 1–4 times per week	High, 1–2/year	1–2 years
Partial-surface vegetation carrier, linear, >50 cm between plant levels			Very well suited: • Climbing plants Well suited: • Surface-covering/overhanging woody plants (full coverage difficult)	Very high, <3 years	Average, 1–4 times per week	High, 1–2/year	2–3 years
Partial-surface vegetation carrier, solitary elements	Trough planters (concrete, steel, plastic) on support frame/mounting plate, with and without climbing aid	Well suited: • Masonry and concrete construction • Exterior insulation and finish systems (structural suitability must be confirmed, poor workmanship can yield thermal bridges) Conditionally suitable: • Rear-ventilated (rainscreen) facade, not suitable for plants with negative phototropism	Very well suited: Climbing plants Suitable: Ground-covering/overhanging woody plants Moderately suited: Grasses, perennials, herbs, and sedum	Very high, <3 years	High, daily	High, 1–2/year	2–3 years

Table 8.7 (Continuation) Overview of ground-based and facade-bound vertical planting systems with regard to use of materials and need for maintenance

9 Recreational Elements

Recreational and leisure activities constitute an essential component in the design of public parks and open spaces. In this regard, playgrounds and sports facilities offer very specific opportunities for use. Relevant to their design are safety aspects as well as the standard sizes of playing fields, and hence the planning must take both into account. Thus for playgrounds, impact attenuation surfacing, fall protection areas, and sufficient safety clearances around the play equipment often determine the final form of the planned facility.

Special uses such as campgrounds and open-air stages are likewise based on minimum dimensions. The applicable requirements and recommended values must be taken into account as part of their planning in order to ensure they function properly. Both safety (e.g. escape routes for outdoor facilities) and aspects pertaining to comfort of use (e.g. space allocations, provision of sanitary facilities) are of key importance.

9.1 Play Areas and Playgrounds

For children's playgrounds adjacent to housing, a minimum setback of 10 m from windows of occupied rooms is generally required. The space needed for different play areas and pieces of playground equipment determines the necessary playground size – or, in other cases, the space available will only permit certain play areas to be created and certain playground equipment to be used.

Elements of playground equipment must be positioned to avoid any overlap of the main circulation routes and equipment play areas as well as obstructions in areas of swinging movement. In addition to these safety areas, the falling space that could be occupied by a user when falling from an elevated part of the equipment must also be taken into consideration.

Type / main user group	Guideline value for urban design	Recommended sizes per playground	Location
Playgrounds in public spaces			
Close to housing / small children up to 6 years	0.5 m²/inhabitant usable play area, 0.75 m²/inhabitant gross area	40–50 m² usable play area, 60–225 m² gross area	Max. walking distance from the dwellings: 100 m
Neighborhood playground / children 6–12 years	2 m²/inhabitant (ÖNORM 2607)	450–800 m² usable play area, 675–1,200 m² gross area	Max. walking distance from the dwellings: 400 m
Village, borough, or district playground / children and youth 12 years and older		600–3,000 m² usable play area, 800–3,750 m² gross area	Max. walking distance from the dwellings: 800–1,000 m
Families/adults	1.5 m²/inhabitant (gross area)	≥ 1,500 m² usable area, ≥ 2,250 m² gross area	Max. walking distance from the dwellings: 800–1,000 m
Playgrounds in residential developments (refer to building code or community statutes and bylaws for applicable local regulations)			
Play areas for small children; in Berlin, when serving 75 or more dwellings: also suitable for older children	Provide 4–6 m² usable play area per dwelling unit for 3 or more dwellings	Minimum 25 m²; Berlin: 50 m², Upper Austria: 100 m²	Max. walking distance from the dwellings: 100 (50) m

Table 9.1 Orientation values: minimum requirements for playground areas (relevant directives and building regulations must be observed) (Sources: German Olympic Society (DOG) guidelines, DIN 18034-1, state building codes, ÖNORM B 2607)

Play area	Minimum size including safety and movement area	Equipment
Sand play	20–35 m^2	Sandbox, sandpit, game table
Stand-alone equipment	6–20 m^2	Spring rocker; seesaw; playhouse; balance beam
Stand-alone equipment	20–30 m^2	Swing; slide; balance station; climbing net, water feature
Composite structures	70–100 m^2	Themed play structure; climber-slide combination; water feature combination
Play on multiple elements	150–500 m^2	Slides, seesaws, swings, climbers and upper body equipment (overhead ladders, rings, etc.), balance beam
Adventure playground	600–800 m^2	Play combination (themed) with surrounding wooded areas
Ball games, running and mobility games	800–1,300 m^2	Small courts; terrain modeling and climbing wall; fitness course
Played with and in water	200–500 m^2	Wading pool; water features
Skate parks	250–400 m^2	Pools, half-pipes, quarter-pipes, etc.

Table 9.2 Minimum sizes for different play areas in public spaces (Source: Gälzer, 2001), supplemented)

<table>
<tr><th>Free height of fall</th><th>Falling space width / width of impact area</th><th>Surfacing</th></tr>
<tr><td>≤0.6 m</td><td>1.5 m</td><td>No impact absorption required</td></tr>
<tr><td>≤1.5 m</td><td>1.5 m</td><td>Protection from falling → Table 9.4</td></tr>
<tr><td colspan="3">Formula for calculating the falling space = free height of fall × 2/3 + 0.5 m</td></tr>
<tr><td>1.65 m</td><td>1.6 m</td><td rowspan="5">Protection from falling → Table 9.4</td></tr>
<tr><td>1.8 m</td><td>1.7 m</td></tr>
<tr><td>2 m</td><td>1.83 m</td></tr>
<tr><td>2.5 m</td><td>2.16 m</td></tr>
<tr><td>3 m</td><td>2.5 m</td></tr>
</table>

Table 9.3 Width of falling space as a function of fall height

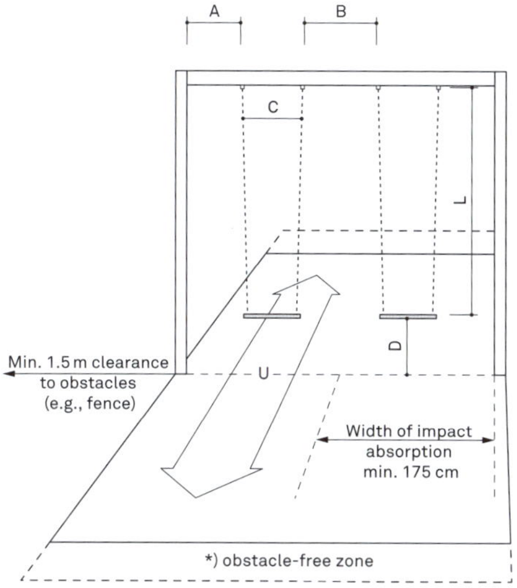

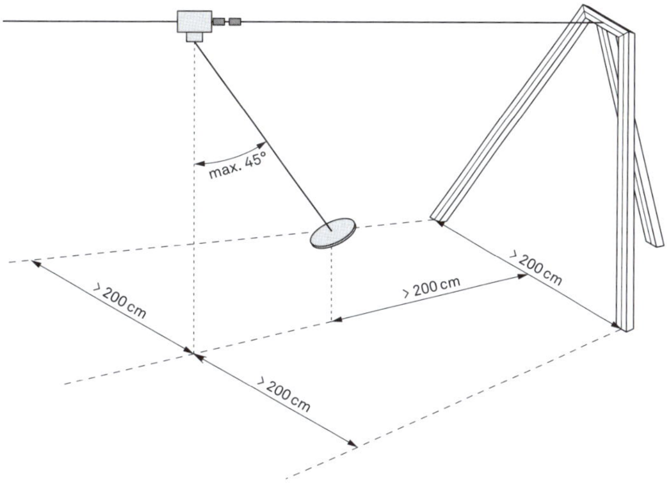

A = minimum clearance to frame = 20 % of L + 20 cm

B = minimum distance between swing seats = 20 % of L + 30 cm

C = V-shaped swing suspension = width of swing seat + 5 % of L

D = clearance beneath swing at rest: standard swing seats = 35 cm / tire and bird's nest seats = 40 cm

L = center of fulcrum (swivel joint) to top edge of seat

U = 2 × (L × 0.867 + 225 cm) impact-absorbing loose material);
for impact-absorbing surfacing (e.g. rubber safety tiles) = 2 × (L × 0,867 + 175 cm) + 50 cm obstacle-free zone *) on both sides

Figure 9.1 Examples for minimum clearances at swings and cableways per EN 1176-1

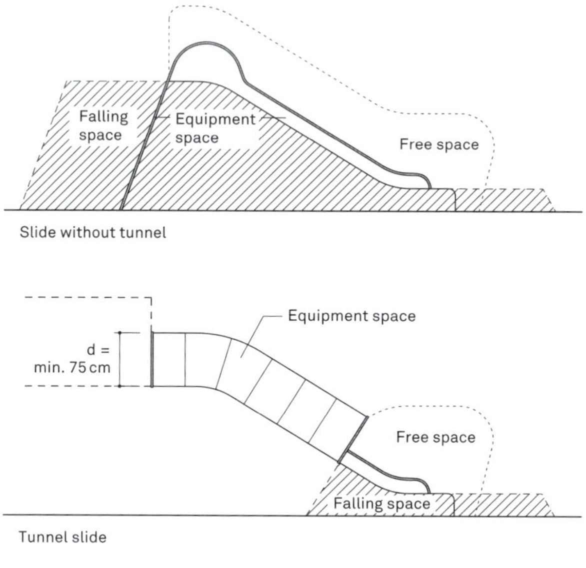

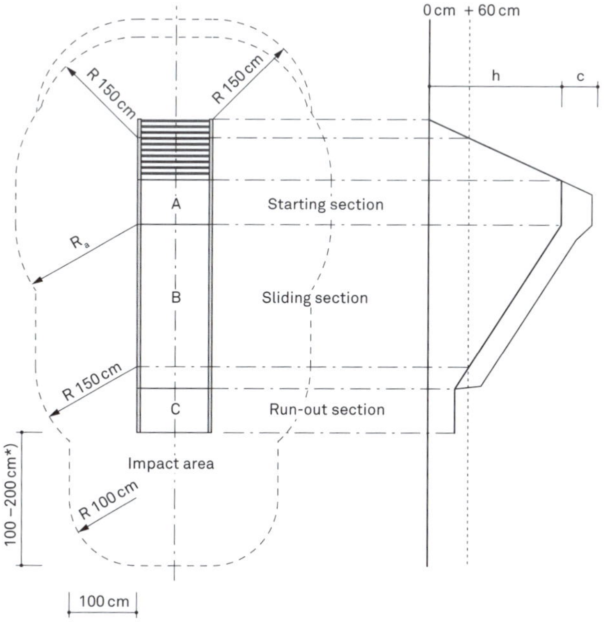

A = the radius is determined by the free fall height h

B = the length of the impact area is dependent on the type of run-out section (per EN 1176-3)

C = the height of the side protection is determined by the free fall height h (e.g., for a free fall height h > 250 cm, c = min. 50 cm)

Figure 9.2 Examples of falling spaces and free spaces for slides

<table>
<tr><th rowspan="2">Platform or landing height</th><th colspan="2">Fall prevention on play equipment</th><th rowspan="2">Surfacing</th></tr>
<tr><th>Easily accessible for all ages (EU)</th><th>Not easily accessible for children under 3 years old / accessible for all ages in DE*</th></tr>
<tr><td><0.6 m</td><td>No requirements</td><td>No requirements</td><td>No requirements (in DE)</td></tr>
<tr><td>0.6 to <1 m</td><td rowspan="3">Protective barrier (to prevent unintentional falls or climbing over or through) required, height ≥0.7 m</td><td>No requirements</td><td>Loose material</td></tr>
<tr><td>1 to <2 m</td><td>Guardrail required, with a height of ≥0.6 m to 0.85 m</td><td>Impact-absorbing surface (up to 1.5 m grass allowed) → Table 9.5</td></tr>
<tr><td>2 m to <3 m</td><td>Protective barrier required, height ≥0.7 m</td><td>Impact-absorbing surface → Table 9.5</td></tr>
</table>

* Deviating rule in Germany due to the legal duty of supervision for children up to 3 years of age

Table 9.4 Required protection against falling from platforms and landings of playground equipment

<table>
<tr><th rowspan="2">Surface material</th><th colspan="5">Maximum fall height per EN 1176-1:2008-08</th><th rowspan="2">Comments</th></tr>
<tr><th>≤60 cm</th><th>≤100 cm</th><th>≤150 cm</th><th>≤200 cm</th><th>≤300 cm</th></tr>
<tr><td>Concrete, stone, bitumen-bound materials</td><td>Only permitted in DE</td><td></td><td></td><td></td><td></td><td>Should only be used in exceptional cases, and not for equipment that causes a forced movement of the user's body, such as slides, swings, or carousels</td></tr>
<tr><td>Topsoil</td><td>x</td><td>x</td><td></td><td></td><td></td><td>No compacted or dried-out earth; not barrier-free</td></tr>
<tr><td>Grass</td><td>x</td><td>x</td><td>Permitted in DE (assuming sod is well maintained)</td><td></td><td></td><td>National regulations and regional climatic conditions must be observed; areas must be protected from drying out; not barrier-free</td></tr>
<tr><td>Wood chips (particle size 5–30 mm)</td><td colspan="4" rowspan="4">Layer thickness ≥20 cm, plus 10 cm to counteract the material's tendency to scatter</td><td rowspan="4">Layer thickness ≥30 cm, plus 10 cm to counteract the material's tendency to scatter</td><td>Must be placed on a well-drained substrate; not barrier-free</td></tr>
<tr><td>Bark mulch (particle size 20–80 mm)</td><td>Must be placed on a well-drained substrate; not barrier-free</td></tr>
<tr><td>Sand (particle size 0.2–2 mm)</td><td rowspan="2">Should not contain any silt or clay, recommended particle size: 1–5 mm, not barrier-free</td></tr>
<tr><td>Gravel (particle size 2–8 mm)</td></tr>
<tr><td>Other materials (e.g., rubber safety tiles, synthetic surfacing)</td><td colspan="5">With adequate HIC test value as per EN 1177</td><td>HIC = Head Injury Criterion</td></tr>
</table>

Table 9.5 Fall heights as a function of the ground material

9.2 Sports Facilities

The type of sports facility being planned and issues related to how it will be used form the basis for its design: the required dimensions and features vary, depending on whether the premises is for public recreation or will be used by a school or a club.

Combined facilities, in which fields for different types of sports are juxtaposed and often superimposed in a minimum amount of space, are particularly attractive for recreational and school sports.

A north-south orientation generally represents the optimal alignment of playing fields and running tracks. The impact of glare on the athletes from high sun angles from the south is significantly lower than it would be in an east-west orientation when the sun is lower in the sky.

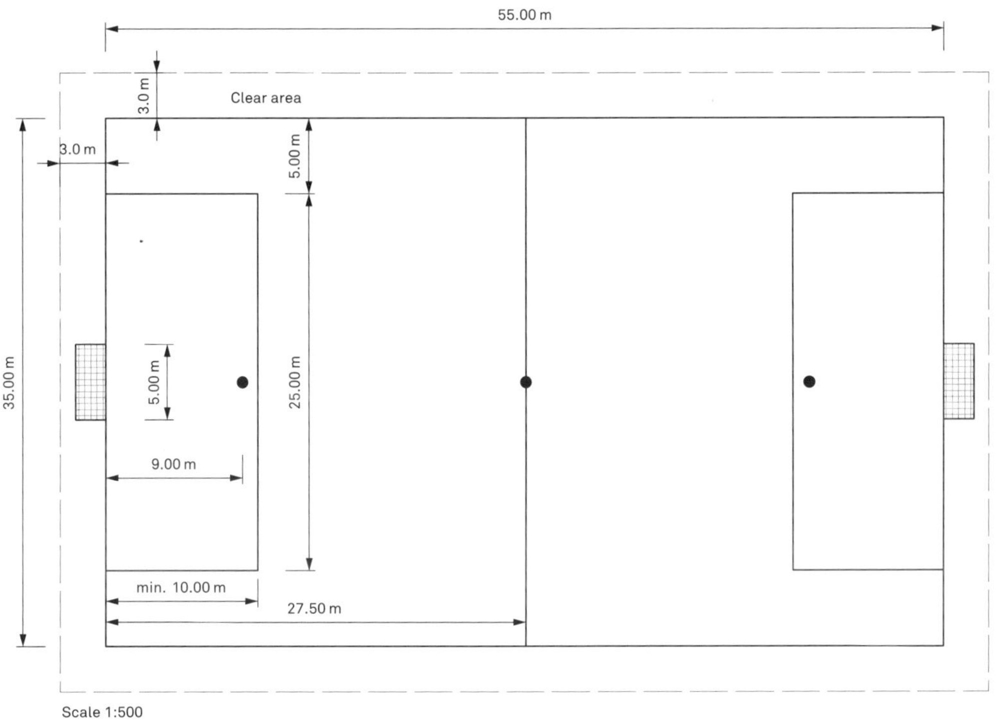

Figure 9.3 Soccer (compact sports field)

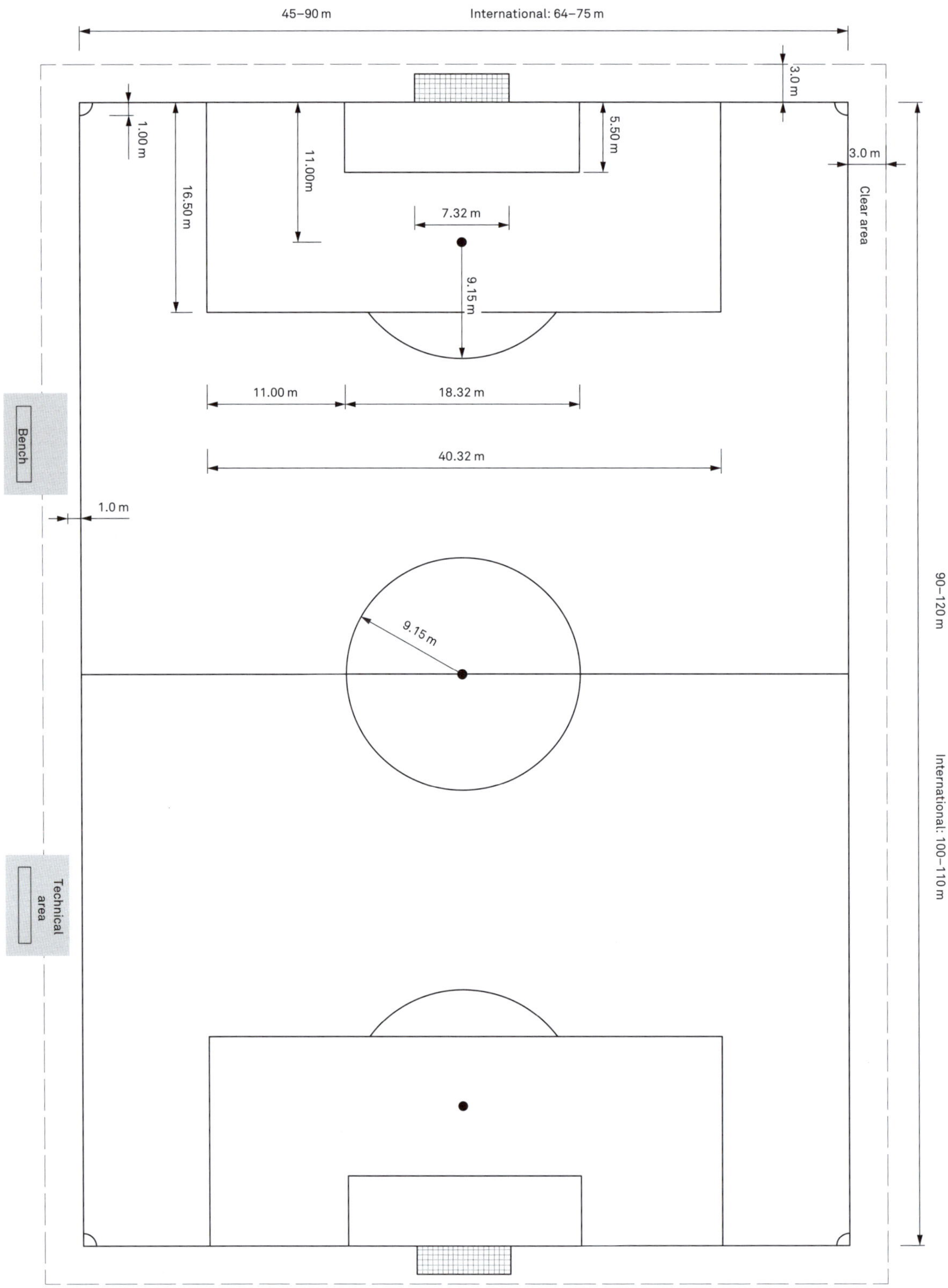

Scale 1:500

Figure 9.4 Soccer (international competition (FIFA))

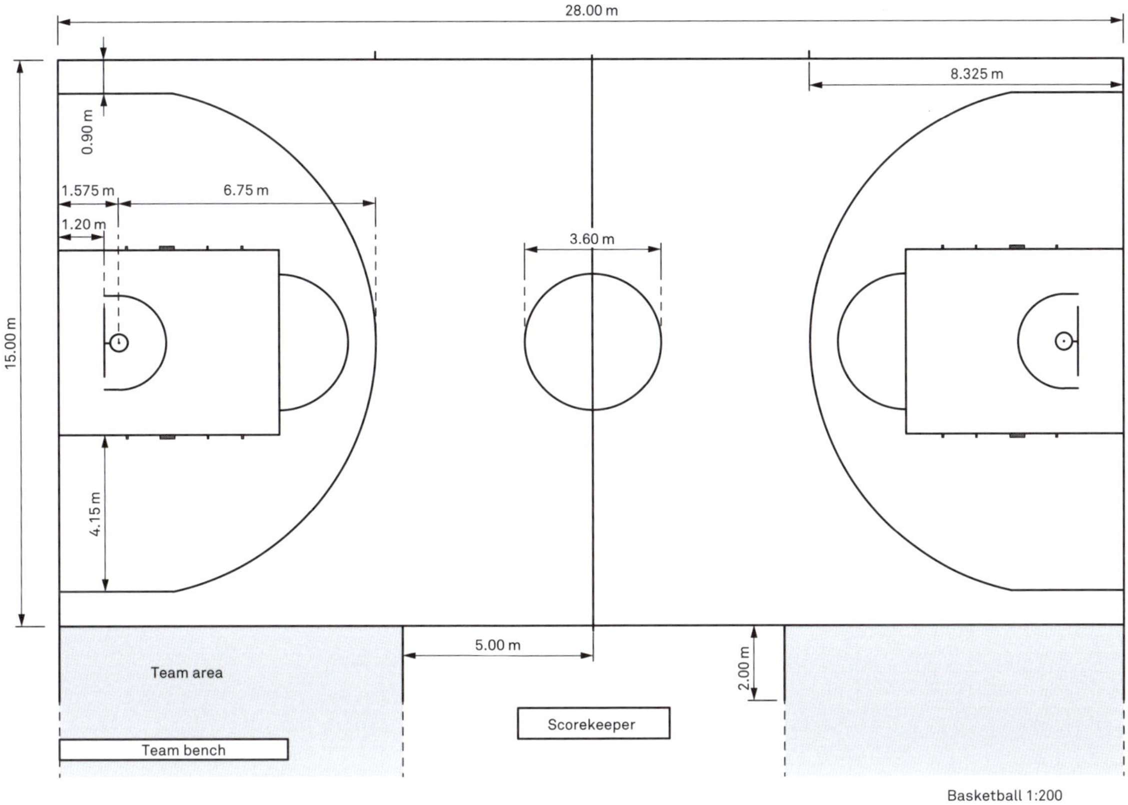

Figure 9.5 Basketball and Streetball

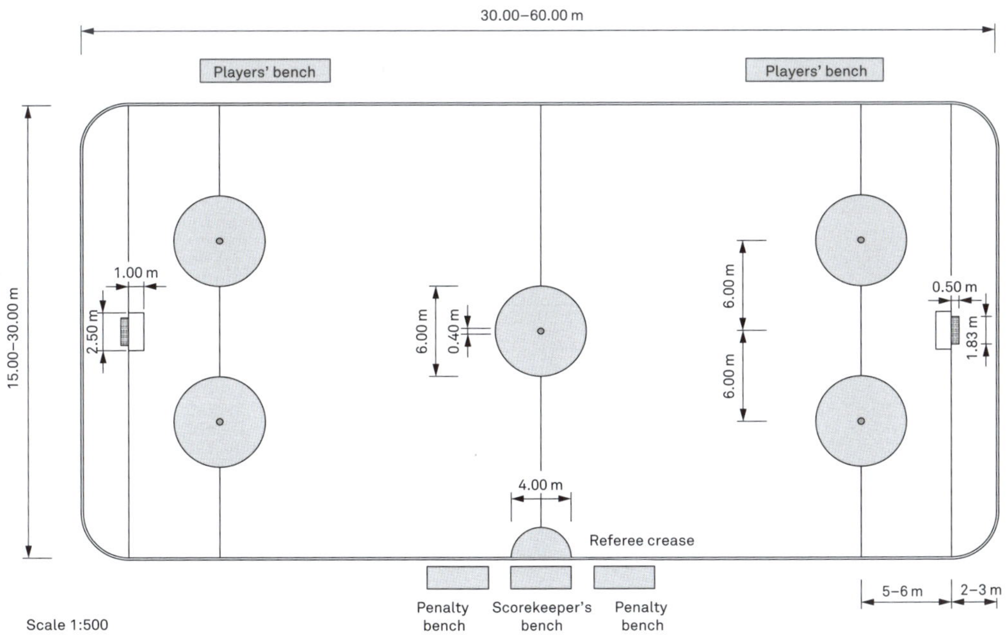

Figure 9.6 Inline hockey

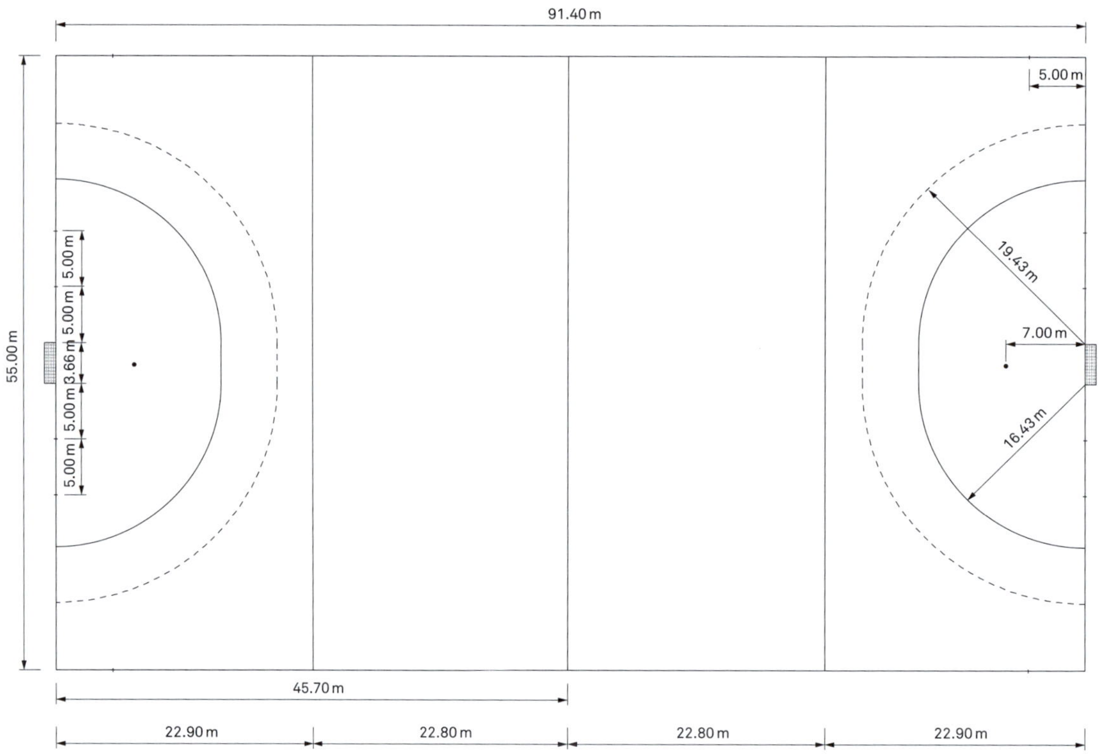

Scale 1:500

Figure 9.7 Field hockey

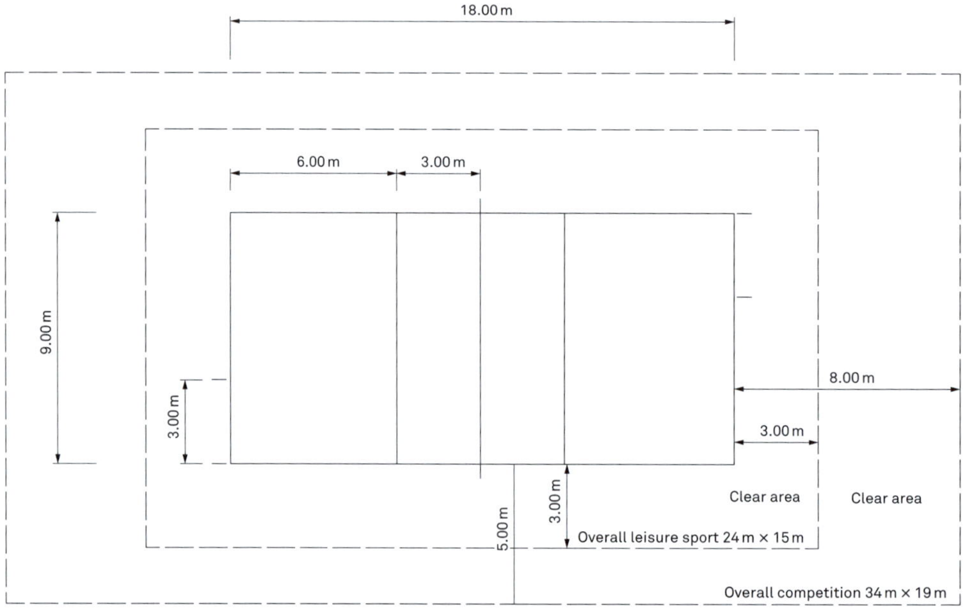

Scale 1:200

Figure 9.8 Volleyball

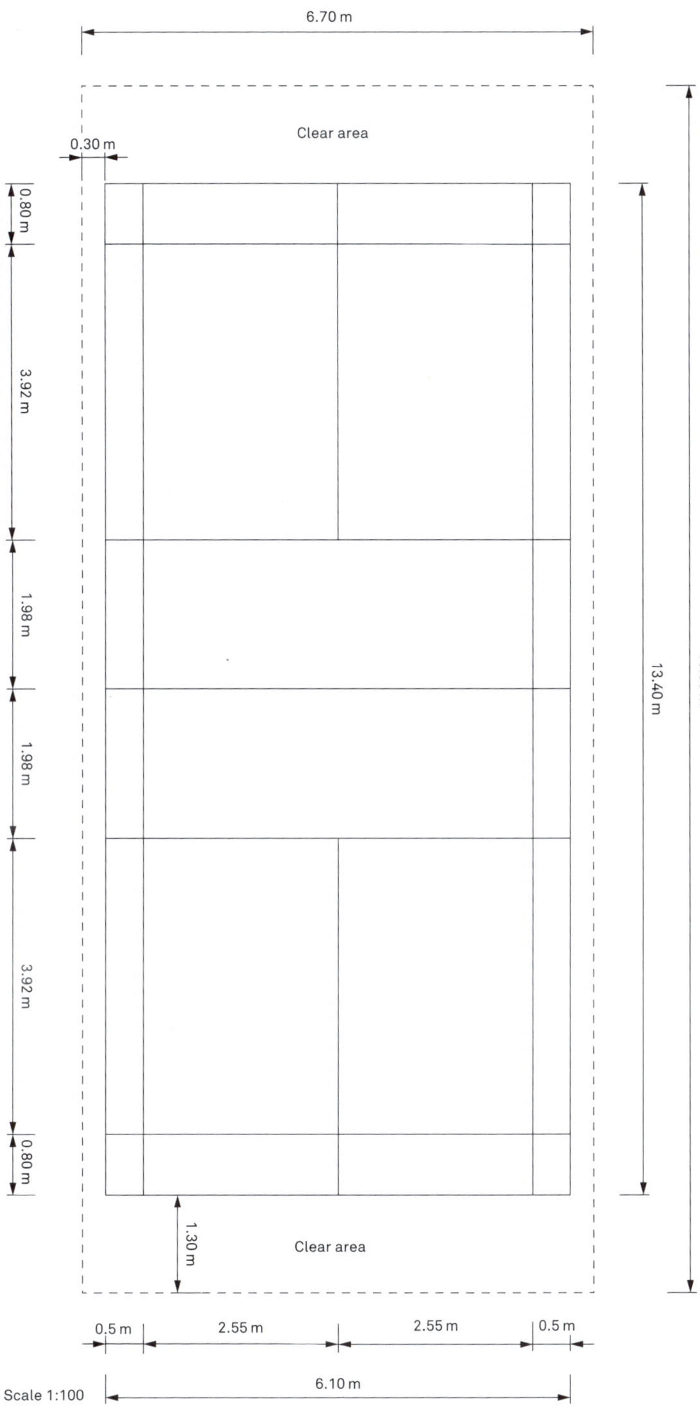

Figure 9.9 Badminton

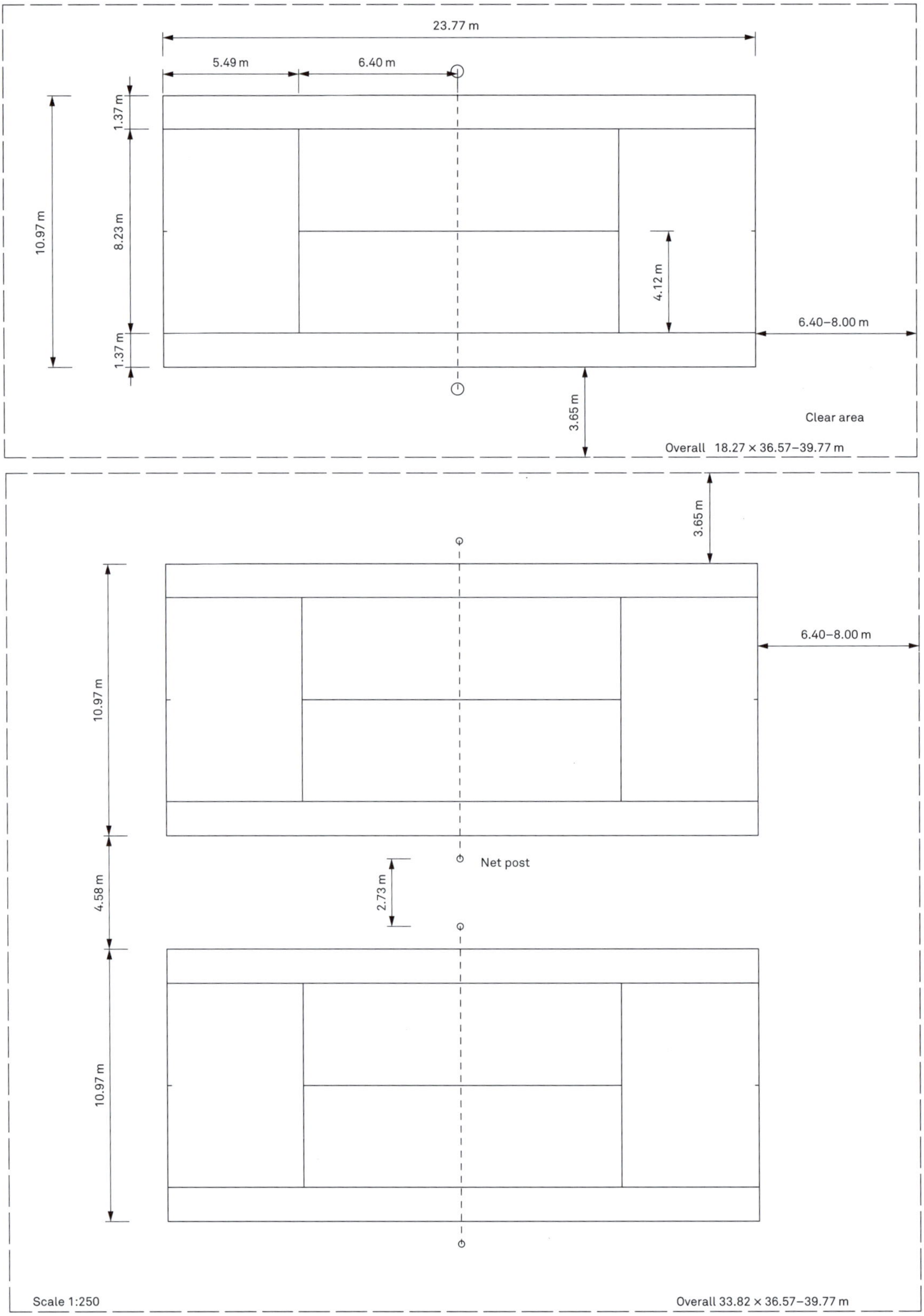

Figure 9.10 Tennis: single court and paired courts

Sport	Length			Width of individual lane	Safety zone along outer lane
	Start area	Distance	Run-out		
Sprint track	3 m	110 m	17 m	1.22 m	0.28 m
Standard track	–	400 m	17 m	1.22 m	0.28 m

Table 9.6 Running Tracks

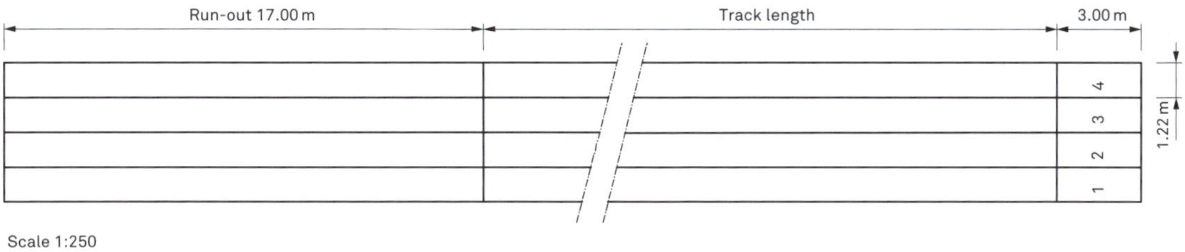

Figure 9.11 Running Tracks

Jumping event	Runway		Landing area	
	Length	Width of single/multiple facilities	Length	Width
Long jump	≥45 m, take-off board ≥2 m in front of the landing area (1 m for top-level competitive sports)	1.22 m / 2 m	Landing area ≥8 m (9 m for top-level competitive sports)	2.75 m
Triple jump	≥45 m, take-off board ≥11 m in front of the landing area	1.22 m / 2 m	Landing area ≥8 m (for youth ≥9 m, for top-ranking athletes ≥13 m)	2.75 m
Pole vault	≥45 m	1.22 m / 2 m	Cushion ≥5 m	≥5 m
High jump	Semicircle with r ≥ 18 m		Cushion ≥4 m	5–6 m

Table 9.7 Jumping Event

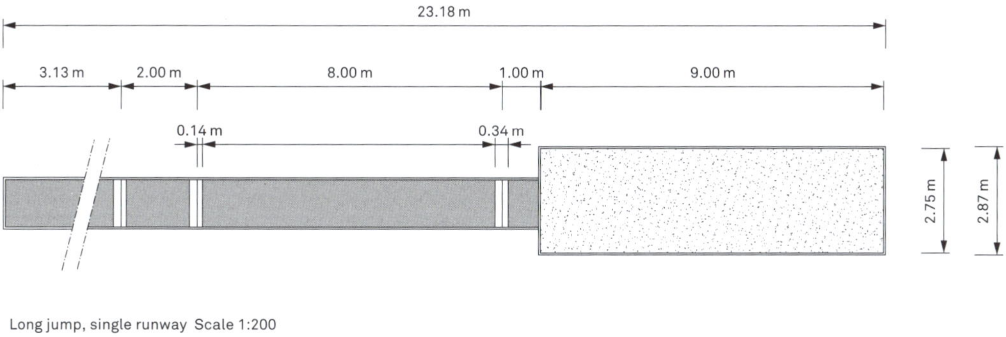

Figure 9.12 Long jump

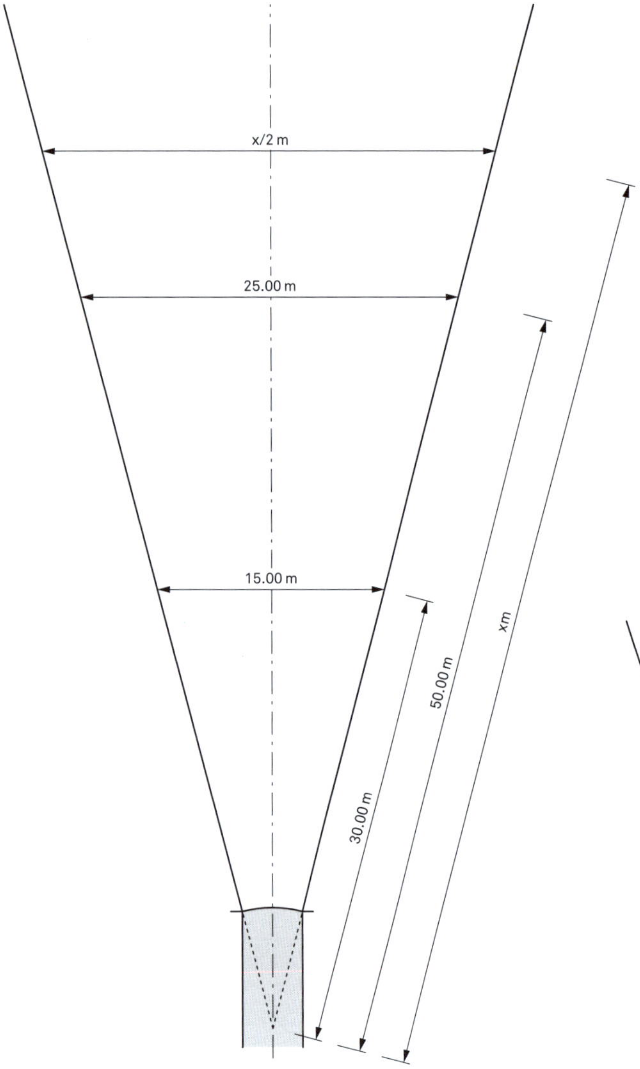

Sector for javelin throw
Scale 1:500

Figure 9.13 Throwing event: Javelin

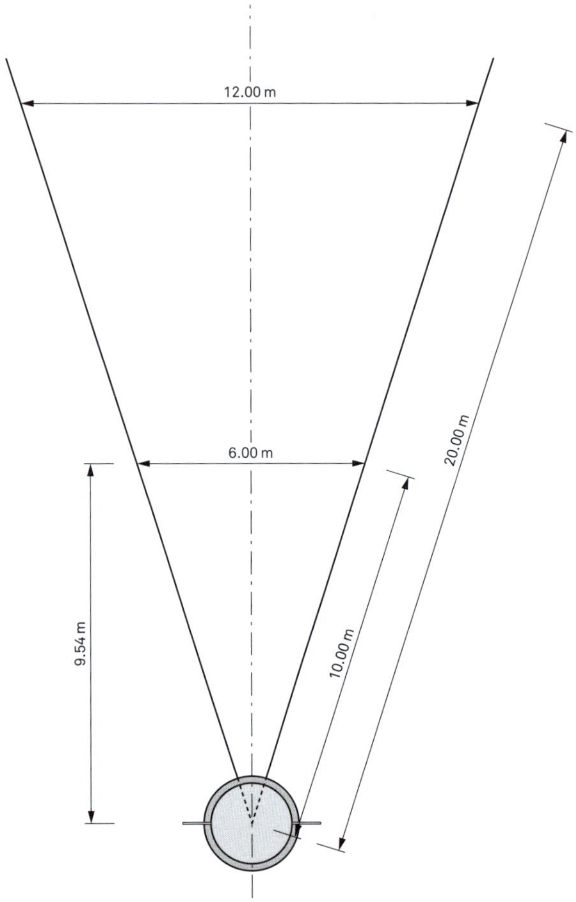

Sector for shot put, discus throw,
and hammer throw
Scale 1:200

Figure 9.14 Throwing events: Shot put, hammer throw, and discus

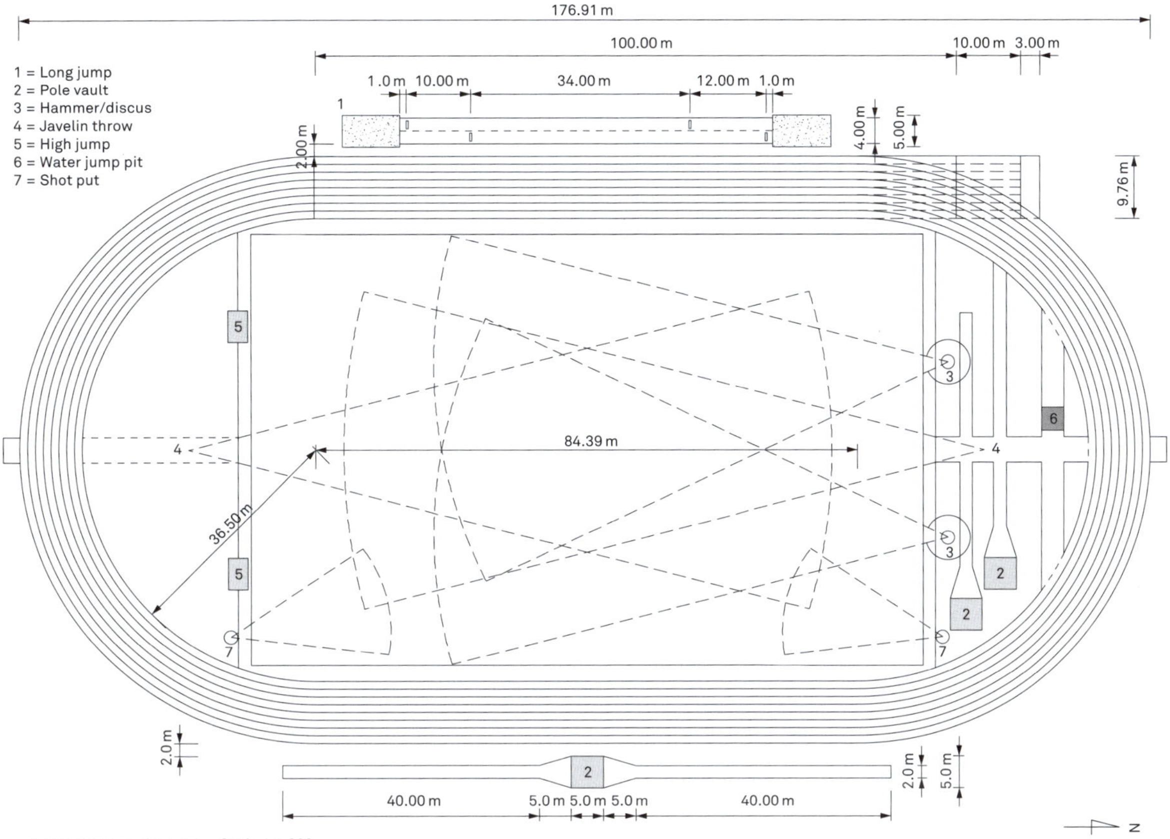

Competition track type A Scale 1:1,000

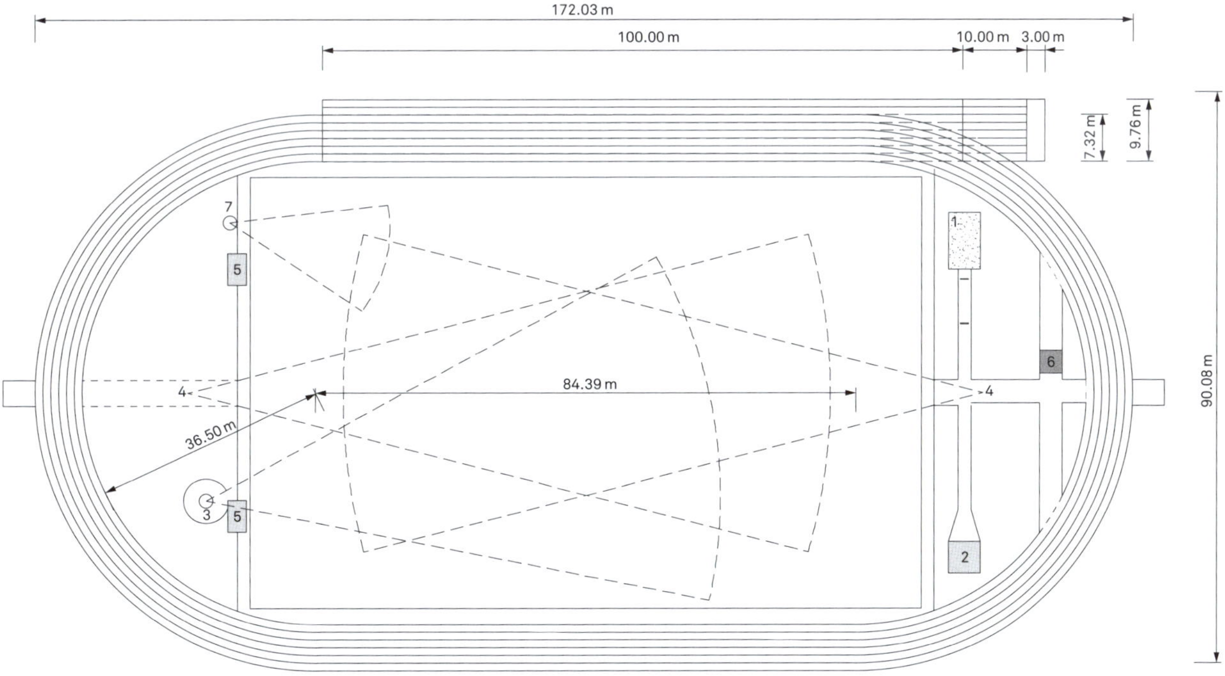

Competition track type B Scale 1:1,000

Figure 9.15 Competition track type A and B

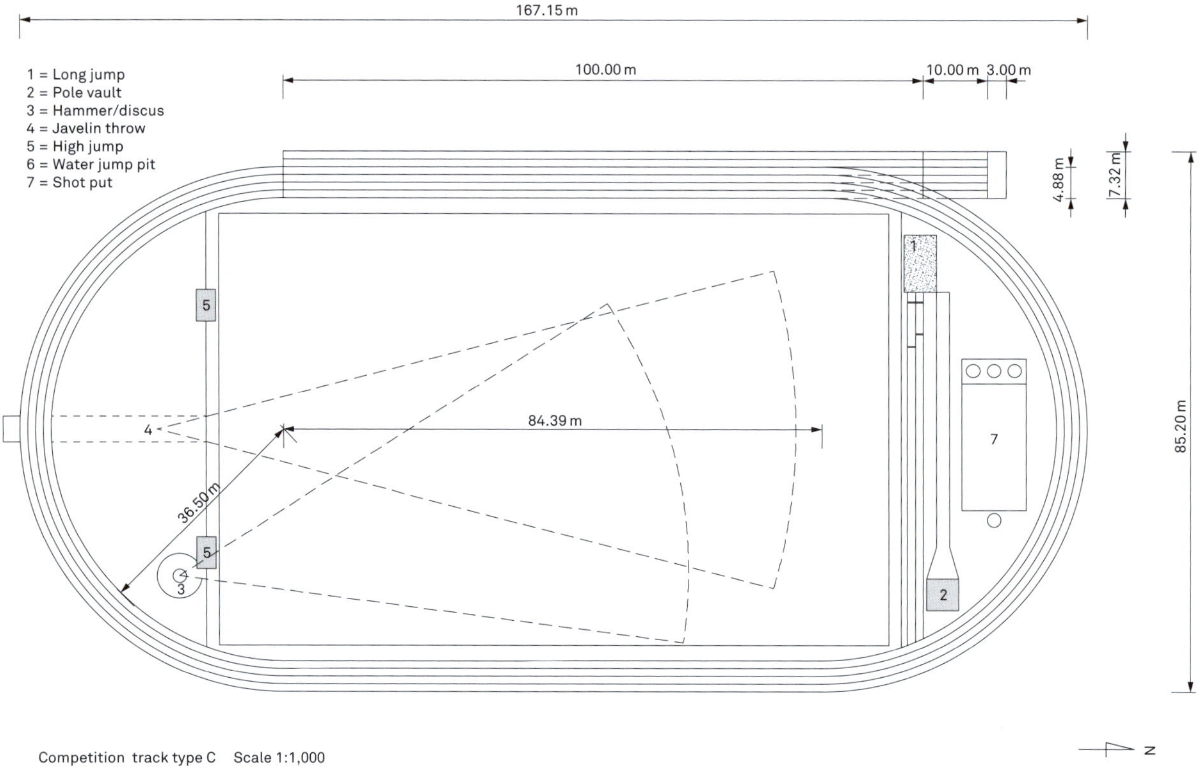

Competition track type C Scale 1:1,000

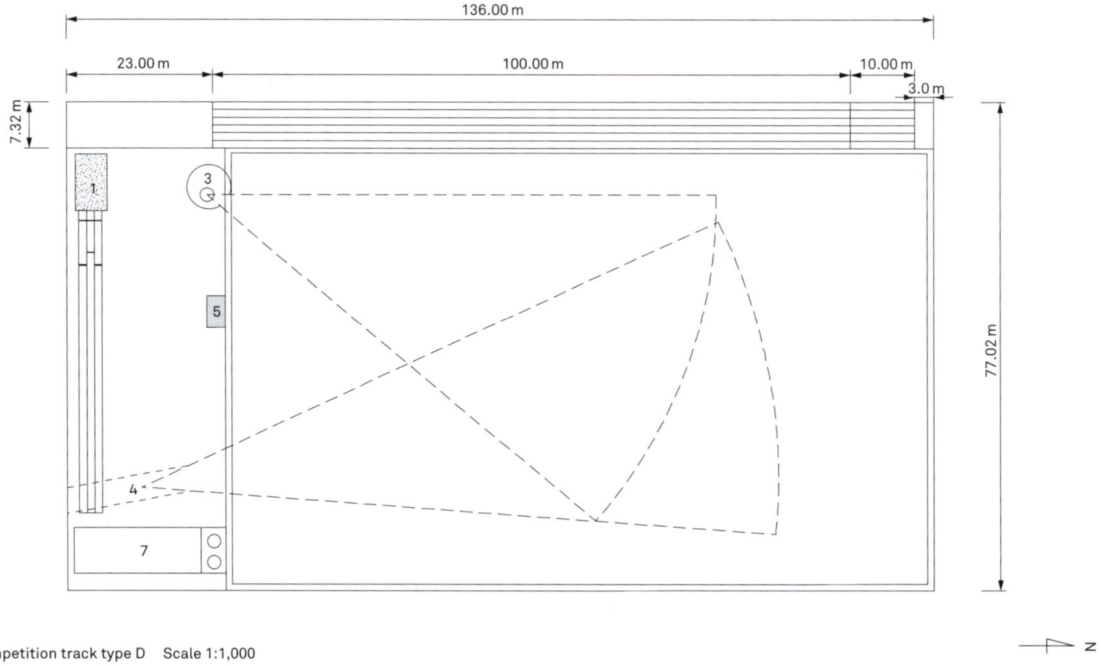

Competition track type D Scale 1:1,000

Figure 9.16 Competition track types C and D

Sport		Playing field/lane	Clearance to side barriers	Surface
Pétanque	International/national competition	Minimum 15 × 4 m		Any ground surface, preferably water-bound paving or a compacted sand/crushed stone mixture
	Leisure sports and other competitions	Minimum 12 × 3 m (12 × 5 m double lane) or terrain libre		
Boule lyonnaise		27.5 × 4 (2.5) m		Any ground surface
Jeu Provençal		24 × 4 m or terrain libre	1.5 m	Any ground surface
Boccia		26.5 m × 4.5 m		Special surface, typically on natural sand lanes
Bowls (lawn bowling)		31–40 m × 4.3–5.8 m		Grass

Table 9.8 Boules

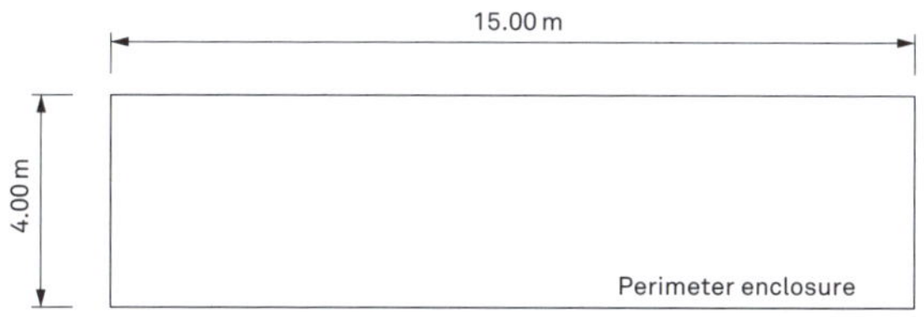

Pétanque international Scale 1:200

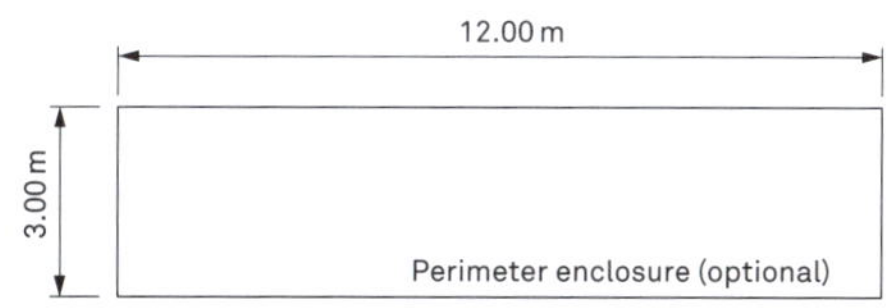

Pétanque leisure sports Scale 1:200
Double lane: 12 m × 5 m

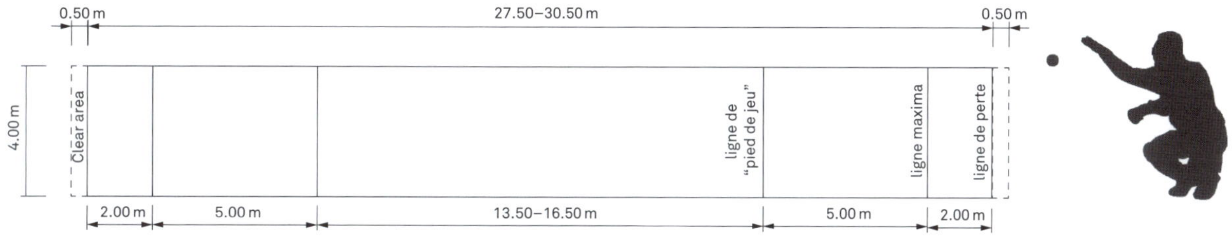

Boule lyonnaise Scale 1:200

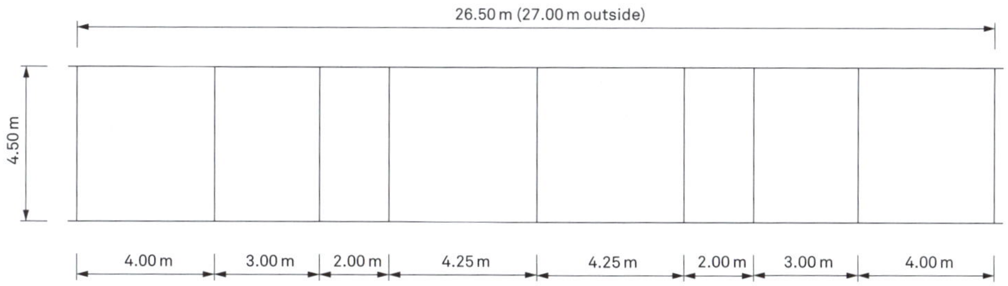

Boccia Scale 1:200

Figure 9.17 Boules

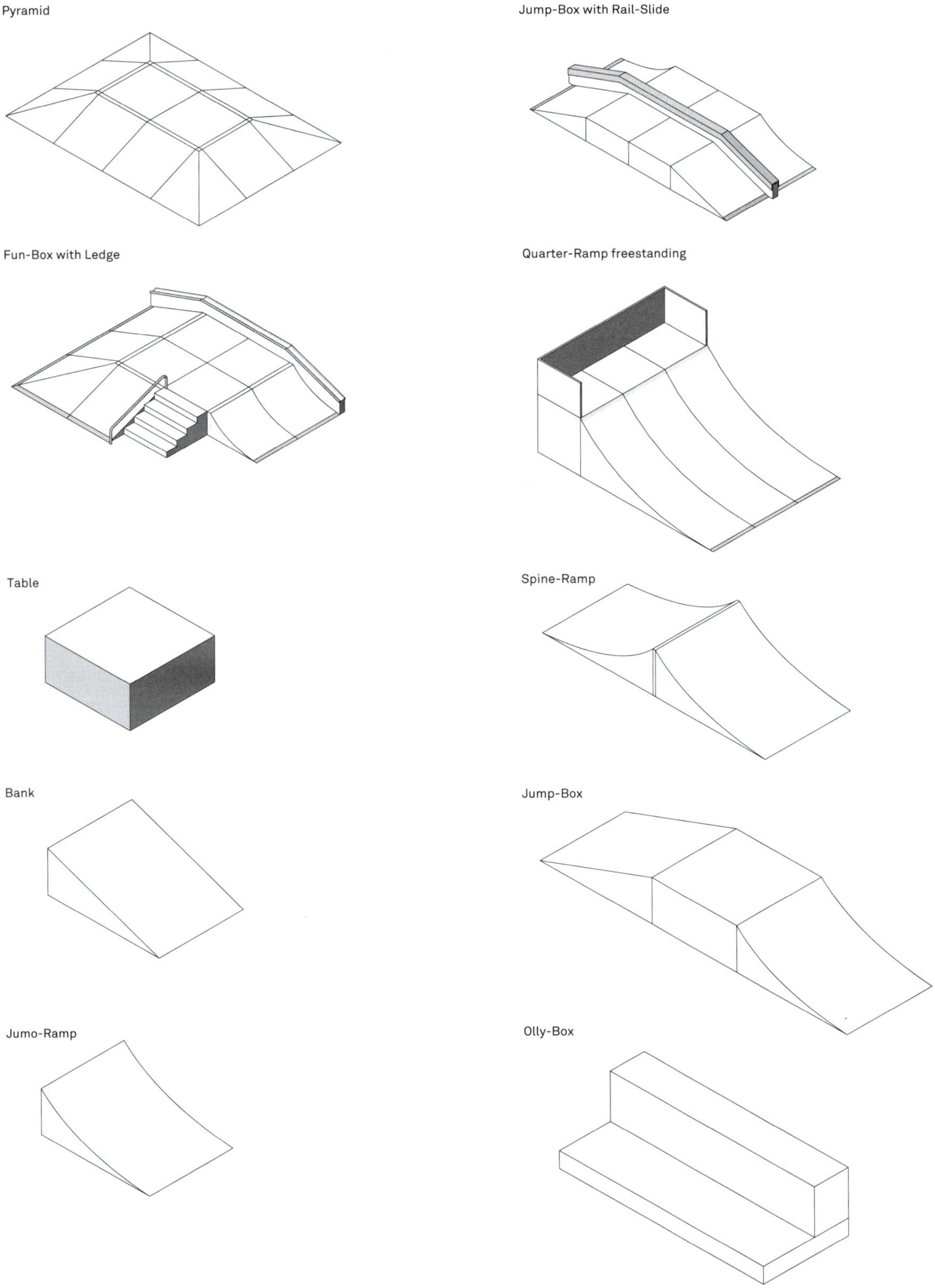

Figure 9.18 Skating facility

Foothold height (height of fall to the ground)	Safety area	Surfacing In safety area	Additional requirements
Boulder walls			
≤0.6 m	–	–	–
>0.6–1 m	2 m	Unbound (grass/topsoil)	–
>1 m–3 m	2 m	Noncohesive sand, water-worn gravel (4–8 mm), wood shavings, bark mulch, or rubber safety tiles	–
Climbing wall with safety rope			
>3 m			Minimum 2 m high fenced enclosure around the grounds or the climbing wall (to prevent unauthorized entry) or, alternatively, no climbing holds (grips) below a height of 2.50 m.

Table 9.9 Sport climbing

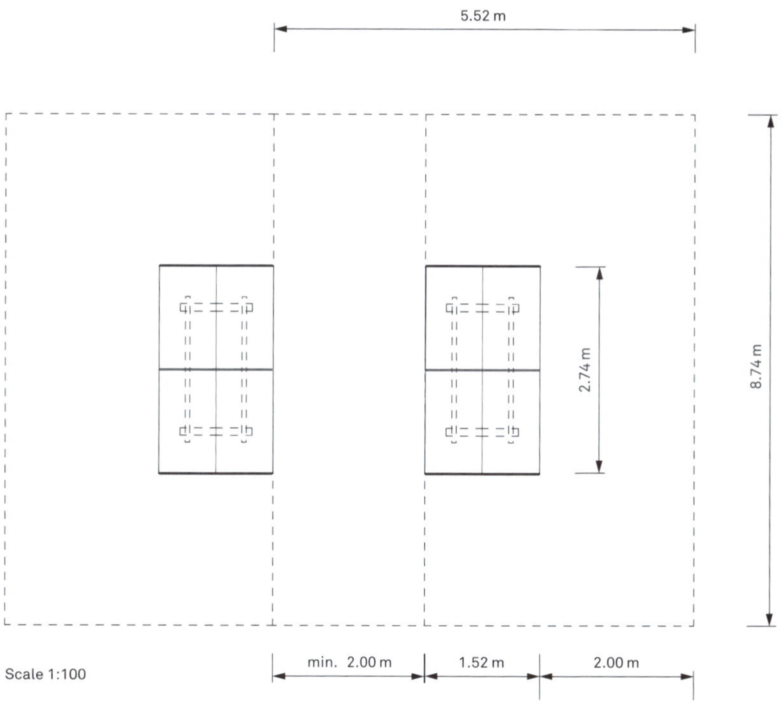

Figure 9.19 Table tennis

Type of sport/riding arena	Dimensions	Surface
Riding arenas in general	Min. 20 × 40 m	
Dressage	Dressage arena for classes A-L: 20 × 40 m International competitions for classes M-S: 20 × 60 m	Quartz sand, sand mixtures (e.g. mixture of sand and sawdust/fleece shreds
Show jumping	Training: Overall size: ≥ 3000 m² Jumping competition: 25 × 50 m	
Western riding	Min. 20 x 40 m, optimal = 30 × 60 m	
Longeing circle	Diameter: minimum 12 m, better 15 m	
Round pen	Diameter: minimum 15 m, better 18–20 m	
Driving	Competition arena: 40 × 80 m	
Icelandic horse riding	Track: 6 × 250 m Oval track: 46 × 79.44 m / 46 × 110.70 m	

Table 9.10 Equestrian sports

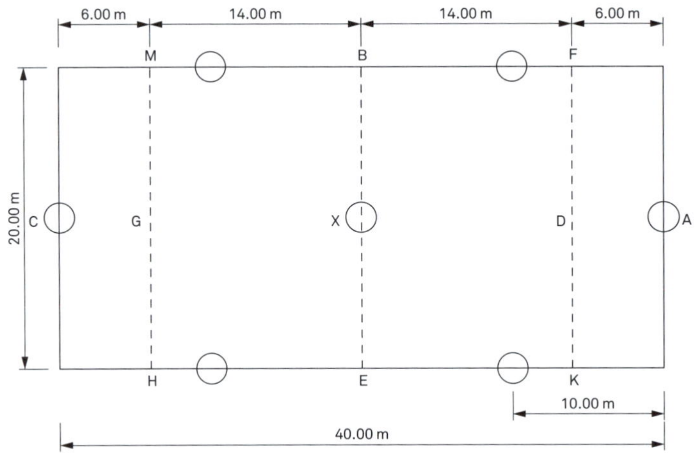

Figure 9.20 Equestrian sports

9.3 Campgrounds

Campgrounds can be separated into short-stay (short visit), vacation, and extended-stay (long-term or seasonal stay) facilities. Extended-stay campgrounds are distinguished by larger and separated individual campsites, whereas vacation and short-stay campgrounds have open sites on camping fields. In the majority of cases, both campsite types are combined. Separated campsite lots are suitable for recreational vehicles (RVs) and larger tents, and usually have integrated parking space for a passenger car. Areas without separation are particularly suitable for tents without an accompanying car. In this case, separate collective parking areas are designated on the periphery of the campground. Camping fields on the whole require less circulation space.

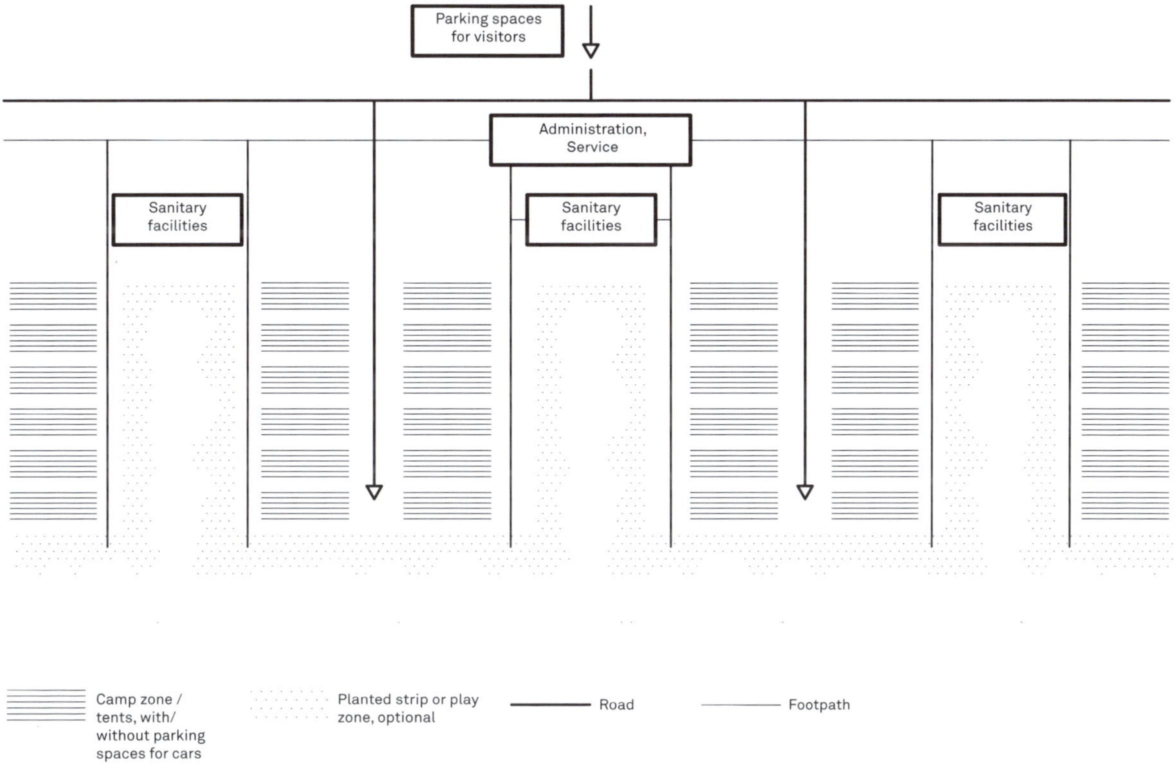

Figure 9.21 Functional diagram of a campground

Type of use	Space needs/dimensions
Campsites	
Small tents on open field	40 m²
Large tents	80 m²
Average space needed per campsite on open field	60–80 m²
Separated campsite lot for RV or large tent with integrated parking for passenger car	100–120 m² (min. 75 m² *)
Separated campsite lot with passenger car in a remote parking area	min. 65 m² *
Separated campsite lot, including ancillary areas (paths and screen planting)	140 m²
Circulation	
Vehicular access and main paths	5.5 m wide
Secondary paths	3–4 m wide
Roadways with one-way traffic	3 m wide
Dead ends not longer than 100 m	3 m wide
Circulation space, total	
Service and circulation areas	50–100 % of the actual campsites

* as per Bavarian campground regulations

Table 9.11 Recommended values for the space needs of campgrounds

		Per 100 campsites	Per 200 campsites
Washing facilities	Washbasins, men	8 washbasins, including 2 in private compartments	Additionally: 1 washbasin and 1 shower, both accessible, suitable for wheelchair users
		4 individual showers	
	Washbasins, women	8 washbasins, including 2 in private compartments	
		4 individual showers	
	Toilets, men	4 toilets and 4 urinals	Additionally: 1 accessible toilet, suitable for wheelchair users
	Toilets, women	8 toilets	
Dishwashing and laundry facilities		2 dishwashing sinks and 1 laundry sink or washing machine	The facilities must be accessible for the disabled
Drinking water taps		4, distributed pragmatically on the site	

Table 9.12 Sanitary facilities at campgrounds (recommended values based on the campground regulations of Baden-Württemberg/Bavaria)

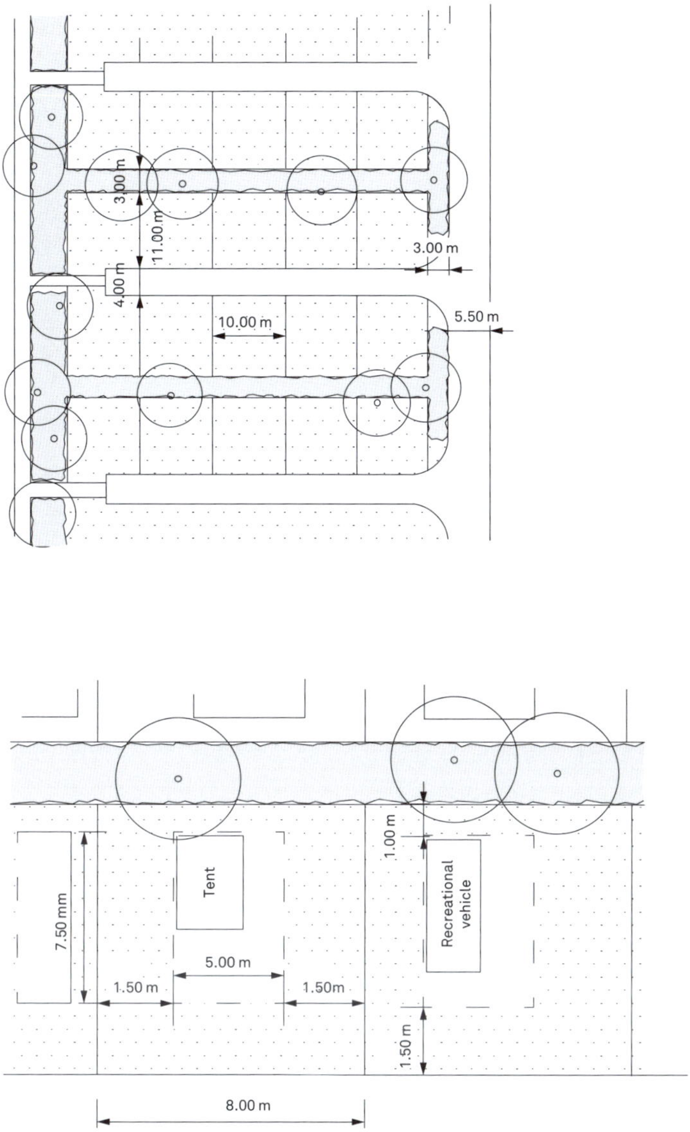

80 m² area for tent / recreational vehicle

Figure 9.22 Dimensions of separated campsite lots

9.4 Outdoor Theaters and Tiered Seating

Outdoor theaters and straight or semicircular arrangements of tiered seating can be constructed in outdoor facilities for various purposes. Stepped constructions alone often serve as seating areas that can be used as outdoor classrooms in schools, for instance, or as simple gathering places in parks.

For outdoor stages that are to serve as event venues (theaters, open-air cinemas, etc.) or for tiered seating at sports facilities, specific requirements must be observed when the visitor area accommodates more than 1,000 persons.

A rough estimate for the number of persons visiting a place of assembly can be made as follows:

- For seats at tables: one person per square meter of ground area
- For seats in rows: two persons per square meter
- For standing areas: two persons per running meter of a tier

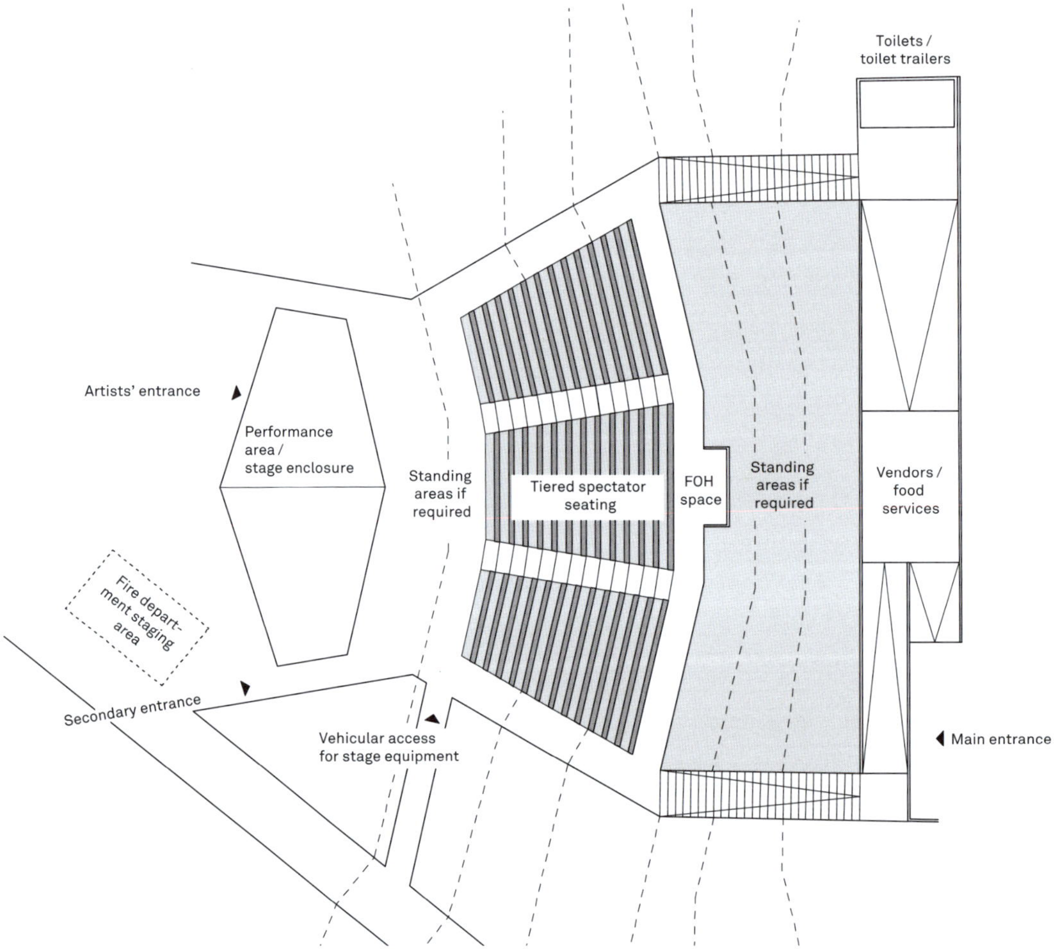

Figure 9.23 Functional and spatial program for an outdoor theater

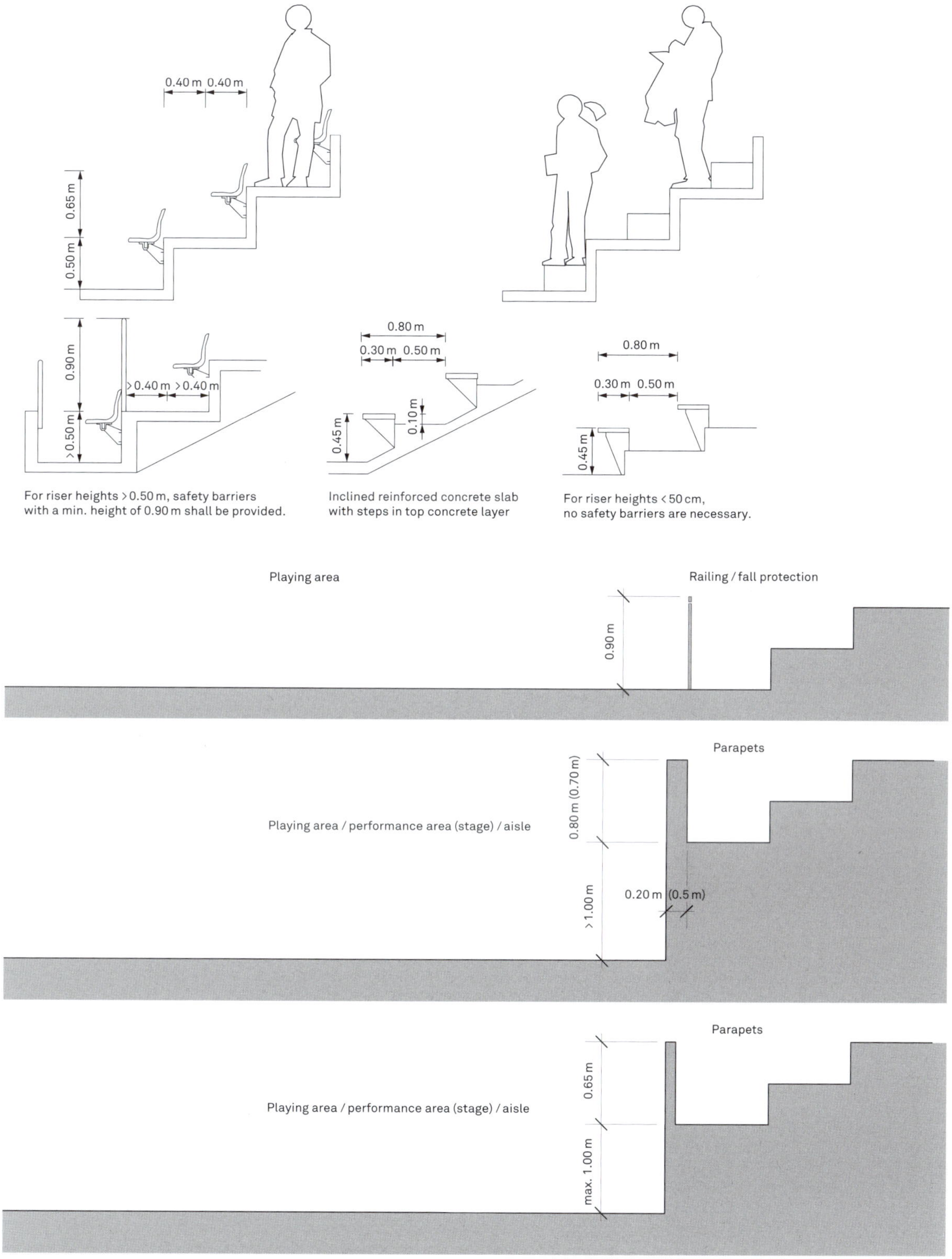

Figure 9.24 Fall protection and dimensions of seating rows and standing areas for outdoor places of assembly

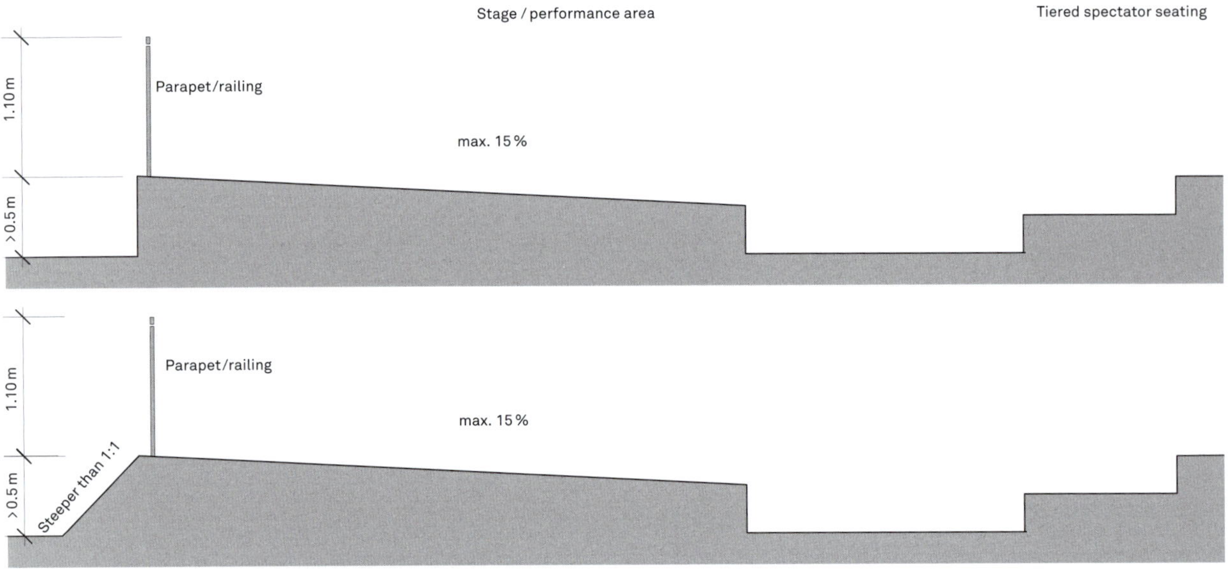

Figure 9.25 Fall protection for performance and playing areas

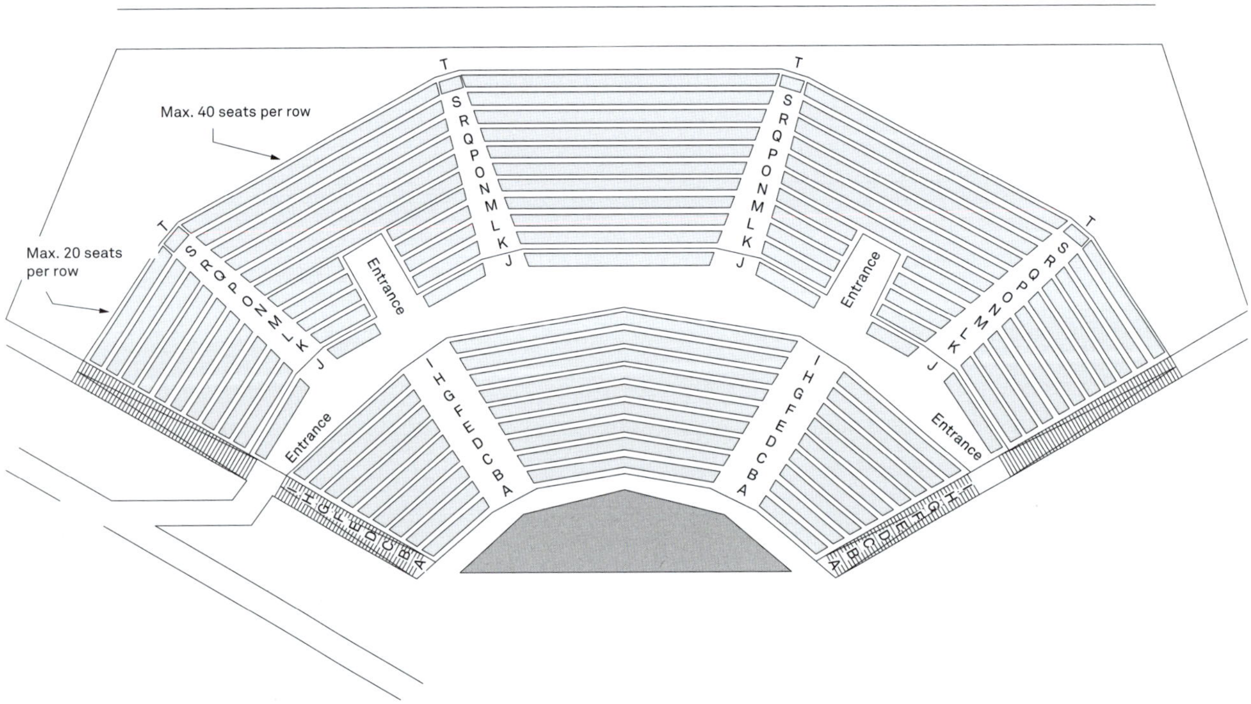

Figure 9.26 Exemplary layout of seating blocks and aisles

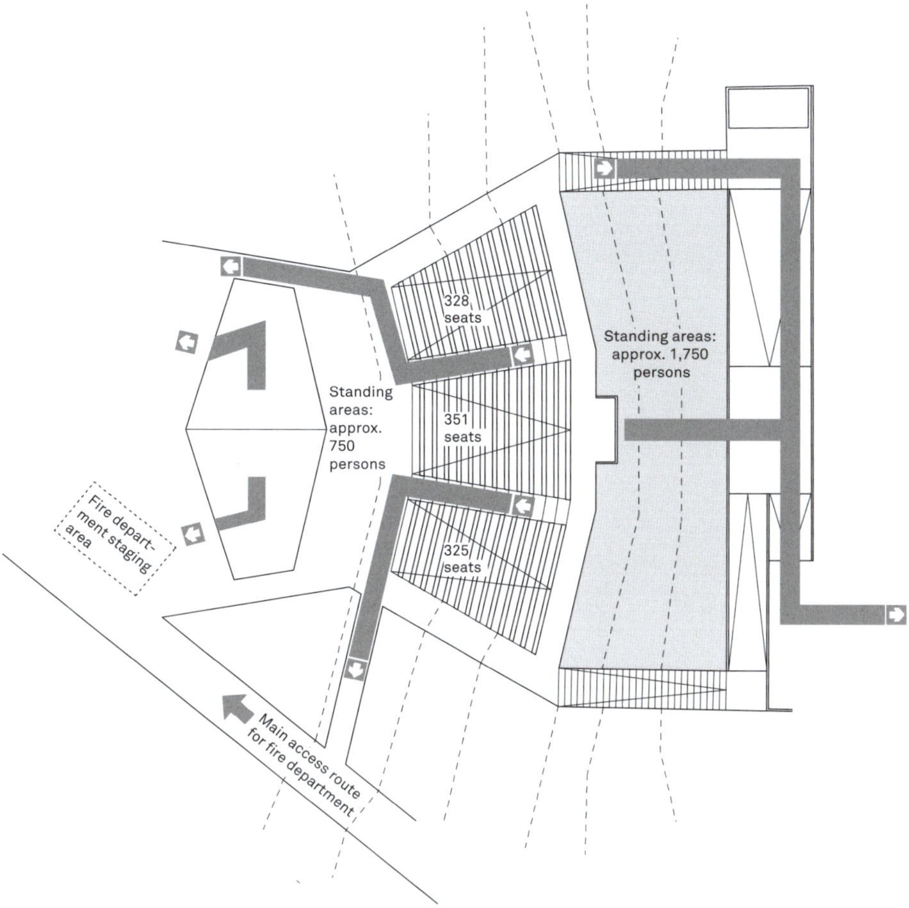

Figure 9.27 Example for an escape route plan, as exemplified by the outdoor theater in Spremberg

Visitor seating	Women Water closets	Men Water closets	Urinals	Wheelchair-accessible toilets
Up to 1,000 visitors				Min. 1 toilet per 10 wheelchair user spaces
Per 100	1.2	0.8	1.2	
More than 1,000 visitors				
Per additional 100	0.8	0.4	0.6	
More than 20,000 visitors				
Per additional 100	0.4	0.3	0.6	

Table 9.13 Quantity of spectator restrooms (per MVStättV)

Selected Reference Books

General References

Bielefeld, Bert and Skiba, Isabella. *Basics Technical Drawing*, 2nd rev. ed. Basel 2009

Bielefeld, Bert (ed.): *Planning Architecture. Dimensions and Typologies.* Basel 2015

Bielefeld, Bert: *Spaces in Architecture, Areas, Distances, Dimensions*. Basel 2018

Brandl, Wolfgang; Schegk, Ingrid: *Baukonstruktionslehre für Landschaftsarchitekten*. Stuttgart 2009

Erhardt, Walter et al.: *Der große Zander. Enzyklopädie der Pflanzennamen. Vol. 1: Familien und Gattungen – Vol. 2: Arten und Sorten*. Stuttgart 2008

Heiss, Oliver, Christine Degenhart, and Johann Ebe. *Barrier-Free Design: Principles, Planning, Examples*. Detail Practice. Basel 2010

Gälzer, Ralph: *Grünplanung für Städte*. Stuttgart 2001

Lay, Bjorn-Holger et al.: *Bauen mit Grün. Die Bau- und Vegetationstechnik des Garten- und Landschaftsbaus.* 4.edition. Stuttgart 2010

Lay, Bjorn-Holger (eds.) et al.:*Lehr – Taschenbuch für den Garten-, Landschafts- und Sportplatzbau*. 7. Edition. Stuttgart 2013

Lohrer, Axel. Basics Designing with Water. Basel 2008

Loidl, Hans and Bernard, Stefan. Open(ing) Spaces: Design as Landscape Architecture. Basel 2014

Margolis, Liat and Alexander Robinson. *Living Systems: Innovative Materials and Technologies for Landscape Architecture*. Basel 2007

Neufert, Ernst and Peter. *Neufert Architects' Data*. 5th Edition. Chichester 2019

Petschek, Peter. *Grading: LandscapingSMART, 3D-Machine Control, Stormwater Management*. 3nd rev. and updated ed. Basel 2019

Petschek, Peter, and Siegfried Gass, (eds.) *Constructing Shadows: Pergolas, Pavilions, Tents, Cables, and Plants*. Basel 2011

Richter, Gerhard: Handbuch Stadtgrün: *Landschaftsarchitektur im städtischen Freiraum*. Munich 1981

Skiba, Isabella and Züger, Rahel. Basics Barrier-Free Planning. Basel 2009

Steenbergen, Clemens. *Composing Landscapes: Analysis, Typology and Experiments for Design*. Basel 2009

Wöhrle, Regine Ellen and Wöhrle, Hans-Jörg. Basics Designing with Plants. Basel 2008

Zimmermann, Astrid (eds.): *Constructing Landscape. Materials, Techniques, Structural Components*. 3rd edition. Basel 2015

Zimmermann, Astrid: *Planning Landscapes. Dimensions, Elements, Typologies*. Basel 2014

Chapter 2 Human Measure

Bogardus, Emory S.: „Measuring Social Distances“, in: *Journal of Applied Sociology* 9 (1925): 299–308

Bundesministerium für Gesundheit: *Handbuch für Planer und Praktiker*. Bad Homburg 1996

Hall, Edward T. *The Hidden Dimension*. New York, 1966.

Hansestadt Hamburg: *Landschaftsprogramm einschließlich Artenschutzprogramm*. Hamburg 1997

Hansestadt Hamburg: *Musterflächenprogramm für allgemeinbildende Schulen in Hamburg*. Hamburg 2011

Gälzer, Ralph: *Grünplanung für Städte*. Stuttgart 2001

Gehl, Jan. *Life Between Buildings: Using Public Space*, translated by Jo Koch. New York, 1987. Originally published as *Livet mellem husene*. Copenhagen, 1971

Le Corbusier: *Le Modulor. Essai sur une mesure harmonique, à l'échelle humaine applicable universellement, à l'architecture et à la mécanique*. Boulogne (Sein) 1952

Richter, Gerhard: Handbuch Stadtgrün: *Landschaftsarchitektur im städtischen Freiraum*. Munich 1981

Stolzenberg, H.; Kahl, H.; Bergmann, K. E.: „Körpermaße bei Kindern und Jugendlichen in Deutschland“, in: *Bundesgesundheitsblatt – Gesundheitsforschung – Gesundheitsschutz*, 50, 2007, 5/6

Chapter 3 Topography

Mader, Günter: *Freiraumplanung: Hausgärten, Grünanlagen, Stadtlandschaften*. Munich 2004

Chapter 4 Circulation

De Groot, Rik: Ontwerpwijzer fietsverkeer, Ede 2006 (= Publicatie; 230)

Deutsche Verkehrswacht e. V.: *Skate & Roll: Inline-Skaten – aber sicher*. Meckenheim 2002

Deutscher Blinden- und Sehbehindertenverband e. V.: *Erkennbarkeit des unteren Aufmerksamkeitsfeldes und der letzten Trittstufenmarkierung bei Treppen*, July 1st 2013. www.dbsv.org

DIN 32984:2011-10

DIN 18040-1:2010-10

EAR 05

ERA 10

Gargulla, Nadja; Geskes, Christof: *Treppen und Rampen in der Landschaftsarchitektur*. Stuttgart 2007

Gerlach, Jürgen et al.: „Sinn und Unsinn von Shared Space – Zur Versachlichung einer populären Gestaltungsphilosophie“, in: *Straßenverkehrstechnik 2*, 2008 (part 1) and 03, 2008 (part 2)

Harris, Charles und Dines, Nicholas: *Time-Saver Standards for Landscape Architecture. Design and Construction Data.* New York et al. 1998

Kalwitzki, Klaus-Peter: „Shared Space – Den Raum miteinander teilen. Von einer Exkursion nach Drachten und Haren/NL“, in: *Verkehrszeichen* 03, 2007

Land Salzburg, Abteilung Soziales: *Barrierefrei Bauen*. Salzburg 2008

Mader, Günter: „Treppenbau, Teil 1: Kleine Mathematik des Treppenbaus", in: *DEGA Galabau*, H. 45, 2002

RASt 06

Robatsch, Klaus: „Geschwindigkeiten, Bremsweg und Breitenbedarf von Inline-Skatern", in: *Zeitschrift für Verkehrssicherheit*, 44, 1998

Mahabadi, Mehdi; Meyer, Alexandra: *Treppen im Freiraum. Planungs- und Baugrundsätze*, Stuttgart 2006

Ministerium für Bau und Verkehr des Landes Sachsen-Anhalt: *Empfehlungen für den Bau und die Unterhaltung von straßenbegleitenden Radverkehrsanlagen in Sachsen-Anhalt*. Magdeburg 1998

Senatsverwaltung für Stadtentwicklung, Berlin: *Fußverkehrsstrategie für Berlin – Ziele, Maßnahmen, Modellprojekte*. Berlin 2011

The Danish Cyclists Federation: *Bicycle parking manual*. Copenhagen 2008

Schuster, Andreas; Sattler, Josef; Hoffmann, Stephan: „Benötigen wir ein neues Pkw-Bemessungsfahrzeug für den Entwurf von Anlagen des ruhenden Verkehrs?", in: *Straßenverkehrstechnik*, 56, 2012, H. 1

Senatsverwaltung für Stadtentwicklung Berlin: *Fahrradparken in Berlin – Leitfaden für die Planung*. Berlin 2008

Chapter 5 Vertical Elements

Bayerisches Landesamt für Umwelt (eds.)/Dr. Katharina Stroh (LfU): *Lärm – Straße und Schiene*, http://www.lfu.bayern.de/umweltwissen/index.htm

DIN 18065:2011-06

Mader, Günter; Zimmermann, Elke: *Zäune und Tore aus Holz und Metall*, Munich 2006

Wirtschaftsministerium Baden-Württemberg: *-Städtebauliche Lärmfibel Online*, Stuttgart 2007: http://www.staedtebauliche-laermfibel.de

Chapter 6 Street Furniture

Abfallwirtschaftsbetrieb Munich: *Müllräume und Müllbehälter – Standplätze – Vorschriften und Hinweise*. Munich 2011

Bauordnung Wien, LGBI. Nr. 11/1930, last amended by LGBI. Nr. 46/2013

Berliner Stadtreinigung: *Grundlagen für die Gestaltung von Standorten und Transportwegen für Abfallbehälter*. Berlin 2011

Beucker, Nicolas; Zurnatzis, Monika: *Stadtmobiliar für Senioren – Ausstattungskriterien für eine altengerechte Stadt. Studienbericht 2011*, http://socialdesign.hs-niederrhein.de

Deutsche Lichttechnische Gesellschaft (LiTG) e. V. „Fachausschuss Außenbeleuchtung" (LiTG); Steck, Bernhard: *Zur Einwirkung von Außenbeleuchtungsanlagen auf nachtaktive Insekten*, Berlin 1997 (= LiTG-Publication; 15)

Deutsche Lichttechnische Gesellschaft (LiTG) e. V. „Fachausschuss Außenbeleuchtung" (LiTG); Eckert, Martin: Straßenbeleuchtung und Sicherheit, Berlin 1998 (= LiTG-Publication; 17)

Gesetz über die Vermeidung und Behandlung von Abfällen und die Einhebung einer hierfür erforderlichen Abgabe im Gebiete des Landes Wien (Wiener Abfallwirtschaftsgesetz), LGBl. für Wien Nr. 13/1994, last amended by Gesetz LGBl. für Wien Nr. 31/2013

Ris, Hans Rudolf: *Beleuchtungstechnik für Praktiker*. Berlin 2008

Stadt Zürich, ERZ Entsorgung + Recycling Zürich: *Wegleitung II: Kostenloser, neuer Kunststoffcontainer*. Zurich 2008

TRILUX-LENZE GmbH + Co KG: *Licht für Europas Straßen – Beleuchtung von Straßen, Wegen und Plätzen nach DIN EN 13 201*. Arnsberg 2005

Chapter 7 Water

Baumhauer, Jörg; Schmidt, Carsten: *Schwimmteichbau: Handbuch für Planung, Technik und Betrieb*. Berlin 2008

Deutsche Gesellschaft für das Badewesen: *Merkblatt 94.05 Verkehrssicherungs- und Aufsichtspflicht in öffentlichen Bädern während des Badebetriebs.* 2008

Deutsche Gesellschaft für das Badewesen: Merkblatt 94.12 Verkehrssicherungs- und Aufsichtspflicht in öffentlichen Naturbädern während des Badebetrieb. 2014

Deutscher Schwimm-Verband e. V.: *Bau- und Ausstattungsanforderungen für wettkampfgerechte Schwimmsportstätten*. 2012

Deutscher Wetterdienst – Institut für Technisch-Wissenschaftliche Hydrologie (Hrsg.): *KOSTRA-DWD 2000: koordinierte Starkniederschlags-Regionalisierungs-Auswertungen*. Offenbach 2006

DIN EN 13451-10

DWA-A 138 – Planung, Bau und Betrieb von Anlagen zur Versickerung von Niederschlagswasser

FLL-Richtlinie Richtlinien für Planung, Bau, Instandhaltung und Betrieb von Freibädern mit biologischer Wasseraufbereitung, 2010

Hansen, Richard, and Friedrich Stahl. *Perennials and Their Garden Habitats*, translated by Richard Ward. Portland, 1993. Originally published as *Die Stauden und ihre Lebensbereiche in Gärten und Grünanlagen*. Stuttgart, 1991

Koordinierungskreis Bäder: *Richtlinien für den Bäderbau (KOK-Richtlinien)*. 2013

Lomer, Wolfgang (ed.): *Garten- und Landschaftsbau*. Stuttgart 2001 (= Der Gärtner; 4)

Mahabadi, Mehdi: *Regenwasserversickerung, Regenwassernutzung. Planungsgrundsätze und Bauweisen*. Stuttgart 2012

Mahabadi, Mehdi; Rohlfing, Ines M.: *Schwimm- und Badeteichanlagen. Planungs- und Baugrundsätze.* Stuttgart 2008
Mahabadi, Mehdi; Rohlfing, Ines M.: *Schwimm- und Badeteichanlagen. Planungs- und Baugrundsätze.* Stuttgart 2005
Niesel, Alfred (ed.): *Grünflächen-Pflegemanagement – dynamische Pflege von Grün.* Stuttgart 2006
Stadt Graz: Barrierefreies Bauen für alle, 2006

Chapter 8 Plants

Deutsche Gartenamtsleiterkonferenz (GALK), Arbeitskreis Stadtbäume: *GALK-Straßenbaumliste*, Revised October 29, 2013. Routinely updated list available online (in German only): http://www.galk.de
Beccaletto, Jacques; Retournard, Denis: *Obstgehölze erziehen und formen: Spaliere, Kordons, Palmetten.* Stuttgart 2007
Beltz, Heinrich: *Spalierobst im Garten – Sorten, Pflege, Schnitt.* Munich 2012
Bundesgesetz über die Regelung des Kleingartenwesens (Kleingartengesetz). [Federal law on the regulation of allotment gardening] (Austria), December 16, 1958, last amended by BGBl. I Nr. 98/2001
Bundeskleingartengesetz [Federal law on allotment gardens] (Germany), February 28, 1983, last amended September 19, 2006
FLL – Empfehlungen für Baumpflanzungen – Teil 2, 2010
Florineth, Florin: *Pflanzen statt Beton.* Berlin 2012
Gaida, Wolfgang; Grothe, Helmut: *Gehölze. Handbuch für Planung und Ausführung.* Berlin 2000
Gälzer, Ralph: *Grünplanung für Städte.* Stuttgart 2001
Großmann, Gerd; Wackwitz, Wolf-Dietmar: *Spalierobst.* Stuttgart 1998
Gunkel, Rita: *Fassadenbegrünung – Kletterpflanzen und Klettergerüste.* Stuttgart 2004
Kaltenbach, Frank: „Lebende Wände, vertikale Gärten – vom Blumentopf zur grünen Systemfassade“, in: Detail, 2008, 12
Köhler, Manfred; Barth, Georg; Brandwein, Thorwald; Gast, Dagmar: *Fassaden- und Dachbegrünung.* Stuttgart 1993
Krupka, Bernd: *Dachbegrünung. Pflanzen- und Vegetationsanwendung an Bauwerken.* Stuttgart 1992
Magistrat der Stadt Wien, Programm für umweltgerechte Leistungen „ÖkoKauf Wien“ (ed.): *Leitfaden Fassadenbegrünung.* Vienna 2013
Petschek, Peter, and Siegfried Gass, eds. *Constructing Shadows: Pergolas, Pavilions, Tents, Cables, and Plants.* Basel 2011
Prinz, Dieter: *Städtebau.* Band 1: *Städtebauliches Entwerfen.* Stuttgart 1995
RAS-LP 4 Richtlinie für die Anlage von Straßen, Teil: Landschaftspflege, Abschnitt 4: Schutz von Baumen, Vegetationsbestanden und Tieren bei Baumaßnahmen, 1999
Richter, Gerhard: *Handbuch Stadtgrün: Landschaftsarchitektur im Städtischen Freiraum.* Munich 1981
Senatsverwaltung für Stadtentwicklung Berlin: *Das bunte Grün – Kleingärten in Berlin.* Berlin 2010
Zentralverband des Deutschen Dachdeckerhandwerks – ZDVH (Hrsg.): Fachregel für Abdichtungen – Flachdachrichtlinien, Cologne 10/2008, changed Dez. 2011
Roloff, Andreas: *Bäume in der Stadt: Besonderheiten, Funktion, Nutzen, Arten, Risiken.* Stuttgart 2013
Straßenbaumliste der Deutschen Gartenamtsleiterkonferenz (GALK) und KLimaArtenMatrix für Stadtbaumarten
Wiener Kleingartengesetz [Vienna allotment garden act]. LGBl. für Wien Nr. 57/1996, last amended by LGBl. für Wien Nr. 35/2013
ZinCo GmbH (ed.): *Planungshilfe „Das grüne Dach“. Standardwerk für Planung und Ausführung genutzter Dachflächen.* Untersingen 1998
ZinCo GmbH (ed.): *Planungshilfe Geh- und Fahrbeläge auf Dächern und Decken.* Untersingen

Chapter 9 Recreational Elements

Bildungswesen (ZNWB): *Arbeitshilfen zum Schulbau.* Berlin 2008
Bundesministerium fur Umwelt, Naturschutz und Reaktorsicherheit: *Liste giftiger Pflanzenarten.* 2000
Dittrich, Gerhard (Hrsg.): *Kinderspielplätze: Analysen, empirische Befunde und Planungsempfehlungen.* Stuttgart 1974
EN 1176-1:2008
EN 1176-3:2008
Forschungsgesellschaft Landschaftsentwicklung Landschaftsbau (FLL), in Kooperation mit der deutschen Reiterlichen Vereinigung (FN): *Empfehlungen für Planung, Bau und Instandhaltung von Reitplätzen.* 2014
Gälzer, Ralph: *Grünplanung für Städte.* Stuttgart 2001
ILA – Institut für Landschaftsarchitektur, Universität für Bodenkultur Wien: *Schul:FREI – Empfehlungen für Schulfreiräume*, Wien 2004, http://www.schulfreiraum.com
Landwirtschaftskammer Nordrhein-Westfalen: *Wege zum Naturverständnis – Pflanzenverwendung in Kindergärten und kinderfreundlichen Anlagen.* 2002
Lorenz von Ehren Nursery. *Planning Tips Trees and Shrubs.* http://lve-baumschule.de/en > Planning tips
Richter, Gerhard: *Handbuch Stadtgrün: Landschaftsarchitektur im Städtischen Freiraum.* Munich 1981
Sekretariat der Kultusministerkonferenz, -Zentralstelle für Normungsfragen und Wirtschaftlichkeit im Natur- und Umweltschutzakademie des Landes NRW (ed.): *Naturspielräume für Kinder – eine Arbeitshilfe zur Gestaltung naturnaher Spielräume an Kindergärten und anderswo.* Recklinghausen 1999
Stürzebecher, Peter; Ulrich, Sigrid: *Architektur für Sport: Neue Konzepte, internationale Projekte für Sport und Freizeit.* Munich 2001

Verband Garten- und Landschaftsbau Rheinland: *Giftige Pflanzen an Kinderspielplätzen*. 1974
Bayerisches Landesamt für Umwelt (LfU): *Geräusche von Trendsportanlagen*. Part 1 and 2, 2005
Verordnung der Wiener Landesregierung, mit der nähere Vorschriften für Kleinkinderspielplätze, Kinder- und Jugendspielplätze und Kinder- und Jugendspielräume erlassen werden (Spielplatzverordnung), 1993
Satzung über die Beschaffenheit und Größe privater Spielplätze für Kleinkinder (Spielplatzsatzung), Jan. 14, 1986

Index

P

Q

R

S

T

U

V

W

Imprint

Author: Dipl.-Ing. Astrid Zimmermann

Drawings: Rike Kirstein, Andreas König, Stefan Wolf, Christian Zimmermann, Christian Schellhorn

Cover: Zplus Landschaftsarchitektur, Outdoor facility daycare in Berlin-Karlshorst (photo Astrid Zimmermann)

Book concept and editing: Annette Gref

Project coordination: Annette Gref, Katharina Kulke

Production: Bettina Chang

Translation: David Koralek/ArchiTrans

Copyediting: Keonaona Peterson

Layout concept: Hug & Eberlein

Composition and Cover: Sven Schrape

Paper: Amber Graphic, 130 g/m²

Printing: Kösel GmbH & Co. KG, Altusried-Krugzell

All CAD drawings were produced and laid out using the Vectorworks program Vectorworks LANDSCHAFT

The technical recommendations contained in this book reflect the current state of technology but expressly require explicit coordination by the responsible specialist planners to ensure compliance with the applicable and current laws, regulations, and standards of the country concerned. Neither the author nor the publisher can be held in any way accountable for the design, planning or execution of faulty work.

Acknowledgements: Here I would like to thank all the institutions and individuals who have contributed to the success of this publication.
Special thanks go to Annette Gref for her support with the book's concept and its content. For technical discussions, research work, and other valued assistance, I also wish to express special thanks to Thilo Folkerts, Ulrike Zimmermann, Inge Zimmermann, Gabriele Schneider, and the Chair of Landscaping and Construction at TU Berlin/Prof. Cordula Loidl-Reisch.

Library of Congress Control Number: 2019942880

Bibliographic information published by the German National Library
The German National Library lists this publication in the Deutsche Nationalbibliografie; detailed bibliographic data are available on the Internet at http://dnb.dnb.de.

This work is subject to copyright. All rights are reserved, whether the whole or part of the material is concerned, specifically the rights of translation, reprinting, re-use of illustrations, recitation, broadcasting, reproduction on microfilms or in other ways, and storage in databases. For any kind of use, permission of the copyright owner must be obtained.

ISBN 978-3-0356-1857-0

This publication is also available in a German language edition (ISBN 978-3-0356-1856-3)

© 2020 Birkhäuser Verlag GmbH, Basel
P.O. Box 44, 4009 Basel, Switzerland
Part of Walter de Gruyter GmbH, Berlin/Boston

9 8 7 6 5 4 3 2 1

www.birkhauser.com